The Feeling of Forgetting

The Feeling
of Forgetting

Christianity, Race, and
Violence in America

JOHN CORRIGAN

The University of Chicago Press
Chicago and London

The University of Chicago Press, Chicago 60637
The University of Chicago Press, Ltd., London
© 2023 by The University of Chicago
Published 2023
Printed in the United States of America

32 31 30 29 28 27 26 25 24 23   1 2 3 4 5

ISBN-13: 978-0-226-82763-6 (cloth)
ISBN-13: 978-0-226-82765-0 (paper)
ISBN-13: 978-0-226-82764-3 (e-book)
DOI: https://doi.org/10.7208/chicago/9780226827643.001.0001

Library of Congress Cataloging-in-Publication Data

Names: Corrigan, John, 1952– author.
Title: The feeling of forgetting : Christianity, race, and violence in America /
    John Corrigan.
Description: Chicago : The University of Chicago Press, 2023. |
    Includes bibliographical references and index.
Identifiers: LCCN 2022052884 | ISBN 9780226827636 (cloth) |
    ISBN 9780226827650 (paperback) | ISBN 9780226827643 (ebook)
Subjects: LCSH: Racism—United States. | White people—Race identity—
    United States. | Church and social problems—United States. | Collective memory—
    United States.
Classification: LCC E184.A1 C64 2023 | DDC 305.800973—dc23/eng/20221107
LC record available at https://lccn.loc.gov/2022052884

♾ This paper meets the requirements of ANSI/NISO Z39.48-1992 (Permanence of Paper).

to David Kirby and Mark Pietralunga
il pranzo mi fa pensare

Contents

Bad Memories

This Sunday's message addressed one of the biggest ways people self-sabotage: They re-live bad memories. It just comes naturally to humans. And yet one of the most important skills to learn is how to erase these memories.

COMPASS CHURCH OF SALINAS[1]

Christianity and Forgetting

Christianity is about forgetting. From the time of Saint Paul's advice to the Philippians to forget what was behind, Christians have devised life in refuge from history. They have invented and continuously reanimated a muscular repertoire of prayers, performances, doctrines, hopes, and rituals to erase the past. The original sin of Adam and Eve is rinsed from the soul in Catholic baptism. The old self is deleted and the new one reborn in Protestant evangelical conversion. Fasting forgets food. Devotional silence forgets words. Saving blood washes away the soul's memory of sins. The eschatological future negates the psychological past. Sermonists beseech congregations to forgive and forget, and, especially, to forget one's own failings. Prayers petition for the end of memory of what is discomfiting. God himself forgets, and that is a good thing.[2] For the Compass Church of Salinas and many other Christians, what "just comes naturally to humans," memory, must be erased.

Christianity also is about remembering. There are religious calendars, rituals of remembering, catechisms, confessions, material mnemonics, bodily exercises, and fierce exhortations to nurture memory. For some scholars, religion itself is fundamentally about remembering. For them, the greatest sin is forgetting. Tradition, the bedrock of religion, is a spectacular performance of memory. Christian tradition celebrates the past even as Christian forgetting effaces it.

Christians who forget and remember are like persons of other faiths. Memory and forgetting are knit together in the lives of all humans, regardless of religion, ideology, or habits of everyday life. Memory and forgetting are always at play, conjoined in shaping what people think and do. Practically speaking, without one there cannot be the other. We forget, nevertheless, that forgetting itself is fundamental to who we are as humans. We forget that we forget. And when we do remember that we have forgotten something, we sometimes may feel blameworthy. Even as Christianity guides some American memory into the waters of Lethe, the river in the underworld named for the Greek spirit of forgetting, Americans may feel bad about forgetting.

American Christians often consciously choose to forget the American past. They have various reasons for that. And although sometimes the past just seems to fade, that, too, can be self-directed, a choice made absent the awareness of choosing. The Christian technologies that foster such forgetting are prominent in the practice of Christian faiths. Most obvious are the exhortations embedded in myriad sermons on Philippians 3:13–14 preached continuously from American pulpits from colonial times to the present. The text is forthright: "but this one thing I do, forgetting those things that are behind, and reaching forth unto those things that are before." Clergy over centuries have spun the meanings of this text in various directions as they have applied it. But interpreters always have embraced its simple core truth, that forgetting is both necessary and good. That belief frames not just a behavior but a mentality, a way of engaging the world, time, and space. It is an expression of a mentality that has flowed from the chapel into the corners of American life and back again into the practice of religion.

The religious practice of forgetting is heavily reinforced by the Christian emphasis on emptiness. American Christianities since the Spanish Main have encouraged persons to pursue the feeling of emptiness, urging them to empty themselves of self and to do so in expectation that only then can they be filled with the grace of God.[3] The practice of self-emptying, which is unceasing because it ultimately is impossible, is a nuclear Christian discipline, a chronic disposition inculcated in various ritual and ideological ways. It is a habit of forgetting the self, and, with the self, much else. It installs forgetting as a norm.

Christian forgetting is further embedded as embodied social behavior. Christian preaching in America since early colonial times characterized various social and political opponents as enemies deserving of annihilation. Picturing foes such as Native Americans as Amalekites—enemies whom the ancient Jews annihilated and "forgot," at God's command—Americans have justified genocide, and other incidences of mass violence, as necessary to moral order. Armed with Scripture, American Christians have insisted that such crusades of extermination, like the groups targeted, ought to be forgotten. Such fully enacted forgettings are additional nodes in the network of religious beliefs and rituals that constitutes a broader American habit of forgetting.

There are other ways in which Christianity, and religion in general, fosters forgetting. I address some of them in this book. The aim of this book is more specific than that, however. The discussion I broach has to do with American forgetting of race, and especially racial violence, and how religion is implicated in that. White Americans have tried for many generations to forget their genocidal campaigns against Native Americans, as well as their enslavement of Africans. They have not been successful in forgetting that brutality, in spite of the fact that their Christianity, also for generations, has trained them in what clergy limn as the art of forgetting. Consequently, white Americans are haunted by their past enactments of racial violence. Efforts to deliberately forget, in the final calculation, have not worked. And white failure to forget has contributed to ongoing cycles of violence toward racial others. While recent scholarship about Christian nationalism and Christian white supremacy has emphasized how some American Christians seek to remember and restore what they believe was an ideal Christian past in the United States,[4] I argue that their effort to forget the past is equally important, and a central component of their white nationalism.

The Trauma of Colonization and the White Perpetrator

Europeans arrived on the shores of the Americas ready to claim the land as its discoverers and its rulers. The North American British colonies strung along the Atlantic seacoast quickly grew westward, displacing Native Americans in a gradual but relentless advance implemented by vicious military interventions, treaties soon broken, and long-term attrition by starvation, transmission of disease, environmental wreckage, and cultural dispossession. With white American settlement of the trans-Mississippi, a growing sense of entitlement interlaced with destiny transmogrified more encounters into massacres. In time, the United States began outlawing Indian religious practices, a tactic that damaged all of Indian life. Other defining aspects of Indian tradition—such as the buffalo hunt for Plains tribes—no longer were possible in the wake of mass white migration. Indian families were coerced into giving their children over to boarding schools, where supervisors attempted to strip from them the remaining markers of their identity. And then the colonial past became a colonial present in which inequalities and injustice remain systemic.

Some Native Americans describe such losses as the enduring wound underlying the post-traumatic stress suffered in their communities. They relate how that haunting cultural trauma has frustrated attempts to grieve. And they report that it has been alive in generations down to the present. Some researchers believe that biological epigenesis plays a role in its transmission. The case is similar with African Americans, who incompletely mourn their losses arising from slavery and its ongoing aftermaths of white violence and cultural assault. There is much to mourn, but the means by which to mourn it are not within easy reach.

Both Native Americans and African Americans, in the face of calamity and amid a continuing predicament, have exhibited resilience. The Indian is not vanished, not a "forgotten race." African Americans have resisted, adapted, and survived. Both traumatized groups unceasingly negotiate cultural space with white power. They remain haunted, and continue to take damage from the cultural traces of colonial pasts as well as the wasting infringements of the present, some members of each group more so than others. Traumas have long-term consequences, and some of those are obvious. Some are not.

Anglophone scholarship has for several decades endeavored in various ways to define trauma and to analyze how it affects groups over time. Theorizing about trauma emerged from several areas of academic inquiry in the latter part of the twentieth century. Holocaust studies, the renewed interest in Sigmund Freud that was abetted by French incorporation of psychoanalysis into culture theory, and the waning spell of deconstructionist theory all played their parts in that endeavor, as did the war in Vietnam. Soldiers returning from the war bore their own baggage, which soon led to the coalescence of a theory of post-traumatic stress disorder (PTSD). Research in these various areas was drawn together in literary trauma theory, an interpretive foray that proved influential but, in the early twenty-first century, was undermined by critical investigation of its questionable domain assumptions and hermeneutical gaps. Widely adopted as an interpretive paradigm by literary scholars, it also proved influential in historical scholarship, religious studies, and the social sciences. Its stark differentiation of victim and perpetrator, and its tardiness in addressing trauma in colonial and postcolonial settings, however, contributed to its decline. In this book, I propose a different way of thinking about trauma by focusing on the perpetrator and the colonial, and by incorporating neuroscientific research and recent psychological studies, as well as anthropological, historical, and philosophical scholarship.

The trauma of the perpetrator is braided with the trauma of the victim. There clearly is a difference between the two, and justice requires that we respect that difference. But trauma is a psychological category, not a moral one. Trauma theory for a period of time did not address the trauma of the perpetrator for fear that it would undo the category of trauma itself, which had emerged as a matter of the victim's experience. Perpetrators may experience violence as its agents, but they experience it nonetheless. And the sequelae of that experience haunt perpetrators as it does victims. We can note that Native

Americans and African Americans report being harrowed by transgenerationally transmitted trauma, alongside present-day wrongs enacted against them. But we can register as well that scholarship has not attended sufficiently to white trauma as the other side of that same coin. White trauma, detectable as an underground river in American culture, where it sometimes is powerfully joined with Christianity and especially evangelical Christianity, surfaces at times in acts of brutality, terrorism, and insurrection. As we come to know more about how that happens, we will be better positioned to address it.

Studies of terrorism, and not of trauma theory, since the 1970s have sought to explain how and why perpetrators of terror behave as they do. That body of research, which grew rapidly in the 1990s and then especially after the 9/11 attacks, was aimed at solving the puzzle of why persons and groups committed atrocities. The sense of urgency to find the psychological key to unlock the process and open it to analysis resulted in an outpouring of research on hate and anger in the behavioral profiles of terrorist groups, as well as a keen focus on ideologies that appeared to foster those emotions. Writers identified extremist ideologies that separated the world into absolute good and evil as prompts to emotions of hate, anger, and fear, and therefore, as they reasoned, to violence. While such research sometimes made intuitive sense, it lacked precision, left gaps, and, while offering seemingly psychological explanations, typically was not well informed by academic research in the field of psychology. Such terrorism scholarship nevertheless eventually helped to shape discussion about the American historical past, as researchers began to inquire into the motivations of those who perpetrated massacres and held slaves.

Ideology and Emotion

The most obvious gap in the terrorism scholarship that sought to explain motivation was the one between ideology and emotion. Many late twentieth-century studies framed terrorism as religious performance, invoking categories drawn from monotheistic theology cum Manicheanism: hard binaries of good and evil, light and darkness, us and them. That approach, which remains a theme in present scholarship, assumed that such ideology, with its fanatical policing of boundaries, situated groups psychologically in profoundly emotional scenes that naturally were steeped in hate, anger, and fear. From there, writers argued that violence, again, was a natural outcome of such positioning. In such a scheme, then, perpetration is born of ideology, which, once digested, is transposed into emotions, and, finally, violent action. That approach is found in other writing about terrorism, war, international relations, colonialism, and racial violence.

I argue in this book that in order to understand racial violence in America, it is important not only to study religion, to understand the transmission of trauma in culture, and to closely examine the experience of the perpetrator, but also to recognize that ideology, even the most extreme, does not naturally lead to specific emotions and certain violence. Ideology is involved, and extremist ideologies especially so. But the process is more complicated than it sometimes might seem. And it is important that we recognize that fact because there is such a thing as a cycle of violence that is grounded in emotional relationships between opposed groups. That cycle often is present in genocide and other forms of mass violence, and there is a crushing need both in America and elsewhere to interrupt it.

I steer discussion away from the idea that there are certain hardwired emotions in humans that are similarly prompted by environmental stimuli across times and spaces, regardless of culture. In other words, extremist ideas do not prompt certain fully formed emotions. The theoretical framework for the hardwired position, basic emotions theory (BET), while informing much research over the last sixty years about how humans feel—and, not coincidentally, exercising a dominant influence on government-funded anti-terrorism research—is no longer persuasive. Research in a range of fields, and especially in anthropology and neuroscience, progressively is undermining the idea that all humans are born with the same fixed repertoire of specific emotions, which they socially deploy in the same manner, no matter the culture.

The ascendant alternative theory, psychological constructionism, denies that emotions are hardwired. It maintains that emotions are made on the fly, as core affect—bodily feelings of agitation or pleasantness/unpleasantness—is interwoven with cognition, in a process involving both body and culture. In such a reading of emotional response, ideology, which is a cognitive map of the world, does not naturally prompt hardwired emotions. Instead, an emotion—hate, love, anger, joy—is the product of a multifaceted process involving the interweaving of affect and cognition. That process, taking place extremely rapidly, assembles a great many component parts that can include ingredients—drawn from personal experience and cultural situatedness—of which the subject may be unaware and that can be incorporated invisibly.

Because of its foregrounding of the fluid and co-constitutive interplay of ideas and feelings, psychological constructionism offers useful perspective on how repressed experience can inform emotion. Let us take the example of repressed experience of trauma. Instead of focusing on repressed emotions themselves—something that might make sense if one were to adopt a BET approach—a constructionist approach can facilitate, among other things, a stronger focus on repressed *memory* of trauma. In so doing, it can leverage memory research that enables conceptualization of memory as both ideological and, in some measure, affectual. But it does not propose that anger repressed at the time of an event reemerges whole at a later date. Neither does it propose that repressed memory of trauma emerges outrightly as fear, or hate, or anger, or any other specific emotion. What it does do is enhance the possibilities for investigative analysis to move from repressed memory to emotion. Emotion, constructed out of core affect somatically experienced and intertwined with mental and cultural materials, can arise from repressed memory. And it does so in a process that does not leave as large a gap between ideology and feeling as does BET.

Such an approach opens possibilities for historians who can track ideas in culture more precisely than feelings. It licenses analytical forays that explore repressed memory as an experience with an affectual dimension, and it can build on that foundation to more complicated understandings of how ideology and feeling collaborate in composing emotions such as anger and hatred. There can be no certainty that specific ideas are naturally joined to distinct emotions. Context, for the individual and the group, will always shape how a memory, including a collective memory, will find expression in emotion. But it is possible to envision how memory of trauma might be culturally, and perhaps also epigenetically, coded and transmitted, in certain contexts, as core affect that presents as anxiety. From there, it might coalesce as a hope or a despondency. The situation of the person or group will be paramount in determining that outcome.

Such an approach to repressed trauma, again, hinges on research reporting that memory has an emotional component. In discussing that research in this book, I also address how memory and forgetting are interrelated, and how deliberate forgetting is pervasive in both personal life and collective life. Just as there are cultures of remembering, there are cultures of forgetting. Just as individuals intentionally forget trauma, groups build cultural technologies to collectively repress those unwanted memories. But memory rarely disappears without a trace, even amid the most determined efforts to erase it. The power of both remembering and forgetting, their durability in culture and personal life, has to do with their imbrication. In Christianity, the force of remembering is made possible by the weight of forgetting.

Again, none of this is to say that hate and anger do not play a role in religiously legitimated violence. The point, rather, is this: hate and anger as manifest in terrorism, in genocide, or in other mass violence do not spring naturally from exposure to ideology that maps an acutely binaried world. In this book about the American scene, where racism and religion are often coconspirators in violent actions, I propose that groups are *drawn* to extremist ideologies for reasons having to do with affect. Emotions such as hate and anger, including collective hate and anger, can be built out of materials that include ideas about absolute good arrayed against absolute evil. But the starting point in my understanding of ongoing racial violence in America, and its connections to Christianity, is not ideology. It is a feeling, which we might in shorthand call anxiety, a core affect, arising from the power of repressed memory of white trauma, the trauma of the perpetrator, to discomfit the white social body.

The fact of whites' recall of events that they previously had attempted to screen from memory vexes and perplexes. It is perplexing because such recall, as memory/affect, is a particularly complicated and hard-to-categorize feeling. It is what in everyday life we refer to as the feeling of forgetting. It is a feeling about not knowing, but at the same time not knowing what one does not know. It is an uncertainty, a sense of being caught between knowing and not knowing. There is something uncanny about it. It is powerful, a noetic feeling, similar to the noetic feelings that are standard in Christianity (and highlighted in evangelicalism), a sensing that something is real, in a profound, foundational way; but it is a sensing as well that is unclear about exactly what that thing is. It can be the experience of deliberate forgetting leaving a trace, a gist, in memory.

Such a feeling can have social consequences. Psychological research emphasizes that the feeling of uncertainty, of simultaneously knowing and not knowing, can undermine identity, and that in turn can have important implications for persons and groups. Social groups that experience severe crises of identity often resort to uncompromising strategies of worldview defense. Those strategies typically involve a heightened sense of boundaries, a strongly reinforced effort to police them, and an embrace of ideology that accentuates difference, locating the group at odds with others. All social groups, regardless of their status, can have that experience. I am interested in examining how a segment of the white population periodically has embraced such a program of worldview defense when they have been uncertain of their place within the society as whole. I am interested in how events occurring in the present—for example, the election of a Black president—can prompt memories of the past, including memories that the group, by cultural means, has tried to deny and bury. Memories such as slavery or the Wounded Knee Massacre, memories of perpetration of violence, still haunt, and groups haunted by them can be said to collectively experience a feeling of forgetting, an experience of uncertainty. They know genocide, but they do not know it. And they wonder about who they are and where they belong. They may drift, and they may grab onto extremist ideas to keep from drifting.

Repressed memory can impose on consciousness in various ways. The past can appear even if it was thought to be forgotten. In America, the past can reappear in the form of the Indian who, imagined as vanishing or gone, haunts white America. White Americans campaigned against Indians for centuries, reasoning that they should exterminate them, and whites legitimated that campaign with arguments derived from their readings of the Bible and other Christian writings. Ever-present in American literature, and occupying center stage in the vast national spectacle of nineteenth-century Spiritualism, the ghost of the "forgotten Indian" appeared to remind white Americans of many things, but especially the colonizers' role in decimating a people.

The Indian continues to haunt, most recently at the insurrection at the U.S. Capitol in early 2021, as we shall see. White American responses to those hauntings, like white responses to slavery, have been of several sorts. But one response has been renewed white commitment to extreme ideology. Hate and anger sometimes have followed, and, then, violence. Christianity has been implicated in that violence, not only for its legitimation of it—for the perpetrators' Christian theologizing of its righteousness—but also, and perhaps more importantly, for American Christianity's urging of forgetting on its membership. And, it has been especially implicated for its urging of Americans to forget painful memories having to do with race.

Approach and Argument

There is abundant detail about human memory, feeling, cognition, and trauma in these pages. There also is historical argument about white perpetration of violence and the ways in which religion has been involved in that, including by fostering a practice of forgetting. I have taken pains to incorporate current thinking in several interrelated areas of academic inquiry—memory studies, social neuroscience, anthropology, philosophy, psychology, and perpetrator studies, among others—and I am aware that such an approach risks, at times, distracting from the historical scene that I am sketching. But I have concluded that in this case historical analysis cannot rely solely on conventional approaches to historical sources. And so I number myself among others who have pursued interdisciplinarity because the theoretical resources and the models of analysis and interpretation within our home fields do not in themselves fit the task of delivering answers to the questions we ask. I identify as a scholar working primarily in the fields of religious studies and history, and I have in mind a readership that is interested in American religious history. But in this book I have tried also to think as I imagine scholars in other fields do when they inquire about these themes in which we share an interest, namely, memory, emotion, and so forth.

I also am aware that I have endeavored in this book to integrate research from areas of academic inquiry that do not share a uniform vocabulary, and

at times do not communicate easily with each other about the epistemological frameworks that frame their respective studies. I have made an effort to
organize my discussions of that research in a way that can maximize possibilities for commonalities to surface, and in a way that permits the assembling
of an argument that will make sense to scholars from each of those fields, but
most especially, scholars interested in religion, race, and violence in America.
I have offered my own translations of meanings of a wide disciplinary array
of academic articles and books, simplifying where I can, hopefully without
misrepresenting, and have engaged in a few places in debates that are important to individual fields. I intersperse historical writing with discussions
about laboratory experiments and philosophical investigations. As a result,
each chapter unfolds not as historical narrative but in the thinking through of
several related aspects of the overall argument of the book, some of which are
historical and some of which are not. I return to discussions of certain topics
in subsequent chapters, refining them with additional information and critical perspective. Emotion, for example, recurs, as do trauma, religion, ideology, and violence. My process has been one of layering rather than linear nar-
ration. I have aimed at keeping one foot in American history and another in
scientific and theoretical literature, although sometimes this might have more
the character of a juggling act than a dance. Bearing that in mind, and in the
interest of mapping what is to come, I offer a spare, unnuanced summary of
the central points of the argument here, in conclusion to this introduction.

   White anxiety about race is fundamental to understanding ongoing white
antipathy to racial minorities. That anxiety runs deep and is inscribed on
the very bones of white American life. It is there because whites have put it
there, in the form of memory of violence they perpetrated against nonwhites.
Whites have repressed memory of that violence, but have failed in their attempts to forget it. Christianity has played an important role in that process
of repression by promoting forgetting as religious practice. In white performances of anger about race matters, Christianity often is strongly present, not only implicitly—because it has fostered repression of memory of
perpetration—but because it sometimes also has explicitly legitimated that
perpetration. Those performances take place as repression becomes expression: white memory of violence haunts, and appears. Anger or hate ensue as
the end products of a process in which repressed memory, as intermixed cognition and affect, is experienced as something like the feeling of forgetting.
It is an experience of simultaneous knowing and not knowing—as, for example, in everyday terms, in knowing one has left the house without accomplishing some important task but being unaware of what that task might be.
It is an epistemic feeling—in this case a feeling about not knowing—that is

experienced collectively, where it can manifest as an uncertainty about identity itself. Amid such uncertainty, whites are primed to defend their worldview, and they can gravitate to extremist ideologies that offer sweeping binaried conceptions of the social world—good versus bad, us versus them—and models of strict policing of boundaries. As that experience of a feeling of forgetting is constructed into emotion within a broader context of affect, memory, and identity, hate and anger emerge as emotional thresholds that can lead to violence. Through all this, whites remain dysfunctionally attached to a group they have victimized, a fact observed even by African American and Native American writers, who, in commenting on their own experience of ongoing transgenerational trauma, have characterized the white predicament as braided with their own. That dysfunctional attachment is a platform for a new episode in a cycle of violence.

I note in closing that I write as a white academic whose ancestry includes soldiers who fought Indians in the colonial-era Northeast and the nineteenth-century West. But I do not need knowledge of such ancestry to recognize my implication in some of the history that I write about here. I discuss the situatedness of the scholar, with regard to this project, a few pages further on, but here I note two things: I recognize how I share in the benefits of whiteness that have arisen in part through whites' historical role in perpetration of violence against nonwhites, and also, I both know and do not know the ways in which my own dilemma as a white American is joined to their trauma.

Colonial Legacies

Land and Progress

The violent attempt to subvert the democratic electoral process that took place at the Capitol on January 6, 2021, attested the conjunction of race, Christianity, and violence in America. Some rioters waved the Confederate flag, which, in the immediately preceding years, had become more explicitly charged with white supremacist intention. Others unfurled Christian banners proclaiming messages such as "Jesus 2020," "In God We Trust," and "Jesus and Trump." One rioter lugged a large wooden cross while others clustered here and there to pray loudly to Jesus. Some in the mob professed anti-Semitic, misogynist, and anti-Asian views. Together they assaulted the Capitol police, causing injury and death in the course of occupying parts of the Capitol. One rioter confronted a Capitol police officer with the words: "Put your gun down and we'll show you what kind of [n——] you are."[1] Texas real estate agent Jenna Ryan, calling for the breaking of the Capitol's windows, rejoiced when the violence commenced, chanting "U-S-A! U-S-A! Here we are in the name of Jesus!"[2] For some, it was "a kind of Christian revolt."[3] In the aftermath of the violence, one of the rioters formed a local militia in Virginia to carry on the revolt. Masquerading as a Bible study group, the conspirators met secretly to assemble a large cache of explosives.[4]

One of the most visible insurrectionists that day and subsequently the most recognized was Jake Chansley (aka Jake Angeli).[5] Eventually convicted of a felony for his role, the so-called QAnon Shaman stood out against the background of rioters for his costume. In a bearskin headdress with horns, his naked torso and arms tattooed, an exotic-looking amulet around his neck, and American-flag warpaint on his face, and brandishing an American flag mounted on a spear, he struck in unwitting parody the figure of a Native American. Part of his day included praying to Jesus at the dais in the Senate.

The Cherokee scholar Joseph Pierce pointed out that while many news bureaus described the costume as "Viking," in fact, given the context of the riot, it was a condensed symbol of white claims to power that were grounded in colonial violence against Indians. Pierce observed: "I want to emphasize that Angeli is not just attempting to replicate an Indian image, but to live in Indianness as a statement of a right to this place, this country." Chansley, playing Indian, evinced a sense of primal attachment to Native Americans and their history, and a sense of ownership of the North American landmass that was bound up in that fantasy. But "what he does not realize is that this claim to aboriginal belonging is only possible because of the violent seizure of indigenous lands by the very government that he now protests." Extending that line of interpretation, Pierce suggested that "storming the Capitol was an expression of the inability to imagine a world in which white people do not automatically and inevitably wield the power over life and death in this country built on genocide and slavery."[6]

The terror wrought by Chansley and his criminal cohort instanced an anxiety that was deeply embedded in white American Christianity and that surfaced in violence on January 6. That anxiety was rooted in the long history of the white brutalization of Native Americans and enslaved Africans. Its formation began with European colonization that proclaimed the Americas a New World and progressed as settlers determined to engineer that world with the point of a sword. This book attends to that multilayered history, examining some of its episodes through a lens ground from insights of humanities scholars and scientists. At the center of that discussion is an invitation to think about religion, race, and violence in America by surveying how the lives of white American Christians and those whom they have oppressed are conjoined. The two groups are attached, one to the other. That attachment has been dysfunctional, angst-ridden, and broadly productive of serial violence. It is, as Philip Deloria wrote, a "paradox: The self-defining pairing of American truth with American freedoms rests on the ability to wield power against Indians—social, military, economic, and political—while simultaneously drawing power from them. . . . Intricate relations between destruction and creativity—for both Indian and non-Indian Americans—are suspended in an uneasy alliance."[7]

Such dysfunctional attachment is manifest especially in what Americans remember and what they forget. When Pierce ventures that Chansley, fantasizing himself an Indian, cannot remember the white seizure of Indigenous lands, the subsequent genocidal campaigns against Native Americans, and the institutionalized inhumanity of slavery, he is foregrounding the complex processes of cultural memory. Those complex processes are equally perceptible in the case of Anna Morgan-Lloyd, the first criminal sentenced in the January 6 insurrection, who related through her attorney presentencing that she had read Dee Brown's *Bury My Heart at Wounded Knee* and felt suddenly informed and remorseful for her role in the attack on the Capitol.[8] It was as if she remembered something that she had forgotten. Like Morgan-Lloyd, many other white Americans are haunted by the Wounded Knee Massacre, which wields its power because of its simultaneous absence and presence in memory.

American cultural memory, for all Americans, arises from a past of colonial exploitation of the land and its native people and that exploitation's extension into the present. From the late fifteenth century on, Europeans arrived in America intending to capitalize on its human and natural resources. As vectors of catastrophically lethal disease, outfitted with armored horses and advanced weaponry, and bearing a religious certainty that the land belonged to them, they set about to build their own worlds on the wreckage of those they destroyed. That grim program of requisition extended from the late fifteenth through the nineteenth and early twentieth centuries, and it has remained visible in regularly occurring acts of violence since that time. Just as importantly, having coalesced as structural violence, the vestiges of settler colonialism remain a cogent, albeit often unacknowledged, framework for white exercise of power. That power is felt in social minorities' experiences of a range of inequalities, in the sequelae of white prosecution of self-interested social and economic agendas.

When Scarlett O'Hara pondered her future in the closing scene of the movie *Gone with the Wind* with the words, "What is there that matters?" she heard the responsive voice of her father. Echoing over the fantasy of a beautiful slave-era South that still informs the fevered dreams of Confederate flag-waving Americans, he answered, "Why, land's the *only* thing that matters."[9] When a recent historical study expresses the standpoint of many scholars who narrate the American West by "placing Indian lands and nations at the story's center,"[10] it in turn signals a truth about the specifically material power of land that scholars of settler colonialism long have embraced in analyzing colonial pasts worldwide. That is, to speak of settler colonialism is always to speak of land, and to speak of land within a Western discourse is to imply its ownership. Land as property was a commodity bought, sold, traded, taken, and lost. For Europeans, such was the forward movement of history.

For the colonial adventurer, land transmissibility and transaction drove history. The forced deliverance of Indian lands into the juridical geographies of settlers acting as agents of the state typically was achieved in obedience to "the concept of empire as a benign and dynamic guarantor of progress."[11] That logic of progress underwrote European dispossession of Native

Americans. The racially charged principle of progress in land transfers was expressed cogently by General William Tecumseh Sherman in addressing the General Council of the Indian Territory in Ocmulgee, Oklahoma, in 1871: "Two races cannot live together in harmony; the weaker race must give way to the stronger; barbarism in this age of steam and progress must retire before advancing civilization."[12] But as Ned Blackhawk has pointed out, Indians such as the Ute initially "remained more than prepared to enter into diplomatic relations with U.S. representatives" over land claims and Indian sovereignties. They "attempted to rein in renegade warriors, to broker and then to uphold teetering agreements, and to convince their people that American promises were not fleeting."[13] In other words, the episodes of mass violence that accompanied white settlement of Indian lands were not inevitable.

In a rolling series of claims spanning centuries, whites took land for its rich agricultural value, its minerals (especially gold and precious metals), its lumber, its animal life, and the access it provided to fisheries. Whites sometimes took land by destroying its potential to support Indian lives. Black Moon, the Miniconjou Lakota leader, summarized the colonial state of affairs while addressing an assembly of Indians and whites in late June 1867: "The whites are cutting through our territory with their big roads of trade and migration. . . . They shoot our game, and more than they need; they are cruel to our people, abusing and killing them given only the slightest provocation. They cut down our forests in spite of our opposition and without offering us compensation. They are completely ruining our land."[14] This was about a century after George Washington had provided the official federal template to Major General John Sullivan on his disembarkment against the Iroquois: "Parties should be detached to lay waste all the settlements around with instructions to do it in the most effectual manner, that the country may not be merely overrun but destroyed." Washington urged that "it will be essential to ruin their crops in the ground" and effect "the total destruction and devastation of their settlements," because the national project depended on "the terror with which the severity of the chastisement they receive will inspire [them]."[15]

Continuing, Black Moon made two statements crucial to understanding relations between Indians and whites in the midst of the violence and rapaciousness that characterized white settlement of the West. For Black Moon, "We were forced against our will to hate the palefaces." He added, then: "Let us hope, let us spread a blanket over that which has passed, and forget it," while endeavoring to find a way to live together with whites.[16]

Suggesting the mingled destinies of whites and Indians, experienced as a sense of connectedness even while hating each other, and proposing that the baleful products of white colonialism be forgotten, Black Moon concisely

signaled the core of the paradoxical relationship between colonists and na-
tives. A convoluted affinity bound each side to the other even as they hated
and fought, a predicament that both sides tried to forget—for different reasons in each case, but ultimately unsuccessfully in both.

The mentality of colonization conflates land with landowner. The taking
of Indian lands was accompanied by the taking of Indian lives. The observation that "the question of genocide is never very far from discussions of settler
colonialism"[17] prompts questions about "the logic of elimination" of the native
in settler colonial enterprises,[18] and it raises the issue of how that logic was expressed in the rhetoric of colonization. For Chris Mato Nunpa, it was, in short,
"the genocidal and imperialistic mind-set present in the Euro-American population."[19] And that mindset was not just an artifact of raw calculation about
land and its possessors, but about the more complex matters of race and religion as well. As Tiffany Hale notes, manifest destiny is "an explicitly racial
concept," and "beliefs about manifest destiny, providence, civilization, and savagery were . . . profoundly spiritual in nature."[20] For Vine Deloria Jr., it boiled
down more pointedly to the fact that Christianity was a colonial institution.[21]

The European settler colonial undertaking in North America, advanced in
racial violence warranted by religious rhetoric, produced results that proved
for many Americans the philosophical truth of manifest destiny and in so
doing fed its ambitions. That project also left fissures, suspicions, and unresolved tensions, until, in time, "at some level, Americans were uneasy about
their position as conquerors who had secured assent only through the threat
of using extreme violence."[22] And that extreme violence was enacted at a great
many sites across the continent, and perhaps most vividly, for many Americans, in the tragic occurrence at Wounded Knee in 1890. The experience reported by convicted insurrectionist Anna Morgan-Lloyd in seeking clemency
before the court exemplified the popular sense that *something happened* at
Wounded Knee. But her reading could not have informed her of the extent
to which the massacre was framed by Christian rhetoric about the necessary
extermination of Indigenous peoples to make way for a Christian nation. The
170 men, women, and children cornered and then murdered from a distance
by soldiers firing Hotchkiss guns (a small canon firing antipersonnel rounds),
on a cold day in late December 1890, long had been essentialized by white
religio-political rhetoric as an impediment to divinely ordained white expansion of empire. White misunderstanding of the Ghost Dance ritual, which
had become popular among the Sioux that year, contributed to the military
escalations that culminated in the slaughter. However, it was the relentless
characterization of Native Americans as un-Christian and inferior, and the
centuries-long trumpeting of white claims of Christian destiny, that set the

frame for what happened on December 29. The Hunkpapa Lakota leader Sitting Bull, who was killed by whites days before the massacre, previously had stated that he "felt the Church was in some way leagued with the U.S. government in crushing the Dakota nationality."[23] His sense of the Sioux predicament was clear-eyed and veracious.

A Religious Enemy

The Columbian voyages began a centuries-long war between Euro-Americans and Native Americans that included a long series of atrocities perpetrated by the Spanish, French, English, and Portuguese and, in an attenuated and less systematic way, by Indians. From the time of the onset of hostilities, the machinery of settler colonialism, with its ambition, politics, technology, numbers, and religious inspiration, all but guaranteed that European claims to the space of the Americas would advance in brutal fashion. In North America the English carried with them into conquest a biblically grounded rationale that structured thinking about those encounters as a meeting with a religious enemy.

Conflict was present from the beginning. The Virginia Company succeeded in carving out a colonial beachhead at Jamestown in 1607, and within two years the English and Powhatans were fighting. Over the next decade, there were continued frictions, but also enough collaboration with Native Americans initially to inspire a congeries of ostensibly affirmative stories that included the confected tale of an angelic Indian maiden who saved the life of a bold and handsome Englishman. Regardless of whether Pocahontas was real or not, on March 22, 1622, after Indians killed about 350 settlers, things changed. In July of the following year, the English slaughtered a large number of Pamunkeys, and after that, the two sides traded murder for murder for decades.

The major Indian wars in New England followed on the heels of the massacres in the Chesapeake. In 1636 the English and their Indian allies began a campaign against the Pequots that reached its fiery apogee in spring 1637 with the burning of between four hundred and seven hundred Indians trapped inside the fortified Indian village of Mystic. Captain John Underhill, widely lauded for his ruthless prosecution of that campaign, shortly thereafter found himself in command of a Dutch force charged with leading two expeditions against Indians around New Amsterdam. His reputation preceding him, he delivered lethal blows to the Indians during Kieft's War, including a reprise of his tactic at Mystic. In winter 1644 he surrounded an array of wigwams near Stamford, burning as many as 500 Tankitetes and Siwanoys in the fire. In the words of a historian of the war, Underhill, like many of the men who had served with him during the Pequot War, exemplified the emergent theme of serial war with Indians: for soldiers who slaughtered Indians, "violence begets violence."[24]

And violence followed. Led on the Indian side by Metacom, the subsequent conflict that was named King Philip's War (1675–78) was the most destructive war in colonial New England. It pitted the Wampanoags and some Narragansetts against an English force of several combined militias and some Indian allies, notably the Mohawks. The losses on both sides were staggering, with many towns and villages destroyed and atrocities throughout. By some reports as much as one-eleventh of able-bodied English males were killed, and the Indian population of southern New England possibly was halved. The English further south meanwhile were battling the Susquehannas, but it was King Philip's War that struck so deeply into the hearts of New Englanders that it earned the descriptor "The First Indian War." From the time it was fought, and for generations following, it was, like the Pequot War, a foundational wound for the colonies that became the United States.[25] The consequences of the war were "upheaval, destruction, the centuries-long fallout of violence, and ongoing colonialism that haunts everyday habits."[26]

Without much of a pause after King Philip's War, Indians were raiding New England towns and colonists were responding, often viciously. Battles likewise continued in other parts of British North America. Bacon's Rebellion (1676) in Virginia brought more woe to the Pamunkeys, and further south, war with the Yamassees and Tuscaroras (1713) likewise ended badly for the Indians. There was the long Seven Years' War (1756–63) with the French and their Indian allies. Pontiac's rebellion (1763–64), spurred in part by the revelations of Neolin, the "Delaware Prophet," took place on the frontier. More importantly, Pontiac's rebellion opened the way for the vigilante violence of the Paxton Boys, a large militia in Pennsylvania that roamed freely through some of the colony's towns, massacring Indians with the intention to "extirpate from earth this Savage race."[27] The cold-blooded murder of ninety-eight peaceful Delaware Christians at Gnadenhutten in the Ohio Country in 1782 ordained the descent of the frontier into a fixed pattern of egregious violence against Native Americans.

In the nineteenth century that violence increasingly evidenced its genocidal intention.[28] The Indian Removal Act (1830) and the consequent Trail of Tears (1830–50) commenced a long series of violent frontier crusades in which Native American men, women, and children were massacred. A partial list of mid-nineteenth-century occurrences includes the Old Shasta Town Massacre (1851), Blue Water Creek Massacre (1855), Spirit Lake Massacre (1857), Jarboe's War (1859–60), Bear River Massacre (1863), Sand Creek Massacre (1864), Battle of Washita (1868), Marias Massacre (1870), Camp Grant Massacre (1871), Skeleton Cave Massacre (1872), Red River War (1874–75), and Fort Robinson Massacre (1879). Dozens of such massacres took place. Some involved hundreds of deaths. A Christian-flavored ideology of extermination underwrote them, until the Native American population, which had numbered 12–15 million at contact, was reduced—by disease, starvation, and war—to 237,000 by 1900.

Emergent U.S. Indian policy rested on the claim that "'wars of extermination' against resisting Indians were not only necessary but ethical and legal."[29] And Christian leaders sometimes took a central role in engineering the violence. John M. Chivington, the ultimately disgraced commander of the force of Colorado Cavalry that killed hundreds of Cheyenne and Arapaho women and children at Sand Creek, was a longtime missionary of the Methodist Church. He had a firsthand appreciation for how whites came to possess the land, and how that possessing abetted the installation of Christianity: "I suppose I was better acquainted in the territory than any man in it at the time. I had been all over it, organized churches, held religious services, appointed ministers and superintended the arrangement of Methodist Church affairs."[30] White possession of the land mattered to him, and like other missionaries, he "came to see the violence as a part of God's redemptive work among Indian nations."[31] If it is true that "without religion, the institution of war could not have thrived in American history,"[32] Chivington and some of his religious contemporaries on the frontier were foot soldiers in that project.

The religious justification of violence against Native Americans was drawn from scriptural passages and other Christian writings. At the outset of the hostilities with Metacom in 1675, with the horror of the Pequot War's human furnace still fresh in their minds, the New England Confederation had determined to wage war on the Narragansetts by appeal to religion.[33] The formal declaration stated that "It clearly appears That God calls the Colonies to a Warr" against an enemy who has joined their tribes together "as of ould Ashur, Amaleck, and the Philistines did confederate against Israel."[34] It appears to have been the first time that colonists justified war against Indians with reference to Amalekites, a people who, according to the Old Testament, had harassed and ambushed the Jews in the desert as they made their way to the Promised Land. Identified as kin to the Jews, the Amalekites raided the Jews continuously, until finally God commanded Moses to destroy them: "Now goe, and smite Amalek, and utterly destroy all that they have, and spare them not; but slay both man and woman, infant and suckling, oxe and sheep, camel and asse" (1 Samuel 15:3).

The Jews were to exterminate the Amalekites, erasing even memory of them: "I will utterly put out the remembrance of Amalek from under heaven" (Exodus 17:16). But at the same time, "The Lord will have warre with Amalek from generation to generation" (Exodus 17:16). And, crucially, the blotting out was also a remembering: "that thou shalt blot out the remembrance of Amalek from under heaven: thou shalt not forget" (Deuteronomy 25:19).[35] To exterminate but always to have war; to forget but to remember—over centuries that Old Testament message has been parsed by exegetes in many ways, but it has remained an abundantly evocative mixed message, and a compelling guide to understanding memory, violence, and religious power in America. I return to this theme later in the book, exploring in greater depth the crux of what one scholar has broached in discussing the Amalek story in Deuteronomy: "When reconstructing the past, we cannot avoid remembering and at the same time forgetting."[36]

The historian of antiquity Jan Assmann has argued that monotheism as a worldview supplied the creeping motivation for religious violence by establishing the practice of fierce denunciations of other religions.[37] Historians of monotheism have well documented how, additionally, such denunciations typically are most vehement when leveled against heretical groups, groups that can appear to be religious kin but are perceived as having turned against the consensus truths of orthodox belief. When religion and race intersect, the situation becomes more complex, but the core principle of kin endures as a component of religiously legitimated violence. It may be the case that "different people are hated and feared, but the timely antipathy against them is nothing compared to the hatreds turned toward the greater menace of the half-different and the partially familiar," who constitute a primal threat to "the tidy, bleached out zones of impossibly pure culture."[38] Roman Catholics and Mormons were pictured in something like those terms by white Protestant Christians through much of American history. Roman Catholics, Mormons, and Protestants, along with other religious groups, all pictured Native Americans in that way from the beginnings of their encounters with them.[39]

Before identifying the Indians as Amalekites, English Protestants had identified Roman Catholics that way. Catholics in England were Christian; that is, they were religious kin. But they differed as well, in a traitorous way. Conflict with Catholics was religious conflict, and English Protestants typically cited the story of the Amalekites with its justification of extermination in ongoing rhetorical jousts—and during some periods of violence—with English Catholics.[40] But once inserted into the conflict with Indians, the story became a standard way of characterizing the constant wars. Captain Samuel Appleton, a commander of the forces arrayed against the Narragansetts in 1675, wrote to a friend: "By the prayers of God's people, our Israel in his time may prevail over this cursed Amalek; against whom I believe the Lord will have war forever until he have destroyed him."[41] In 1689, preaching to soldiers setting off to fight Indians, Cotton Mather exhorted them, "Turn not back until they are consumed." He advised: "Tho' they Cry; let there be none to save them; But beat them small as the Dust before the Wind." We pray, he said, for "vengeance . . . against the Amalek that is now annoying this Israel in the wilderness."[42] In relating details of the "fight at Piggwacket" in 1725, Rev. Thomas Symmes sermonized that Captain John Lovewell, who lost his life, the battle, and a majority of his force while bounty-hunting Indian scalps, resembled Joshua, Moses's "renowned general, in his wars with the Aborigines of Canaan," the Amalekites.[43]

Jonathan Edwards, Charles Grandison Finney, Alexander Campbell, Ellen Gould White, Robert Louis Dabney, and many other religious and civil leaders of the eighteenth and nineteenth centuries wrote and preached about the Amalekites and their erasure. By the mid-nineteenth century, historians and journalists took it as a commonplace that Euro-Americans justified their wars against the Indians as an extermination modeled after the Jews' destruction of the Amalekites. *Putnam's Magazine* observed in 1857 that Christians in colonial North America treated Indians "as the Amalekites and Canaanites had been treated by the Hebrews." George Bancroft, in his monumental *History of the United States*, discerned that New Englanders assumed that they had "a right to treat the Indians on the footing of Canaanites or Amalekites." The *North American Review*, remarking on seventeenth-century English encounters with Indians in the Northeast, concluded: "Heathen they were in the eyes of the good people of Plymouth Colony, but nations of heathen, without question, as truly were the Amalekites."[44]

King Philip's War in the 1670s remained a profoundly formative experience for New Englanders and their descendants through the middle of the nineteenth century and beyond. It was a catastrophe that shaped identity.[45] But in America in retrospect it was the slaughter at "Mystick" in 1637 that increasingly came to the forefront of discussion about triumph and atrocity in war with the Indians. Edward Eggleston looked back in 1883 on the "scenes of savage cruelty" at Mystic in 1637, an atrocity, he added, that was so appalling to some of the English soldiers that "even the citation of Joshua's destruction of the Canaanites could not allay" their revulsion. Eggleston, like many other commenters, presumably had read veteran Major John Mason's *Brief History of the Pequot War*, which Thomas Prince had published in 1736 and which was republished in the late nineteenth century in a collection with several other accounts of the war edited by the Ohioan Charles Orr. Mason exulted: "Our Mouths were filled with Laughter and our Tongues with Singing." The delivery of the faithful to victory was plain: "Was not the Finger of God in all of this?"[46]

Mystic was, as historian Bernard Bailyn wrote, "holy war."[47] It was a battle, recalled Rev. Thomas Shepard of Cambridge, in which the English triumphed because of their Christian faith: "the Providence of God guided them to . . . the divine slaughter."[48] And the spectacle of human agony indeed was biblical. Captain John Underhill, one of the leaders of the attack on Mystic, reported that the greener soldiers blanched at how "great and doleful was the bloody sight . . . to see so many souls lie gasping on the ground, so thick, in some places, that you could hardly pass along."[49] The Indian allies of the English, said Underhill, cried out that the burning of the Pequot was no good, because "it is too furious and slays too many men."[50] When *The Living Age* in 1871 observed of the slaughter, "As the Israelites slew the Amalekites, so did the Pilgrims slay the Pequot," it was signaling a barely thinkable catastrophe, "the conflagration at Mystick," that nevertheless had taken up deep residence in American memory.[51]

Extermination of the Indians, a religiously justified undertaking, could take on the character of an ethical duty. Even for the explorer Peter Skene Ogden (from a family relocated from Long Island to Canada), who explored the American West and married a Nez Perce woman, Christianity and genocide ran together. He reported in the journal of his Snake River expedition of 1827–1828: "I would willingly sacrifice a year or two to exterminate the whole Snake tribe, women and children excepted. In so doing I could fully justify myself before God and man."[52] Justification soon overlapped with motive. And as the religious framing of war with Indians became a *doxa*, "exterminate" and "extirpate," in reference to Indians, became shorthand for the religiously inspired erasure of North American Amalekites.[53]

In early colonial America, the term *extirpate* was deployed largely in writing that referred to religious enemies, as in Cotton Mather's discussion of the French Royalist attempts to extirpate the Waldenses in the sixteenth and seventeenth centuries.[54] By the early nineteenth century, according to one observer, those who advocated extermination were impelled by "the doctrine they heretofore had held, viz.: that the Indians were the Canaanites, who by God's commandment were to be destroyed."[55] Indeed, in some cases Indians were thought to be actual descendants of the Canaanites—the Lost Tribes myth still holding sway in the nineteenth century[56]—and therefore a deserving target, "under the idea that they were the descendants of the Canaanites, who, by God's commandment, were to be cut off from the face of the earth."[57] When, in a gallows speech in 1766, the Indian murderer James Anen confessed that "he thought it a duty to extirpate the Heathen," he borrowed from the circulating notion of extirpation as a specifically religious duty.[58] When Henry Knox, the first U.S. secretary of war, ordered a 2,000-strong federal force into the Ohio country to punish the Wabash for their attacks on set-tlers, authorizing that force to "extirpate, utterly" the Wabash and other na-tions who were impeding settlement, his thinking, too, had been shaped by a religious logic that advocated "conquering those Philistines [i.e., people of Canaan] who have come up against us."[59]

Historian Jeffrey Ostler, in his detailed chronicling of the use of the term *extirpate*, discussed how Thomas Jefferson thought extirpation a policy op-tion, and how persons throughout government embraced it, and especially so as settlers moved westward.[60] General Sherman, writing President Grant from the frontier, accordingly urged that "we must act with vindictive ear-nestness against the Sioux, even to their extermination, men, women, and children."[61] Americans, said a writer in 1876, had set a course "to pursue them with exterminating vengeance."[62] And it was with faith in a divinely ordained scheme of things that General Jeffrey Amherst wrote to Henry Bouquet in 1763 to "try Every other method, that can serve to extirpate this execrable race.—I should be very glad your Scheme for Hunting them down like Dogs could take Effect."[63] Americans, said a Topeka newspaper, made a prayer of it: "a set of miserable, dirty, lousy, blanketed, thieving, lying, smoking, mur-dering, graceless, faithless, gut-eating skunks . . . whose immediate and final extermination all men, except Indian agents and traders, should pray for." In-dians were "the secret Enemy of Christ."[64] Or perhaps they were not so secret. William Hubbard, author of *A Narrative of the Troubles with the Indians in New England*, had scrutinized the behavior of the Indians in 1677 and discov-ered "hatred of our Religion therein revealed."[65]

In the record of violence against Indians, there is genocide, and it was plainly obvious to Indians as well as to those who prosecuted it.[66] But the na-ture of relations between Indians and Euro-Americans was, as D. H. Law-rence suggested in 1923, always paradoxical: "There has been, all the time, in the white American soul, a dual feeling about the Indian. . . . The desire to extirpate the Indian. And the contradictory desire to glorify him. Both are rampant still, today."[67] Historically there has been a dysfunctional attachment between Native Americans and Euro-Americans. Dysfunctional attachment as a concept that appears in psychological research offers some advantages for analysis when applied to the study of social groups.[68] Social groups can be said to be dysfunctionally attached when they are relationally situated to each other in a way that discloses both the connections between them—the shared norms, ideas, experiences, and goals—and the differences that cause friction between them. In some cases, there are feelings of connectedness alongside feelings of fear and distrust, a sense of kinship alongside a sense of opposite-ness. Dysfunctional attachment can manifest in various ways. In American history, the dysfunctional attachment between Native Americans and Euro-Americans manifested, at one level, as haunting.[69] And there have been other manifestations, including ongoing structural violence against Indians.

The Colonial Present

In 1960 the UN General Assembly's "Declaration on the Granting of Independence to Colonial Countries and Peoples" condemned colonialism as the "subjection of peoples to alien subjugation, domination and exploitation" and to "a denial of fundamental human rights." It likewise ratified economic self-determination, political sovereignty, and cultural freedom for all social and governmental communities.[70] Such a resolution might suggest that there is such a thing as a colonial past that can recede into invisibility. Like all legal or paralegal pronouncements concerned with social justice, it bespeaks a certain amount of reification of social processes in the depiction of colonialism as an event, a point located on a historical line, which is given shape by jurisprudential reasoning and consigned to a prison of its own toxic moment of historical occurrence.

But there is a colonial present as well as a colonial past. And that colonial present powerfully shapes the social possibilities (including the attendant material and psychological statuses) for peoples who grappled directly with the vicious tactics of colonization when the project of settlement was explicit and broadly acknowledged. The colonial present follows on that. It is a structural colonialism that survives in the aftermath of the official closing of the frontier and the resettlement of indigenes. Its pernicious effects are why Waziyatawin Angela Wilson seeks to "wake people up to the extent to which colonization and oppression of Dakota People are ongoing, even in our ancient homeland."[71]

One way of glimpsing the machinery that sustains the colonial present is to consider the simple material aftermath of the Wounded Knee Massacre, in which the ongoing dispossession of Sioux land punctuated the insatiability of imperial ambition. As much as Americans imagined the massacre as a closure of the conflict between whites and Indians, rendering Native Americans as "ghosts that haunt the American mind," the Indian did not disappear. Nevertheless, the "long sentence of pain and dispossession" continued even as Indians demonstrated resilience and skill in adapting to new circumstances.[72] The Dawes Act of 1887 ensured that land transfer from Native Americans to whites would continue in a steady stream of transactions, so that in the half century following Dawes, Indian land holdings dropped from 138 million acres to 48 million.[73] In 2013, the white owner of the site of the massacre itself placed it on the market for an asking price of $4.9 million, pointedly demonstrating the intersectionality of market capitalism and dispossession in the colonial present.[74]

Such land dispossession is one aspect of structural violence that is common to postcolonial societies, taking a variety of forms along a spectrum of material and psychological manifestations. Those range from actual state policies, as, for example, in Argentina,[75] to insidious processes of identity erasure, as in Rwanda,[76] or in the United States, where the nineteenth-century call to erase Indian identity ("Kill the Indian, save the man") was carried forward structurally into succeeding generations by the Indian boarding school system, characterized by David Treuer as "federally funded religious schools."[77] The endgame of the North American boarding schools as a colonialist machinery was, according to one scholar, not difficult to envision: "U.S. boarding schools for Indians had a hidden agenda: stealing land."[78] That judgment fits into a broader picture of the means of subjugation of peoples in colonized spaces in Africa and elsewhere.[79] Regardless of the forms it takes, such a colonial heritage is rooted in a fantasy that colonization has ended, and that the violence of colonialism accordingly is no more. And with that fantasy come the various processes of obscuration, including disavowals of violence in the past.

So, for example, the long history of conflicts between whites and Indians is not a part of a popular founding story about America. There is no popular lesson of struggle and redemption. With respect to the violence of colonial encounter, white Americans "prefer to contain it within the category of 'Indian wars,' rather than allow it to infect the grand narratives of the American Iliad."[80] And this is not to mention the deep shadow cast over the history of Indian wars by the Civil War memory industry.

Such suppression is equally apparent in the construction of Native Americans as a "vanishing race,"[81] a rhetorical turn that effectively belies the legacies of colonial violence against Native Americans. Such adumbrations frustrate understanding of the enduring structural violence of colonialism, which effects material inequalities, legal injustices, and cultural dislocations, and is manifested especially as "environmental racism and ecological genocide."[82] Glen Coultard, reflecting on the policy consequences of that sleight-of-hand, writes that "if there is no colonial present . . . but only a colonial past that continues to have adverse effects on Indigenous people and communities, then the federal government need not take the actions to transform the current institutions and social relationships that have been shown to produce the suffering we see . . . across Indigenous communities today."[83] In other words, the adverse effects of colonialism are not a reified legacy, an inherited illness that sickens the descendants of those who originally contracted it. They are much

more than that. They have become a condition of the present induced by enduring schemata that are active, dynamic, and continuous.

Indians built empires in North America. They conquered and subjugated
tribes with whom they competed for resources, they practiced slavery, they
fashioned geographically expansive cultures, and they battled colonizing
Euro-Americans for land rights and natural resources. Accordingly, they also
played a central role in the development of the empire built by those settler-
colonists, by participating substantially in the forging of the economies, politics, material culture, and lifeways of what was to become America.[84]

But unlike the case in many other regions of the world where Europeans
established colonial presences, settler colonialism in what became the United
States did not offer the possibility for decolonizing gestures because the European settlers retained power. In the extractive colonialism in South Asia,
South America, and parts of Africa—represented vividly by the mines in
the Belgian Congo and the Dutch sugar operations in Java—decolonization
amounted to a loss of the colony, notwithstanding ongoing European influence, and one that could be catastrophic for investors, brokers, settlers, and
governments' dreams. In British colonies in North America, Australia, and
New Zealand, there was no gesture of decolonization, no postcolonial moment to fix in narrative. There was instead permanent dislocation of indigenes and little motive to negotiate new relationships with them. In settler-
descended nations such as the United States, then, "as a result, the structures,
and structural violence, of settler colonialism continue to dominate the lived
experience of Indigenous populations."[85]

Certainly there is, to use a term popularized by Achille Mbembe, a *postcolony* experience of ongoing social and political decomposition and violence in states that were not established as settler colonial projects.[86] There
are structural lineages that worsen the predicament of Indigenous populations in such places just as there are in Australia or the United States. But the
character of the ongoing violence differs in some ways, and not least in that
the ordeal of Indigenous peoples in settler colonial–descended states such as
the United States is a constant witness to the brutality of the colonizer who
now holds power as resident ruler.

Resilience

Native Americans who escaped the exterminating angel of American imperialism invented ways in which to move forward as communities while located
in uneasy relationships with whites. A striking instance of survival of Native
American worldviews and cultures is the recent history of precisely that place

where white Americans previously had pronounced their requiems for Native American ways of life. The dramatic two-month occupation of the Wounded Knee site, on the Pine Ridge reservation, by a group of Oglala Lakotas and members of the American Indian movement in 1973 evidenced the durability and determination of a Native American culture that many Americans believed had passed into historical obscurity.

Wounded Knee subsequently became a symbol of Native American resistance and activism, inspiring other movements in the decades since. A central component of that resistance has been the Native American struggle to gain control of public narratives about their history. One such illustrative instance, which represents a broader array of events, involved the statue of the Spanish conquistador Juan de Onate that was installed at a New Mexico Heritage Center in Alcade in 1994. Onate, who led the Spanish colonization and oversaw the Catholic indoctrination of the Pueblos and other native peoples in the region, commissioned the military action that led to the massacre in 1599 of hundreds of Acomas, including 300 women and children. Ongoing protests from the Keres Acoma Nation and other native communities led to the removal of the statue in 2020. Native American resistance likewise forced the removal of a large statue of Onate in Albuquerque that same year, from a site that already had been undergoing transformation since installation there in 2005 of Nora Naranjo Morse's landscape sculpture *Numbe Whageh* (Our Center Place). In a United States that has become increasingly dialed in to the meanings of monuments—a "memorial mania" according to one writer[87]—and in a parlous and dug-in political environment where battles for control of national narratives rage, Native Americans in these instances prevailed. Four hundred years after the Acoma massacre, Onate and his horse were vanquished.

The persistence of Native Americans in surviving and resisting—what Gerald Vizenor has called "survivance," a "sense of native presence and actuality over absence, nihility, and victimry"—echoes in the words of Indian leaders over centuries.[88] That persistence is founded in an Indian determination to refuse objectification as victim and to insist on recognition as complexly human. In 1879, Chief Standing Bear, the leader of a small band of Poncas (whose own statue was unveiled in the U.S. Capitol in 2019), stood before the judge in his trial and in the course of a moving speech asserted: "I am a man."[89] The judge in the case, who had wept at Standing Bear's words, subsequently agreed "That an Indian is a PERSON within the meaning of the laws of the United States," and thus eligible to sue the state.[90] That it took such an exercise to secure the freedom of Standing Bear and his people bespeaks not only the enduring power of the racist and colonialist mentality that necessitated the trial,[91] but equally the "survivance" of Native Americans who had been fighting for such recognition for generations.[92]

What Joseph M. Marshall calls "the art of perseverance" among Native Americans is visible in a multitude of ways throughout North American history,[93] including in continuities in archaeological evidence.[94] North American history was not "made by white people and done to Indian people."[95] That history was made together, albeit between parties in a dysfunctional relationship, because of Indian persistence.

Indians survived by adaptation. As in all colonial contexts, there was hybridity. But Native American cultures, "dynamic, pluralistic, and enduring,"[96] often held their own in negotiating terms of adaptation, informed by what Ella C. Deloria called "a native shrewdness in meeting new conditions."[97] And they were braced as well by a deliberating approach to cultural change: "Traditions die hard and innovation comes hard. Indians have survived for thousands of years in all kinds of conditions. They do not fly from fad to fad seeking novelty. That is what makes them Indian."[98] Western theories about the consequences of mass violence, about genocide and especially as it has occurred in Africa, Australia, New Zealand, and the Americas, tend to "neglect the agency, resistance, resilience, and creativity" of peoples who have suffered that violence.[99] Theory, for example, that has diagnosed the late colonial and postcolonial condition depicted in Aboriginal and Maori literature has missed the point when characterizing that condition as "a serious ailment when in fact it has given birth to strong-lived visions of cultural recuperations."[100] That recuperative agency and resilience are most visible in how Indigenous peoples negotiate the practicalities of survival, the requirements for staying alive, protecting family and community, and communicating ideas and feelings. There has been a pragmatism to Native American adaptation.

Pragmatism underlay, for example, the Plains Indians' development from scratch of a horse culture. Reintroduced to North America by Europeans after becoming extinct about the time of the Ice Age, the horse was bred, trained, and exploited—most impressively by the Comanches—to enable Indians to compete more efficaciously with Europeans for resources. In North America, and "in the Plains in particular, tribes showed supreme adaptability, resourcefulness, and creative syncretization. They took what Europeans had and made it wholly their own." In this process of pragmatic negotiation, "the horse was the key," and facilitated a "renaissance in Plains cultures."[101] The broader cultural resonances of that pragmatism and persistence are redolent in a wide range of Indian literatures, material culture, and political organization. Writers such as Louise Erdrich, Sherman Alexie, N. Scott Momaday, Leslie Silko, and Nora Marks Dauenhauer have foregrounded it, and they, along with many other Native American writers, have braided it with commentary about healing and spirituality.[102]

Some of the most striking examples of adaptation are found in religion. For the Lakotas, engagements with Roman Catholicism were complex and enduring. Lakotas drew on the social and political infrastructures of the Catholic missions to organize resistance to land theft by whites, to cobble economic support for communities that were severely disadvantaged, and to keep their families intact. But Sicangu Lakota digestion of Catholic missionizing on the Rosebud reservation in South Dakota amounted to a restatement of Catholic doctrines and rituals "in terms of basic categories of Lakota thought and ritual." In general, Sicangus adopted "various forms of the 'white man's prayer' in purely utilitarian terms." Some converted to Catholicism while secretly holding fast to Sicangu religious tradition, while others displayed more openly their ambiguous connections with Catholic orthodoxy by pursuing their own, customized relationships with Catholic spiritual powers. Give-and-take was ongoing until Sicangus burned down the mission in 1916.[103]

The case was largely the same with the Kiowas in the latter part of the nineteenth century. They also drew options from newly introduced white inventories of spiritual practices and belief in seeking a pathway to survive in the midst of drastic changes to their way of life.[104] For many Indians, religion, in short, was a means of locating and capitalizing on spiritual, material, and cultural resources that would enhance the likelihood of survival. It often was a contest of competing spiritual visions. But, as David Martinez writes, "The conflict between Christianity and Indian religions was, on the one hand, a battle for America's soul, while, on the other, it forged a new identity for tribes seeking ways to endure as tribal peoples."[105]

Religious hybridity was especially obvious in the Ghost Dance, a ritual practiced most notably by Plains Indians and also by other tribes further west and south. Christian symbology, linguistic and material, was interwoven in the dance. Its performance expressed Native American anxieties about cultural change, hope for the future, and a sense of connectedness with, but also distance from, the U.S. government. It was partly a religious response to colonialism, an enactment of the suffering brought by colonialism but at the same time a display of adaptation and persistence. The Ghost Dance, like other religious practices, was a "central medium" through which defiance was expressed and assimilation contested.[106] The U.S. government and many white settlers found it threatening for its seemingly millenarian orientation as well as because of its growing popularity among the Lakotas. Such fears led to the Wounded Knee Massacre in winter 1890.

Historical lessons regarding the Ghost Dance and Wounded Knee include the central place of spiritual concerns in Lakota life and the fraught process of cultural amalgamation, but especially the example of persistence and survival. The massacre at Wounded Knee has long served in public imagination as the quintessential witness to the bloody vindictiveness of the settler colonial venture in North America. It became, for many Americans, "a touchstone of Indian suffering, a benchmark of American brutality, and a symbol of the end of Indian life, the end of the frontier." But it was also "the beginning of modern America" and the beginning of a path on which Native Americans embarked with a determination to remain vital and engaged. "Wounded Knee, in other words, stands for an end, and a beginning," and as such, it represents the ongoing "heartbeat" of Native America.[107] It represents survival. "Rather than submit to the negative legacy of the massacre," Michelle Pesantubbee observes, "native people have recast Wounded Knee as a symbol of resistance to historical and contemporary colonization. They have appropriated Wounded Knee as a powerful symbol for the cultural rebirth of the Lakota."[108]

The fact of Native American resilience, including the pragmatic adaptations that Indians made of white Christianity, is fundamental to understanding white American anxiety about race. Resilience has meant that Indians have survived as Indians: they are not a "vanished race." That reality reminds Americans of Indian presence that increasingly is visible—and not just to those who visit casinos or engage in debates about their legal status. Indian survival is a witnessing both of resilience and of near erasure by whites. As much as Americans may wish to forget Indians, they are prompted to remember them because of Native American survivance. The fact that, moreover, Native Americans adapted Christianity to suit the conditions of their survivance is more than just a footnote to that reality. For white Americans who have embraced a comparatively rigid Christian orthodoxy over several centuries, it has been a signal of something troubling about Indians, namely, that they both are and are not Christians. They are religious kin but equally not kin.

The Situation of the Scholar

In this book I discuss relations between white Christians and both Native Americans and African Americans. As a white scholar steeped in Western conceptualizations of academic enterprise, I recognize that I speak from an impure positioning when undertaking such a project. I do not presume to objectively define the experiences of Indians or Blacks. Nor do I intend to intrude on the authority of Indian or Black writers in broaching an interpretation of a violent American historical past and its legacies in the present. My perspective as a researcher, moreover, is in some measure influenced by my lifelong diet of historical and theoretical literature, which occasionally has rested on inapposite assumptions regarding colonial subalterns or subjected populations.

In the mid-twentieth century, the French psychiatrist Frantz Fanon resigned his hospital position treating Algerian torture victims, reporting that he found that the therapeutic practice he had learned in France made little sense in the context of colonial Africa. The therapeutics of the West, in other words, were not easily fitted to a colonial world where the political and social predicaments of the colonized framed self and identity differently than did the culture of the colonizer.[109] In subsequent decades, the core claim of that argument was progressively extended and sharpened by Indigenous writers, and applied to the enterprise of research itself. By the end of the century the Maori scholar Linda Tuhiwai Smith had articulated, in *Decolonizing Methodologies* (1999), an approach to the study of Indigenous communities that rejected research incursions by non-Indigenous scholars, who, according to Smith, were chained to categories and methods that were so Eurocentrically charged as to blind those researchers to the realities of indigenes' lives. For Smith, "the word research is probably one of the dirtiest words in the indigenous world's vocabulary."[110] In the United States, such a view, while finding a measure of traction among theorists and ethnographers who previously had warned about the research risk of desubjectification, has been visible largely in its application to the practical agenda of indigenizing the academy.[111]

Academics' thoughtfulness about the means and ends of research on colonialism, and, as I will discuss in the next chapter, about the enduring residuum of colonialism, constitutes a part of the broader "ethical turn" in academic writing since the 1980s. That turn has been felt in many disciplines, and with regard to academic investigation of many topics. It includes reflection on the position of the scholar and especially on privileged situations of scholars in their investigations of historical and cultural conflict.

One way of assaying such positionality is to draw on an approach suggesting how persons—scholars or not—can be "beneficiaries" in the sense that their comfort and security rely on the vassalage and discomfiture of others. More importantly for researchers, it is the discourse of the beneficiaries that positions them in relation to those over whom they have an advantage. Writing as an intellectual addressing intellectuals, Bruce Robbins recognizes his own entanglements with inequities of power worldwide that erase the tracks back to the distressed labor that delivers commodities to him and many others. He asks: "Who is a beneficiary?" and answers: "You are, probably." In other words, in aiming to cancel the gravity of a compromised discourse that

potentially distorts our perceptions of our research subjects, we look for of-
fenders, and "the target has to include ourselves."[112]

A related articulation of the problem of the situated scholar is Michael
Rothberg's notion of the "implicated subject." Developed out of Rothberg's
professional practice as a literature scholar and his particular interest in the
Holocaust and genocide, his broaching of the term "implicated subject" bears
the marks of the debates that have been churning within that field for decades. For Rothberg, the categories of victim, perpetrator, and bystander are
largely artifacts of a twentieth-century project to interpret the Holocaust, and
have less applicability to the topic of the colony and postcolony, which has so
impressively aroused the interest of scholars in recent decades. He offers "implicated subject" as a term that he believes more accurately captures the complex web of relationships, with their ambiguities, reversals, and contradictions, of communities that stand in fraught relationships with each other. For
Rothberg, *victim*, then, is a desubjectifying term, just as is *perpetrator*. And
while he does not advocate a dismissal of issues of justice and reparation, he
pleads for a more cosmopolitan and generic understanding of the conditions
of suffering and violence, and the roles of those actors who are in one way or
another, directly or indirectly, embedded in them. When he writes that he
intends to examine the role of persons who "occupy positions aligned with
power and privilege without being themselves directly agents of harm," he
reiterates to some extent the concerns of Robbins, but he frames his theory
more in terms of a language that responds directly to issues of oppression that
is purposeful and violent, and often involves the state.[113]

In thinking about the situatedness of the scholar, it is useful to recognize
that Robbins and Rothberg, and a number of other theorists in different fields
who have forayed in the same direction, center their critique on positionality that goes unrecognized—on scholarly unfamiliarity with legacy, benefit,
implication, and participation. Such critiques repeatedly force the issue of
the purpose of scholarship, and in the context of the ethical turn, that purpose is sometimes writ large as a matter of restorative and even, in some instances, retributive justice. The issue has been especially crucial to academic
debates about the study of trauma, including mass trauma such as genocides,
the structural violence of the postcolony, and transmitted psychological harm
of traumatic violence. But there are other reasons to think about benefit and
suffering. A potential case for reparations is not the only reason.

Investigative pathways and themes generated within the broader Western
and largely white scholarly literature of trauma and its representation—which,
as we shall see, overlap in significant ways with writing by Native Americans and African Americans about their own suffering—in some measure

have conditioned discussion about how academics approach the lives of those about whom they write. There exists a likelihood that the subsequent compromised "recovery of the voices of traumatized testifiers and texts may be at the expense of those for whom trauma criticism claims to speak."[114] In other words, how does the historian negotiate the felt duty to describe the genocidal trauma of others while avoiding burying the subjectivities of the traumatized beneath a Western discourse likely to present problems of analytical and epistemological fit?

And just as crucially, how does the white historian, as an inheritor of an anxiety about trauma that took place in the distant past, find a pathway to a standpoint that, on balance, yields compassionate and reflexive perspective alongside critical and analytical precision? White anxiety is a crucial but often overlooked part of the tangle of trauma born of violence perpetrated by whites against Native Americans and African Americans. It is an anxiety with a long arc. It is a racial anxiety, specifically constituted by a process of remembering and forgetting, of erasing and reengaging, a violent past. It is the anxiety of Jake Chansley's charade. And it is the anxiety of the other January 6 insurrectionists, with their prayers, crosses, and Confederate flags.

Trauma

Transmission of Trauma

The colonial present is constituted in social structure and in cultural ballast that weighs on American lives. It is visible in the unequal status of Native Americans, African Americans, and other groups; in the privileges of whiteness and the privations of people of color. Its injuries typically are measured in tiers of life expectancy, educational achievement, earning power, and other categories of data rendered numerically. Those data, however, are part of a larger matrix of factors, some of which are obscure. One of those additional factors is psychological cost. That cost is located among the obstacles communities must overcome in order to make their way forward in the colonial present while escaping the distress of the colonial past. Resilience is crucial to that project, but in order to understand resilience as a dynamic, variable, and sometimes ambiguous response to colonial demands for acculturation, we must dig deeper. It is paramount to consider resilience as determination to overcome governmental and social impedances to equitable sharing of material resources. It also is a project, internal to the community, designed to defeat the colonial inheritances that cause psychological harm.

The massacres at Wounded Knee and many other places, the decades-long Indian wars, and the forced migrations and starvations, among other devastations inflicted by white colonial rule, all bore psychological aftereffects. In the 1990s the psychologist Maria Yellow Horse Braveheart began describing the experience of her own community in recognizing and addressing that harm, arguing that "the Lakota (Teton Sioux) suffer from impaired grief of an enduring and pervasive quality. Impaired grief results from massive cumulative trauma associated with such cataclysmic events as the assassination of Sitting Bull, the Wounded Knee Massacre, and the forced removal of Lakota children to boarding schools." That "historical trauma," a condition transmitted "across generations," amounted to an "unsettled bereavement" of losses incurred over centuries by Lakotas.[1] It was manifest in ongoing fracturing of identity for members of the community: "The process of colonization and varying degrees of assimilation into the dominant cultural value system have resulted in altered states of an Indian sense of self."[2]

Braveheart and her collaborators drew on the upsurge in research about PTSD and the proliferating literature about the Holocaust as trauma to posit a kind of chronic trauma, "historical unresolved grief," that was "passed from generation to generation" among Indians.[3] While the "constructed 'pastness' of Native American trauma seems to make it a non-issue for many,"[4] the catalog of addictions, violence, suicide, and other destructive behaviors in Braveheart's studies evidence for her the loss of a sense of belonging, a profound rupture in the foundations of Native American community. Pursuing that theme, she proposed that Indians remained mired in grief partly because they had lost the means to heal it through spiritual exercises that had been central to their religious traditions. Those means had faded from practice as some Indian rituals were outlawed and the pressures of assimilation frustrated intentions to preserve others. Ongoing racism and oppression, moreover, made that grief always palpable. The return to traditional rituals, such as the sweat lodge and other practices, was an act of recovering identity that was thought efficacious in healing grief.[5]

Colonialism installed a system that entailed long-term psychological consequences for African Americans as well as Indians. Some scholars believe that African Americans experience the "painful—and intergenerationally transmitted and internalized—wounds caused by racist oppression" similarly to Native Americans.[6] That "woundedness of African American life" bespeaks a Black culture that might be "a traumatized site of radical dislocation and pathology." It might also be the case that such a wound lies open within "a well-functioning culture with adaptive capacities that are fundamentally healthy."[7] Or it may be that pathology and adaptation are enmeshed. Later in this book I address recent scholarly discussion about African American trauma with respect to feelings of grief and melancholy. For now, I note that much writing about African American trauma concerns itself—like scholarship on Native Americans—with the intergenerational transmission of trauma.

The broader context for intergenerational trauma includes the examples of other states besides the United States where settler colonialism was characterized by racial violence, creating painful pasts that remain to besiege the present. In South Africa, in the wake of apartheid, "unresolved trauma continues to be transmitted to the next generation."[8] There, "the piercing of communities in the past forms a transferable historical trauma leading from them to their descendants."[9] Accordingly, "much of the present understanding of historical trauma centres on the challenges necessary to disengage the interlocking components of historical trauma by seeking to understand the mechanisms through which it is transmitted and how it works."[10] In Australia, "dysfunctional community syndrome,"[11] a type of post-traumatic or "mass depression" syndrome among Aborigines is understood as the consequence of the trauma of colonization, transmitted across six generations of Aboriginal people,[12] resulting in "cumulative inter-generational impacts of trauma on trauma on trauma, expressing themselves in present generations as violence on self and others."[13] In Israel, the "trans-generational trauma" experienced by the Mizrahi minority (i.e., Jews from the "East" and especially the Middle East, as distinguished from Jews returned to Israel from diaspora in the West) mirrors the predicament of other groups in postcolonial situations, as those predicaments have gained clarity in a range of scholarly studies.[14] Scholars of colonialism have multiplied such examples many times.

For African Americans, trauma is "transmitted transgenerationally" in various ways, not least through "cryptic conversations," a means of communication that paradoxically both reveals and conceals suffering and injustice.[15] Such trauma is said to take the form of a "transgenerational haunting,"[16] arising from a "transhistorical identification with slavery and its afterlife."[17] In early statements of trauma theory, such intergenerational activity was termed "transposition, meaning that the trauma experience was transposed from one generation to another," such as from Holocaust survivors to their children, and to their grandchildren.[18] In the wake of postcolonial studies research, and with the recent ascent of fields such as African American literary history, it can appear that "the multigenerational experience of trauma across groups who experienced mass trauma is a universal phenomenon."[19] Where earlier theories of transmitted trauma focused on the Holocaust, current research centers on the aftermaths of colonialism. In other words, to return to the example of Wounded Knee, "the colonization and oppression of Dakota People are ongoing," both in the sense of structural violence and of transmitted trauma.[20] In America, it has been the trauma of race that especially has drawn scholars' attention, and, more specifically, it is the trauma of race that is experienced by all: "race in America, with all its visible and invisible history must live in part as secretly unmetabolizable trauma in any contemporary persons."[21]

In the midst of the research that finds intergenerational transmission of trauma, there have been a few studies that fail to find it. One study involving the children of Holocaust survivors found no evidence of intergenerational transmission of the parents' Holocaust experiences; children did not appear to bear the ordeal of their parents' trauma.[22] Other research in recent decades about Holocaust-related trauma likewise has been critical of claims of transmissibility for various reasons, including political reasons. In other words, there has been debate, and that debate at its most productive has led to fresh questions about how trauma can be theorized. Researchers debate how it should be defined, the extent to which it is individual or collective, its representability in literature, its theorization in humanities scholarship versus scientific studies, and the responsibilities and intentions of those who study it. It also has prompted thinking about how the experience of trauma in Native American and African American communities can be a guide to what trauma might be like for other communities, including whites who have perpetrated trauma.

Repression of Trauma

The term *trauma* is widespread in Native American and African American writing about those communities. It typically is deployed as a way of capturing something of the horror of the events that have marked the histories of those communities under white oppression and as a prompt to think about the aftermaths of those events. It is language that serves as a condensed symbolic rendering of human suffering, injustice, violence, resilience, and potential recovery. It is also a term that is heavily freighted with meanings coded in academic writing of the last half century. The term *trauma*, while continuing to demonstrate some level of serviceability in narratives about religion, race, and violence in America, is also a highly politicized icon representing vigorous debates among scholars in a range of fields.

The stars aligned for those debates in the late twentieth century for a number of reasons, and the results have ranged from researchers' flat-out exasperation with their colleagues' continued use of the term to an assortment of efforts to rehabilitate or adapt it to more precise usages in fresh contexts of scientific and humanistic research. I incline to the latter project, which I think is important because there currently are opportunities for advancing understanding of what we mean by *trauma* by examining its events and conditions in novel interdisciplinary ways. Moreover, if we were to realize any intellectual profit from canceling the study of religio-racial trauma,[23] we would have to be willing to withdraw not only from conversation in a public arena that appears content with its investment in the term *trauma*, but from engagements with current scholarly ventures, especially by African American and Native American scholars, that are bending the term to their own political purposes.[24] And the upshot of that withdrawal, if the recent past serves as any guide, moreover, could be the contrivance of a new secret language to replace it, a neoteric discourse tilting badly from discipline-specific jargon, that carries forward equally freighted notions of identity, victim, agency, and responsibility with regard to mass violence and genocide.

The problem with trauma, as some critics have enunciated it, is trauma theory. Trauma theory was an important and influential perspective taken by literary scholars beginning in the late twentieth century. Roughly coemergent with communications media fascinations with stories of childhood sexual abuse that were suddenly remembered; with a multiplying scholarship on the Holocaust and other subsequent genocides; and with widely reported discoveries of PTSD, trauma theory ascended rapidly in the topical agendas of academic societies. By the early twenty-first century, however, some scholars, sensing that "'trauma' and 'trauma studies' is pretty much exhausted as a term," began steering away from it.[25] Humanities research and especially literary studies were "seen as a kind of 'faddish' interest in trauma, or a collapsing of everything into trauma."[26] Trauma was said to be a "tangled assemblage" of interests and research programs that drew on many disciplines but had not found its root or center.[27] That seeming shortcoming (i.e., its cross-disciplinary complications) ironically might prove in the long view to have been an advantage, if discussion of traumatic events is to remain a viable component of humanistic discourse. But there was much dissatisfaction with trauma theory, much criticism not only of its sometimes skewed renderings of affect, memory, and representation, but of its strained ethical positionings as well.

For all the recent criticism of trauma theory—much of which is deserved—the fact remains that the facts remain. There are genocides and other instances of mass violence. There is suffering. There is the testimony of "a deeply subjective inner voice that *'something has happened.'*"[28] There is "an emotional response to a terrible event."[29] After genocide there is an "affective afterlife."[30] There occurs "a person's emotional response to an overwhelming event that disrupts previous ideas of an individual's sense of self and the standards by which one evaluates society."[31] Traumatization is an "objective fact."[32] And then there is the additional fact of the pervasiveness of academic discourses about historical trauma that inspire strong affirmations of its centrality to scholarship: "Trauma has become established as a unique way of appropriating the traces of history and one of the dominant modes of representing our relationship with the past."[33] If trauma, then, is one of the ways we have come to think about the past, the fact of its many historical forms and contexts suggests that we would choose well in taking a pluralistic approach in investigating it. That approach would "acknowledge both the neurobiological and social contexts of the experience, response, and narratives, as well as the possibilities that language can convey the variable meanings of trauma," and in a way that "does not exclude the fact that social, semantic, political, and economic factors are present in the experience and recollection of trauma."[34]

Trauma studies initially appeared as a theory about shock, memory, emotion, and representation grounded in theses advanced by Freud, the nineteenth-century American psychologist Morton Prince, and the psychoanalyst Sandor Ferenczi, among others, who explored the ways in which repressed memories of terrible experiences remained present in the emotional lives and everyday behaviors of people. But the central figure always has been Freud.

Research on trauma is strongly influenced by Freud's ideas about memory and its repression. Freud's study of "Anna O.," coauthored in 1895 with Josef Breuer, the physician who had treated her, aimed at understanding the origins of hysteria in trauma. Arising from Freud's pondering on that case was his preliminary articulation of the process of how the traumatic event was forgotten, became buried in memory, and after a time surfaced in a way that resulted in psychological difficulties and physical suffering for the subject.[35] For Freud, accordingly, "the hysteric suffers mainly from reminiscences."[36] By that he meant that buried trauma returned periodically as affect manifested in physical symptoms, ranging from the wiggling of arms and legs to paralysis, insomnia, language and eating disorders, and compulsive repetitions, to name just a few of the bodily signs of trauma that Freud regarded.

Fundamental to Freud's thinking about trauma and its return was his theory about repression. Freud, in fact, claimed that "the theory of repression is the cornerstone on which the whole structure of psychoanalysis rests."[37] Its essence "lies simply in turning something away, and keeping it at a distance, from the conscious."[38] Repression accordingly "is brought to bear invariably on ideas which evoke a distressing effect (unpleasure) in the ego."[39] Freud's explicit delineations of the process of repression, like his writing about many aspects of psychic life, turned on a hydraulic metaphor: "The repressions behave like the dams against the pressure of water."[40] Psychic material or, in more recent neuropsychological terms, an engram, a kind of memory, might seem beyond the reach of language, insusceptible to representation, and for that reason fugitive, unrevealed, and eerie. Freud was certain that such material was extant, however, albeit buried below the surface of consciousness, where it might build up pressure and push against the metaphorical walls that contained and sequestered it. Sometimes such material somatically confessed itself, perhaps in a slip of the tongue or a tic, even as the individual failed to consciously recognize its presence.

Before Freud, Johann Hebart (d. 1841), a German pioneer of scientific psychology, had proposed that ideas competed for attention in consciousness, with some ideas inhibiting the awareness of other ideas.[41] Accordingly, some ideas fell below the threshold of consciousness as part of that process. Freud extended Hebart's theory as he joined it to the Parisian Jean-Martin Charcot's research about the neurology of hysteria,[42] eventually arriving at the term "repression" (and the mostly interchangeable term, for Freud, "suppression")[43] to describe a process of psychic life involving a certain kind of forgetting of painful events. Framed preliminarily in collaboration with Breuer, that theory, "an extension of the concept of the traumatic hysteric,"[44] addressed the problem of "patients [who] have not reacted to a psychical trauma because the nature of the trauma excluded a reaction, as in the case of the apparently irreparable loss of a loved person or"—and this is important for understanding the inhibitive potentiality in social institutions and customs—"because social circumstances made a reaction impossible."[45] And then, Freud concluded, there was another possible reason: "or because it was a question of things the patient wished to forget, and therefore intentionally repressed from his conscious thought."[46] That last option has been especially germane to subsequent research.

Freud's theory of repression included the foundational provision that a person did not actually delete an experience from memory. And a repressed memory might sometimes burst through the dam of repression and find its way into behavior, characteristically through bodily expression, in fits or aches, dizziness, or unwonted speech. But patients labored to prevent such breaches, by practicing a routine of mental hygiene that later brain science confirmed as common: "One phenomenon that is not in dispute in the disputatious literature on traumatic memory is that patients vigorously try to avoid thinking of traumatic materials."[47] Yet what is left in the unconscious in such cases? What arises from repressed trauma to prompt behaviors that often do not comport with recognized standards of thinking, feeling, and doing?

People are wired with "motivated forgetting systems" that reduce expressions of memory. There are neurobiological models for that process. For now, it is useful to keep in mind that there is a growing body of scientific research that tracks the pathways between the neocortex—the "rational" or "thinking" region—which is located across the upper parts of the brain, and the limbic system, including the hippocampus and amygdala—sometimes called the "emotional" or "feeling" brain—which is positioned below the neocortex. Such research is often conducted with functional magnetic resonance imaging (fMRI) technology, which allows glimpses of increases and decreases of blood flow in the various parts of the brain. Sometimes positron emission tomography (PET) scans, which map, especially, metabolism of some sugars, are involved. That research has delivered evidence of adaptive behavior

involving suppression of memory of experiences through tracking of neurological communications between and across the neocortex and the hippocampus. Some research in that area, for example, has focused on the subgenual anterior cingulate in Brodmann Area 25 of the cerebral cortex—a part
of the brain on the underside of the cortex proximate to the amygdala and
hippocampus—revealing evidence that the area is a sort of governor of the
limbic system,[48] a field manager and coordinator of affect and thoughts, and
"centrally involved in repression."[49] Along with the ventromedial prefrontal
cortex and the orbital frontal cortex (located in the frontal lobes of the brain),
the subgenual cingulate is involved especially in "suppressing primitive affect."[50] The research in this area is extensive, but in short it is fair to say that
emergent science regarding the workings of interrelated brain structures offers important support for Freud's theory of repression.

Put in lay terms, the thinking brain and the feeling brain (a distinction
that in itself is of limited usefulness) talk to each other in managing traumatic
memory. Accordingly, "in healthy individuals, modulating hippocampal activity during suppression might disrupt conscious memory, leaving perceptual, affective, and even conceptual elements of an experience intact," as "unconscious remnants of a suppressed memory," which "may persist and harm
mental health." That is, the cortex and limbic systems are systematically interrelated in such a way that core aspects of an experience, while not available
to consciousness, remain active as suppressed memory in the unconscious.
It is possible as well, however, that such adaptive behavior includes a longer-
term process for increasingly powerful inhibitory control of suppressed material through activation of mechanisms that are set in motion by cues from
a person's environment. Something like a picture of a loved one, a performed
song, or the smell of gunpowder might cue the process of regulation to more
forcibly repress memory. Such mechanisms suggest "the existence of an inhibitory control process that directly targets neocortical traces reactivated by
cues and that may undermine unconscious expressions of memory." That is,
the brain might in some cases achieve an assemblage of neural pathways between the neocortex and limbic system that effectively defangs the process in
which traces of trauma are "bursting through the dam."[51] The brain can build
the dam stronger.

But again, what remains in the unconscious during repression? What are
"traces" of perceptions, of memory, of feeling? There are different kinds of
evidence of each of these types of traces, and that includes neuroscientific
studies that focus on emotion alongside cognition. Indeed, the extant traces
might be composite constructions: studies increasingly point to such traces
as amalgams or *assemblages* of cognitions and feelings. In view of the fact that

scientific "evidence that unconscious emotion exists, at least in some forms, is now fairly strong,"[52] it is possible to appreciate that while common thinking about emotion considers it a highly visible, highly perceptible experience that might lead one to jump for joy, crumple in heartbreak, or fight in anger, cognitive neuroscience has shown that implicit processes—that is, camouflaged processes—that involve cognition also are present in emotional life.[53]

To speak of implicit knowledge—such as knowing how to ride a bicycle, or, for sociologists, for example, how culture is implicit in social networks[54]— is a way of saying that "we know more than we can tell."[55] It is a concept that has been fundamental in neuroscience research and has been adapted by humanities researchers and social scientists to their own agendas in recent decades. Emotion by the same token can be something like "implicit." The same networks of brain activity involved in implicit knowledge also are involved in tacit emotion. There can be collaborations between hidden knowledge and hidden feeling. What is repressed is not just a cognition, and not just an emotion, but an amalgam of the two.

People can be anxious, angry, or afraid and not be conscious of that. People can feel more than they can tell because they experience "unconsciously generated emotion."[56] Similarly, people may not remember something that has been repressed, yet experience an emotion in connection with implicit memory of it. In other words, "emotional response can serve as an index of implicit memory. That is, subjects can display emotional responses attributable to some event in their past they do not remember."[57] The unconscious emotion people experience and the cognitions they repress both are part of a process by which people construct their lives, how they make stories of who they are, and why they do what they do. Life is invented on the run and repressed material shapes self-consciousness and self-expression as parts of that process of invention. "The laboratory and the clinic have converged on a simple but fundamental insight" about repression: "We structure our fragmentary reality by omitting from and elaborating on our meager scraps" of information and feeling.[58] Emotions, like cognitions, are shaped and reshaped, consciously and unconsciously, as environmental stimuli prompt adaptive behaviors. Repression is a regulatory mechanism that abets that adaptation.

Trauma Theory

The theory of repression was a keystone concept for Holocaust studies of the late twentieth century that focused on trauma. But such studies were less interested in repression as a process involving ceaseless innovation and reconstructions as persons made their lives than as a means of preserving an experience in amber. Scientific investigations of repression—its processes, causes, effects, and linkages to other mental mechanisms—had a different agenda than the work of Holocaust historians and interpreters of its aftermath. The latter fashioned theory about violence, memory, and repression in investigating Nazi-era genocide and other instances of mass violence in places such as Armenia, the Belgian Congo, Uganda, the Balkans, and Cambodia. Groundbreaking historical research on the Holocaust and memory by Dominick LaCapra, Shoshana Felman, and Saul Friedlander, together with the subsequent "colonial turn in Holocaust studies,"[59] was creative and provocative, and especially so when it drew on the psychoanalytic and deconstructionist writings of theorists such as Jacques Lacan and Jacques Derrida.[60] Such trauma scholarship was clustered, initially, around a therapeutic approach to trauma, and included for some a rethinking of empathy—"a term that has a history both in historiography (or metahistory) and psychoanalytical literature"[61]—as a narrative strategy that represented the nearness of a subject yet insisted on distance.[62] That therapeutic approach, which influenced the work of historians, was itself indebted specifically to the emergence of paradigms for PTSD that were developed in concert with medical programs for treating traumatized individuals.

The diagnostic term *post-traumatic stress disorder*, a condition now broadly applied to psychological trauma patients, arose in clinical practice involving soldiers returning from war.[63] Soldiers suffering from PTSD spoke of it as a haunting, a trace of something they experienced in war that is present in memory but, as research for decades asserted, can barely, if at all, be spoken of. The concept has been in circulation for over a century, elaborated largely with regard to the experience of soldiers in combat. In World War I it was called "shell shock," in World War II, "combat fatigue," and in 1980 the American Psychiatric Association, in referring to the psychological state of Vietnam War veterans, began to call it post-traumatic stress disorder (*Diagnostic and Statistical Manual [DSM]–III*). The study of PTSD in Vietnam War veterans focused especially on the delay between the traumatic event and its subsequent effects on behavior—PTSD was for a time called "delayed-stress syndrome"—and how combatants experienced repression of the memory of the catastrophic event.[64] In the 1990s, the extension of the term to describe the suffering of child abuse, rape, and incest victims, as well as others who had experienced physical violation, led to the coalescence of trauma studies as a subfield pertinent to research in a range of academic specialties.[65]

The American research venture (subsequently haphazardly exported to other English-language nations) that came to be known as trauma studies emerged from the background of Holocaust and genocide studies, PTSD research, and psychoanalytical theories of hysteria and repression. Its nativity in literary studies ensured also that it was steeped in some of the methods and approaches current in that field at the time. Its rapid ascent to strong visibility in panels at meetings of academic societies, in conferences built around its agendas, and in university curriculums and the training of doctoral students, evidenced its strong pull on a generation of scholars who were at the same time discovering that they were uneasy with the deconstructive theory that had swept through English departments in the United States in the latter part of the twentieth century.

The thinking of Paul de Man, Lacan, Derrida, and other European deconstructionists increasingly appeared to offer a rather limited horizon of possibility for scholars who bore a sense of duty to construct as well as deconstruct. That is, there was an "ethical turn" taking place in many fields that was predicated on commitments to civic engagement and political relevance.[66] It grew out of an assortment of intellectual and political backgrounds, including the development of a more robust identity politics in academia, which abetted the project of speaking for one's community, of resisting untruth and inequality, but also demanding that certain concepts of justice, fairness, respect, and even empathy be rehabilitated within academic discourse.[67] The ethical turn questioned the relativist, textualist, and anti-subjectivist perspective of deconstructive critical theory, and weighed the meanings of Martin Heidegger's Nazism, and de Man's anti-Semitism, which was discovered in 1987. It was "a move away from 'theory for theory's sake,' and made the argument that theory 'should mean something.'"[68] It asked, "Can the Subaltern Speak?" and was a part of the rise of postcolonial studies in particular and the morphing of critical literary theory into an ethical-political discourse.[69] The burgeoning scholarship on the Holocaust was one marker of that ethical turn. So also was the rising concern about repressed trauma, which was thought in many cases to reveal an injustice that had occurred, and called for a project not only to enable healing in the traumatized but also to enable communities to confront their traumatizers.

In a perverted performance of those ethical impulses, the frenzy about satanic child abuse of the 1980s,[70] which featured harrowing tales of recovered memories of sexual assault, burst into the media and burned brightly before academic research eventually demonstrated the spurious foundations of many of those cases.[71] That development, however, also prompted within academia (and to some extent outside of it) the devolution of debate into all-or-nothing positions regarding trauma and repressed memory, so that hard lines sometimes were drawn between those who found evidence of repression of memory persuasive and those who did not. Scientific evidence was marshaled on each side.[72] That evidence eventually ranged from neuroscientific and epidemiological research suggesting that most people exposed to trauma do not develop PTSD[73]—and that PTSD was not a "discovery" but a construction[74]—to reinforced calls for a phenomenology of repression in which "the body keeps the score."[75]

But some also importuned that "it is unfortunate that the war over so-called repressed or recovered memories has forced the two sides into such irreconcilable positions" and urged that "finding the middle ground is the only way there will be justice for all."[76] In the upshot, the topic of repressed trauma and the search for justice that was related to it (but not always legibly) remained appealing to scholars for its expansibility to topics within their fields, and because it appeared to offer at least partial escape from the ethical ennui begat by deconstructive critical theory.

Against this background, trauma theory formed within literary studies. Its herald was Cathy Caruth, who complained that "recent literary criticism has shown an increasing concern that the epistemological problems raised by poststructuralist criticism, in particular deconstruction, necessarily lead to political and ethical paralysis."[77] Caruth introduced the term "trauma theory,"[78] and, drawing on a range of psychoanalytic literature and deconstructive criticism and on Holocaust studies such as Felman's, observed of trauma how "its very unassimilated nature—the way it was precisely not known in the first instance—returns to haunt the survivor later on."[79] For Caruth, persons suffering from trauma were unable to integrate their experience into consciousness. Trauma, which was never properly registered in conscious memory, lay buried in the unconscious, breaking forth occasionally to cause trouble and pain. Trauma was "an overwhelming experience of sudden or catastrophic events in which the response to the event" is profound and typically "delayed, uncontrolled, and repetitive."[80] Such an approach reiterated parts of definitions offered by prior theorists of trauma, including the psychoanalytical affirmation that trauma is "an event in the subject's life, defined by its intensity, by the subject's incapacity to respond adequately to it and by the upheaval and longlasting effects that it brings about in the psychical organization."[81]

Building out the concerns native to her area of academic expertise (literary criticism and the poetry of William Wordsworth) Caruth focused her attention on the representability of trauma. She held that unassimilated trauma—meaning a failure to cognitively formulate and remember it as an event—posed difficult problems for the critic because trauma as such resisted representation. How could one talk about it? How could one write about it? How did the critic identify it in literature? How does an author relate it in fiction? Her model of trauma accordingly emphasized the mimetic, meaning that trauma, while not integrated into the cognitive system and therefore un-representable in language, is detectable in mimesis, the imitative repeating or "reliving" of the source event. That imitation, which is another way of saying that the body "kept the score," disclosing the event in various species of so-matic display, might take the form of fidgeting, hiccups, trembling, insom-nia, addictive behaviors, erratic speech, or—Caruth draws here especially on PTSD research—flashbacks, hallucinations, and nightmares. In such a way trauma defeats its own narrativization, as mimetic representation replaces an understanding of trauma as available to memory through conscious imaging and language.

There are several issues that have come to the forefront of academic de-bates about trauma theory that matter for my general discussion of the allied topics of affect, memory, and violence. Attending here to those issues can an-ticipate how my subsequent related discussions about memory and forget-ting, individual and collective trauma, perpetrator and victim, and cognition and emotion have faced similar challenges in theorizing.

First, there is the matter of the relation of affect to cognition. A recurring criticism of trauma theory is that it tended "to reject the idea that trauma and the affects involve any kind of cognition and to treat them instead as physiological processes of the body." Trauma theory was grounded in the trust (subsequently reinforced by emerging "affect theory") that "the affects are fundamentally independent of intention and meaning because they are material processes of the body" within an interpretative scheme that pos-its "a radical separation between the affect system on the one hand, and in-tention or meaning or cognition on the other." For scholars seeking a way in which to ensure that ideas and meaning remained at the center of scholar-ship, trauma theory—in spite of the protests to the contrary by some of its early practitioners—thus operated contrary to what they thought theoreti-cally useful, by encouraging research "to shift attention from the level of polit-ical debate or ideology to the level of the person's subliminal or sub-personal material-affective responses."[82] Such criticism, focused on trauma theory's re-fusal to allow for conscious memory of trauma, gestured to an alternative. It teased about the possibility of a foundational linkage between hidden feel-ings associated with trauma and conscious recounting of the experience of trauma.[83] Writing about trauma subsequently began an irregular retreat from the radical distinction between affect and cognition. That occurred even as a particular kind of "affect theory" itself began to surge, bringing with it a will-ingness to think of affect as prelinguistic and somatic, separate from ideol-ogy.[84] The point here, for now, is that there is a pathway to rethinking how the experience of trauma can involve an interrelationship between cognition and feeling. There is a middle ground for thinking about trauma, perceptible in neuroscientific studies as well as in sociological and historical research.

Second, trauma theory offered a view of a traumatic event frozen in time. The intensity of the experience and the failure to cognize it, to cognitively record it in a way that enabled conscious recall and reflection, ensured that the event itself was held in the psyche in a pristine condition and would break through into behavior somatically in the form of various kinds of physical disturbances now and again. The "memory" of trauma, then, sequestered from other memories and immune to weathering and alteration arising from contact with other cognitions, theoretically remained intact, unaltered by the dynamic interaction between memories, ideas, and feelings that conditioned other memories and that shaped and reshaped memory as a whole over time. That claim, advanced in several disciplines, has been highly contested: "How victims remember—or forget—their most horrific experiences lies at the heart of the most bitter controversy in psychiatry and psychology in recent times."[85] That controversy was warmed by research since the 1990s that evidences that many sufferers of PTSD in fact can remember the events that were traumatizing to them. A major psychological study concluded that "people remember horrific experiences all too well. Victims are seldom incapable of remembering their trauma."[86] Persons can have trouble remembering traumatic events, and can experience pain in so doing, but research on PTSD, for example with Vietnam War veterans, has offered strong evidence for remembering rather than amnesia.[87] Trauma, moreover, has been characterized less as an involuntary amnesia than "as a *process* of active forgetting."[88] When traumatic experience is imagined as stuck in a moment of its happening, its aftermath can have no "after," except as mimesis, so that, "put another way, the privileging of trauma precludes the historicisation of memory."[89] It takes trauma out of the picture for historians and others who endeavor to make sense of its role in shaping events in the present. Again, there is the question of representation: If there is no memory of trauma, how can we write about it? How can it be situated in a history of a people or place if it is outside history? How can we understand how memory of trauma and construction of its meanings might change over time?

Third, trauma theory of the sort born of literary studies in the 1990s was geared to critical analyses of literary texts. It broached a way of reading novels, essays, poetry, and memoir. And it shaped the concerns of the American novel.[90] It foregrounded the psychological aspect of trauma—the experience of trauma as something "real," as something, to borrow from Lacan, "which resists symbolization absolutely."[91] Or put another way, in terms of critical theory, " 'real' refers to the state of nature from which we have been forever severed by our entrance into language."[92] The occult psychological was for trauma the locus of the reality of trauma, where it rested frozen and unrepresentable. Such a view, however, caused problems for research that sought to cleave to the spirit of the ethical turn because it severed trauma from political realities that conditioned the worlds in which trauma sufferers lived. How could trauma be relevant to praxis if it was unrepresentable? The Caruthian trauma paradigm "tends to psychologize, and therefore, potentially, depoliticize the discussion and analysis of socio-historical phenomena and their representation."[93] It slips the particularities of lives and the variegated social-historical contexts that frame loss and in so doing risks making all of history trauma, a universal experience of wounding.[94] It deauthorizes exploration of the ways in which trauma is mediated by shifting discourses, material inventions, and the gravity of institutions. It likewise bears the mark of a Western way of thinking about trauma that elevates "individual psychology and intrapsychic conflict" over environmental factors, social and historical factors, and "the collective or sociosomatic self often found outside the West."[95]

The preoccupation with the fugitive psychological in trauma theory, moreover, risked overlooking "insidious trauma," or "structural trauma," which is a chronic condition of suffering, as distinguished from "punctual trauma," which is acute and located in a single event.[96] Insidious trauma is "a continuing background noise rather than an unusual event."[97] Just as there is a structural colonialism that makes a colonial present, there is traumatic experience that is not limited to a moment, not engraved on the body in a flash of affliction and then lost to amnesia. It is possible to speak of "a spectrum of traumatic disorders, ranging from the effects of a single overwhelming event to the more complicated effects of prolonged and repeated abuse."[98] When an obscure psychological condition is made the marker of a pristine and ahistorical trauma (and therefore, as noted, a universal for history), the chronic suffering is evacuated from the theory: "Routinely ignored or dismissed in trauma research, the chronic psychic suffering produced by the structural violence of racial, gender, sexual, class, and other inequities has yet to be fully accounted for." That badly undermines "the usefulness of trauma theory as we know it for understanding colonial traumas such as dispossession, forced migration, diaspora, slavery, segregation, racism, political violence, and genocide."[99]

Understanding insidious trauma, similarly to understanding ongoing colonial trauma, requires the kind of distanced empathy that I have mentioned previously. But more than empathy is required. There is the fundamental question of how to speak for the traumatized in a way that does not discursively deauthenticate them as subjects. If trauma theory emerged in part from academic yearning for ethically oriented "theory that mattered" that could support a range of political agendas (a bridge too far for it in the end), it stumbled in coming to terms with the quandary of how the voices of those who experienced trauma could be both heard and uncensored in representation wrought by the hearer. There are questions about how trauma research grounded in the trauma paradigm of late twentieth-century American literary studies, which participates in a discourse of power that may hurt those it studies, could ethically progress. There is a confound in that such research "can easily appear callous and unethical in a context where the audience is being asked to bear witness to unspeakable sufferings,"[100] where "survivors are pathologized as victims without political agency, sufferers from an 'illness' that can be 'cured' within existing structures" of institutionalized medicine that speak, themselves, the language of dominant power.[101] There is concern about how "the survivor's experience has been completely replaced by the experience of those who come into contact with the survivor's testimony," so that "the appropriation of survivor experience and its reduction to metaphor is a crucial component of the process of depoliticizing the survivor and then medicalizing her condition."[102]

These concerns bring us back to the discussion of trauma among Native Americans. That trauma, begun virtually at contact, intensified throughout the colonial period and extended into the present. Native American scholars and activists have employed *trauma* widely as a term that helps to construct the meanings of suffering and resilience, subjection and liberation. The term also occurs widely in the historical writing of African Americans. Clearly, it expresses something crucial to those communities' self-understandings. Accordingly, it is important for a researcher like myself to find a critical threshold from which to step forward into understanding those meanings in a way that does not invoke the problematic baggage of trauma theory. My description here of some of the problems involved in that is a pathway toward indicating that my own discussion of trauma will depart considerably from the Caruthian model, which has held sway in the humanities for an extended period of time. My reconsideration of trauma theory draws on my awareness of the contexts in which Native American and African American writers and activists have deployed the term, and it borrows from their insights about repressed grief, melancholy, and violence that arise from their lives within those communities. I take a "pluralistic approach" to trauma theory that acknowledges "both the neurological and social contexts of the experience, response, and narratives, as well as the possibilities that language can convey the variable meanings of trauma."[103]

Perpetrators

Understanding something of the trauma of Native Americans and African Americans, and surveying theory that can be useful in that venture, comprise the first step toward investigating white racial trauma. That investigation can be grounded in the observations of Indian, Black, and white writers alike that whites remain attached to groups they have dominated and traumatized, and that such attachment is dysfunctional and can prompt repeated episodes of violence toward Indians and Blacks. Such investigation, while attending closely to feeling and cognition, also must take seriously the process of repression and, as part of that effort, directly address the topics of remembering and forgetting.

One leitmotif in literary trauma theory studies is that a traumatized person is stranded between forgetting and remembering. Unable to articulate in words the traumatic experience, a person performs a memory of it in an affect-rich communication. There is a paradoxical relationship between mimesis and antimimesis, between self-aware representation of the traumatic event in language and its presence in memory as mediated by feeling behavior that unconsciously imitates or identifies with the event. Traumatic memory evidences the complex, even paradoxical, relationships between representation and affect, presence and absence in memory, and past and present. Another motif in late twentieth-century trauma theory is that the perpetrator is all but erased from the calculation of suffering.

A critical reconsideration of trauma theory raises the issue of the role of the perpetrator. In twentieth-century Holocaust histories and literary studies the common distinction was between victim, perpetrator, and bystander. That scheme has been challenged by scholars working in a number of areas, including postcolonial studies scholars, who have emphasized the role of structural trauma that is wired into the social system and continues to do harm in the postcolonial setting. Some literary studies researchers have integrated that insight into their own method, resulting in fresh terms, such as "implicated subject," to identify the range of parties involved in various ways in punctual and insidious trauma.[104]

Vine Deloria Jr.'s remark that Indians and whites "were somehow destined to be each other's victims" prompts reflection about the way in which the different parties involved in traumatic events and aftermaths are engaged.[105] Specifically, it begs the question of how a perpetrator experiences those events in relation to how the victim experiences them. Such a question, and other related ones, are at the core of perpetrator studies as it has emerged in recent years as a field of academic research.

As publications in the field mount, it appears that "perpetrator-centered research is truly having a moment."[106] In a wave of books and articles, including in the *Journal of Perpetrator Research*, which was founded in 2017, scholars have broached new interpretations of the motives and behavior of perpetrators. They have investigated the actions of perpetrators with respect to contexts previously neglected, and in so doing have overturned previous approaches that centered the moral status of the perpetrator. It is fair to claim that "the emerging multidisciplinary field of perpetrator studies promises to deepen our understandings of the psychology, sociology, politics, and ethics of perpetrator accountability and restoration."[107] Perpetrator studies has affirmed that "the time has come to discard any seemingly unambivalent dividing line between 'perpetrators' and 'victims' that seeks to enable distinct categorization," and to embrace "a transgressive model of perpetration."[108]

The new focus on the perpetrator has begun to influence thinking about trauma. For example, the historian Dominick LaCapra, who is known for his studies of the Holocaust, violence, and trauma, initially was reluctant to broach narrative that would give the appearance of recognizing the trauma of the perpetrator. He argued initially that the "undercutting of binary oppositions is insufficient" because it would entail "deconstructing the opposition . . . between perpetrator and victim."[109] Writing a decade later, in 2004, he asserted that "Nazi ideology and practice were geared to creating perpetrators able to combine extreme, traumatizing, radically aggressive acts of violence with hardness that . . . foreclosed traumatization of the perpetrator."[110] LaCapra nevertheless at the same time was beginning to lean toward the "possibility of perpetrator trauma,"[111] and by 2016 was complaining that "the transgenerational transmission of trauma to descendants and intimates of both survivors and perpetrators" was "under-investigated."[112] His intellectual evolution, which was a zigzag line more than a linear development,[113] was influenced[114] by research published in 2010 that detailed how trauma was transmitted intergenerationally to perpetrators of mass violence.[115] In the meantime, other scholars were variously advancing the case for studying perpetrator trauma in the spirit of resistance to the "Manicheanism which underpins the culture within which trauma has gained ground—a culture of pure innocence and pure evil and of the 'War Against Evil.'"[116] Scholars called for a "long-overdue conversation about perpetrator trauma" that "recognizes trauma as a neutral, human trait, divorced from morality."[117]

In *Moses and Monotheism* (1939), Freud argued that those who followed Moses out of Egypt murdered him—another figure taking his place eventually as a second Moses—and that the perpetrators suffered guilt passed down through generations as a result.[118] One interpreter of Freud has summarized

that interpretation as Freud's lesson in "the traumatization of the perpetrator."[119] It is a lesson that was lost in the war years immediately following publication of *Moses and Monotheism* and in the outpouring of studies of the
Holocaust in the decades after the war. But the idea of the traumatized perpetrator recurred, so that by 1995 Desmond Tutu could address the South African Truth and Reconciliation Commission and observe that "every South
African has to some extent or other been traumatized. We are a wounded
people . . . we all stand in need of healing." Recognizing such a truth was a
necessary first step to ensure that "the ghosts of the past will not return to
haunt us."[120]

Some academics invested in the study of Holocaust trauma resisted, as
noted previously, the characterization of the perpetrator as a traumatized
person. The politically fraught context of trauma studies was so imposing
that "one might well ask if there exists an unwritten but nevertheless powerful taboo that prohibits or at least regulates representations of perpetration."[121] Most conceptualizations of trauma were committed to a view of it
as the experience of a victim, and were focused on finding ways to enable
trauma victims to voice their role as witness to the event. To facilitate the
voice of the perpetrator seemed wrong for a tangle of reasons, including the
risk that it would place the perpetrator on an even status with the victim and
in so doing diminish the significance of the victim's voice and trauma. The
constructed role of the researcher was, for many, enmeshed with the predicament of the victim, so that allowing a perpetrator to speak "violates their
solidarity with the victim."[122] There was concern, moreover, that a broader
equalization of the moral statuses of perpetrator and victim could take place,
presumably entailing consequences for determining accountability and ad-
ministering justice.

In treating trauma as a psychological category rather than a moral one,
new scholarship on trauma offered a number of insights into why in practice that approach was preferable to one that sharply distinguished perpetrator from victim. A study of the Khmer Rouge torture center S-21 concluded
that the characterization of the perpetrator as a "monster" tends to "natural-
ize" genocidal violence, casting it as the handiwork of a subhuman creature
or the sadistic practice of an extreme psychological deviant.[123] That tendency,
present in "Manichean" approaches to trauma studies, can arise from monotheistic conceptualizations of good and evil.[124] (Partly for that reason, many
perpetrator studies addressing mass violence—which thoroughly distinguish
the perpetrator from the victim—have been strongly shaped by their focus
on religious terrorism.)[125] But instead of constructing the perpetrator as a

monster, a "consensus in the interdisciplinary literature has emerged that the participants in genocide are neither demographically nor psychologically aberrant, they are *ordinary*."[126] Accordingly a growing number of studies argue that perpetrators, with occasional exceptions, are best approached as "ordinary people."[127] The purpose is "not to exculpate but to understand them."[128] Perpetrators are "complex humans" living complex historical scenarios.[129] That complexity must be acknowledged and moral judgment must be at least temporarily bracketed because "it is difficult to understand any human phenomenon at the same time that one is condemning it."[130] But one must proceed with caution, because there nevertheless is "ample reason to fear that understanding can promote forgiving" of a sort that could lead to the loss of crucial lessons about accountability and justice.[131]

The ongoing conversation about condemning versus morally bracketing perpetration of mass violence raises a further issue. If a white scholar like myself approaches the history of violence against Native Americans and African Americans abundantly fortified with empathy for the victim, are there costs in terms of intellectual honesty or research ethics? That is, do "we effectively deny our own complicity in violent histories and our own capacity for evil" when "we only ever identify with victims"?[132] Do we risk, at the very least, rigging a research agenda founded in an essentialized understanding of victim that distracts us from our own agency and potential status as a beneficiary of historical genocide?[133] When we overlook the perpetrator do we overlook ourselves?

Ambiguating the categories of victim and perpetrator is not an entirely new project. Auschwitz survivor Primo Levi wrote that "the network of human relationships" inside the concentration camps "was not simple: it could not be reduced to two blocs, victims and perpetrators."[134] Studies of postcolonial territories worldwide have detailed how child soldiers themselves are the victims of terrifying and psychologically disfiguring coercion, how in contemporary Africa, insidious and intergenerationally transmitted trauma precipitates cyclic perpetration of mass violence,[135] and there is the oft-cited example of the African American Buffalo Soldiers, who comprised as much as a fifth of the troops in the West who fought for a government intent on seizing Native American lands. It is becoming increasingly clear that if "the categories of victim and perpetrator are not easily distinguishable in trauma narratives,"[136] then "we need trauma discourses that look at the dynamic between victims and perpetrators and see that both of them are suffering from the psychic deformations of violent histories, albeit in different ways."[137] Researchers responding to that call are beginning to populate a spectrum of definitions of trauma with increasingly more complex interpretations of mass violence and its legacies. At one end of the spectrum, the "trauma of perpetrators goes largely suppressed and denied,"[138] as, for example, denial of intergenerational Holocaust trauma that affected the Jewish perpetrators of massacres at the Sabra and Shatilas refugee camps during the Lebanon War in 1982.[139] At the other end is the claim of Tutu that all are traumatized.

Reconsiderations of the predicament of the perpetrator were prompted especially by research focused on the psychological status of American soldiers returning from Vietnam. In the mid-1980s, clinicians treating Vietnam veterans described symptom patterns recognizable as PTSD, but they also dug into the psychology of killing itself, searching for ways in which to understand how killing led to such psychological suffering.[140] That inquiry into the pain of traumatized war veterans soon was followed by study of nonmilitary perpetrators of violent acts, including homicide. In those studies evidence likewise began to accumulate that reinforced the theory that serious psychological problems followed from "the trauma of being violent."[141] A cohort of researchers took note of the presence of PTSD in murderers just as others were digging into the trauma suffered by Vietnam veterans.[142] They eventually concluded, as did studies of veterans, that such perpetrators could develop PTSD.[143] The authors of a survey of violent crime and wartime killing coined the term "perpetration-induced traumatic stress" to identify a cluster of "psychological consequences" experienced by persons who had a history of that kind of trauma. Those consequences included anxiety, panic, depression, a sense of disintegration, amnesia, and evidence, at least in some, of the inability to recall clearly the traumatic event. It paid particular attention to the consequences of killing civilians in Vietnam.[144]

Scholarship about the trauma of perpetrators has offered various explanations for their psychological problems. Oftentimes the discussion of those causes was joined to an effort to determine why some perpetrators engaged in additional violence at some point after they had returned from war. In the wake of war in the Balkans, mass killing in Rwanda, and large-scale atrocities in other places, that is, as genocidal violence became a more urgent research concern, investigators looked more closely at perpetrators' histories as they pursued answers to questions about the instigation and execution of genocide. "Participation in mass violence also creates trauma," wrote Ervin Staub, adding that "those who execute genocide routinely engage in atrocities."[145] That is, such perpetrators were involved in serial violence. Explanations for that pattern ranged from the determinative role of perpetrators' guilt or shame,[146] to just "problems getting in touch with their feelings."[147] In the case of Vietnam veterans, there also was the additional problem of American dislike of the war and veterans' sense that Americans back home did not want to hear about what the soldiers had done, a complication that reinforced repression of trauma.[148] Many explanations emphasized how traumatized soldiers kept reliving their trauma in a terrifyingly hazy way, caught between the past and the present, in "flashbacks."[149]

Arising from the criticism that twentieth-century trauma theory is founded in a "category error" that "elides the category of victim with that of the traumatized subject,"[150] new scholarship on perpetrator trauma has coalesced as a specifically interdisciplinary undertaking. While there are contending definitions of trauma, and different characterizations of the experiences of perpetrators, there also is significant collaboration across fields of study. It is manifestly true that "without a multidisciplinary knowledge, there can only be an unappetizing competition between disciplines to impose their specific conceptions of trauma."[151]

That multidisciplinarity extends to historical fiction writing. Scholars have pointed out that recent fiction has centered perpetrators and, to varying extents, made them ordinary and "rendered them in affective terms."[152] The examples of Native American and African American authors such as Toni Morrison, Edward Jones, and Sherman Alexie, or of South African novelist Sindiwe Magona, for example, offer ways of reading perpetrator characters, as Morrison would say, altruistically.[153] Magona's *Mother to Mother* (1998), a fictionalized account of the killing of white anti-apartheid activist Amy Biehl by four Black youths, while presenting the crime in all its unvarnished horror and pain, was a deliberate attempt to cultivate understanding for the world of the perpetrators: "And yet, are there no lessons to be had from knowing something of the other world?" That other world was "the world of those, young as she was young, whose environment failed to nurture them in the higher ideals of humanity and who, instead, became lost creatures of malice and destruction."[154] Structural trauma, an aspect of the colonial present, shaped such degradation of the cultural environment and framed persons in a way that pointed them to violence. The case in the American South was similarly written in stories by Flannery O'Connor, Eudora Welty, and others who depicted how, as one scholar has put it, "in each generation the trauma of slavery was injected into slaveholder children."[155] Such projects evidence how "reconfiguring victims and perpetrators in this manner substitutes historically specific scenarios for empathy for exportable textual formula" drawn from overly broad, even universalizing, theories of trauma.[156] Perpetrator trauma, which can be a matter of structural trauma, transmitted trauma, or both, has many different looks and historical contexts.

The questions then arise: What the does the perpetrator remember about the historical past? What has the perpetrator repressed, consciously or unconsciously? How does their trauma—perhaps transmitted to them over generations, or kept alive in them through medial triggers—affect their orientations to their social, political, religious, and racial environments? Is perpetrator trauma involved in cycles of violence? And, importantly, what does the perpetrator feel? And how is religion involved?

3

Emotion

Tears and Massacres

The mass murder of Native Americans at Wounded Knee took place in the midst of much national attention to the Ghost Dance. The dance seems to have emerged among the Pauites in 1870 and then more conspicuously in 1889 among Northern Pauite people who followed the religious visionary Wovoka.[1] Danced in connection with the millennialist belief that white rule of Indian lands was about to end, it likewise incorporated advocacy for what missionaries had called Christian virtues, such as honesty, hard work, and a "moral life." The presence of spirits in Native American religions and the character of the visions to Wovoka—spirits were to assist in the renewal of the world—led to the descriptor "Spirit Dance," which soon became, for speakers of English, the "Ghost Dance."

Government officials and settlers, as well as missionaries and journalists, watched as the ritual spread to the Sioux. Reaching for categories by which to understand it, officials envisaged it as a species of Spiritualism. Abby A. Judson of the Minneapolis Association of Spiritualists, explaining *Why She Became a Spiritualist* (1892), stated matter-of-factly: "Some Spiritualists express themselves by the Indian Ghost dance," meaning that Ghost Dancers were Spiritualists. That made them much like the Shakers, "the 'most radical spiritualists of the day.'"[2] In Armstrong and Wentworth's *Early Life among the Indians* (1892), "spiritualism had its origin with the Indians."[3] Students of Native American life were likely to agree that "as late as 1890 something very like spiritualism was in a state of active existence" among the Indians.[4] And for the scientifically minded Spiritualists (as well as Christian Scientists and evangelical revivalists), Native Americans, as naive scientists, had learned to generate "magnetic force" in their spiritualist rituals: "The magnetic power is as fully generated in an Indian ghost dance as in any Christian revival."[5]

As newspapers such as the *New York World* expressed the opinion that the Ghost Dance was an even more powerful means to communication with spirits than a medium at work in a Spiritualist séance, others warned that things were not right.[6] Sensing that Indian spiritualism was an encroachment on the Christian-scented Spiritualism of middle-class parlors, they denigrated the Ghost Dance as "a crude form of Spiritualism."[7] More pointedly, the aide-de-camp to General Nelson A. Miles, under whose command the Wounded Knee Massacre took place, wrote that it was "a perversion of the Christian religion as taught by missionaries."[8] Speaking directly to the Ghost Dance, a later commentator offered the more far-reaching conclusion that "the manifestations of Spiritualism in the heathen world" were so perverse as to demonstrate that "Spiritualism and Christianity are antagonistic."[9]

Euro-Americans, perpetrators of massacres reaching back into the earliest British colonial settlements, were actors within "the long history of conquest and colonialism that led the Sioux people to turn to the Ghost Dance in the first place."[10] The tragedy at "Wounded Knee was not made up of a series of discrete unconnected events. Instead, from the disarming to the burial of the dead, it consisted of a series of events held together by an underlying logic of racist domination." That dynamic of domination nevertheless required that whites remain in a perverse way attached to Indians. But when the Ghost Dance with its messianism and its likeness to Spiritualism appeared among the Lakotas, that was too close a connection and a triggering event: Americans sensed that a boundary had been crossed. Indians did not fit into a rendering of a white social group based on an ideology of character, yet they seemed to have penetrated the religious culture of Christians. That made them especially dangerous. Thus "the ghost dance became a kind of 'ideological conductor' for the angsts" of whites.[11]

Historical scholarship has shown how the workings of government agencies, the interests of speculators and investors, the personalities of military leaders, and other factors led to the massacre at Wounded Knee.[12] But questions linger: Why would a large American military force attack and slaughter scores of men, women, and children who posed no threat, on a very cold December day, at a location far from any kind of vital national interest? How does such violence, abetted by religious ideas, happen? What made the event so abundantly meaningful that eighteen American soldiers—including the four who had manned the deadly Hotchkiss guns that from a distance sprayed the ravine where women and children took refuge—were awarded the Congressional Medal of Honor for their actions that day? The Wounded Knee Massacre was not simply the tragic outcome of misunderstanding between local settlers (most of whom who saw no threat from the Lakotas), government and military leaders, and Indians. It was an instance of serial genocidal violence, triggered by white Christian concerns about the Ghost Dance, but arising equally from deep wells of affect. White Americans, in a time of massive immigration and continental migration, technological upheaval, breakneck urbanization, deep racial turmoil, and sharpening class antagonisms, were struggling to understand who they were, and in the course of that affect-saturated effort, and with reference to an ideology that drew sharp lines between Native Americans and Euro-Americans, they chose violence.

Nineteenth-century white Americans had mixed feeling about massacres such as Wounded Knee and Sand Creek. Many, and especially those in the West, regarded such catastrophes as part of the colonial project, as generally unfortunate but often necessary events marking the unstoppable march of civilization. Newspapers in the West often justified the slaughter of Native Americans,[13] many cast them as "sub-human,"[14] and some offered cynical resignation: At Sand Creek "that horrible butchery of friendly Indians by Colonel Chivington did not mend matters much. We must now have a war of extermination, I suppose."[15] Some individuals took a more aggressive and ruthless view, applauding the "blood lust" that Americans manifested in their massacres of Indians.[16] Some expressed their patriotism in supporting actions of government entities such as the Congress, which awarded the Medals of Honor to the white soldiers (and, some eighty-five years later, in approving the Department of Defense report denying that the massacre was anything other than a "heated battle").[17]

On the other hand, historians long have noted that there were always whites who condemned the violence and scolded a government that appeared to do little to stop it. Journalists' reports of soldiers in full murderous riot were backed up by testimony from settlers, traders, missionaries, and other white observers, and by testimony of military personnel. Some of that writing was starkly emotional. Some was detached, a blank and numb voice, the "emotionless language of military history."[18] Some witnesses' accounts could take the tone of a stony courtroom exchange of the sort recorded when the trader and interpreter John S. Smith testified before Congress in 1865. Smith answered questions about what he saw as a special military agent at Sand Creek, where his half-Cheyenne son Jack, after having given himself up, was murdered by a soldier the next day while in custody. The questions included: "Were the women and children slaughtered indiscriminately?"; "Were there any acts of barbarity perpetrated there?"; "Did you see them when they were mutilated?"; "Did you see it done?"; and "By whom they were mutilated?" He answered: "Yes; yes; yes; yes"; and "By the United States troops."[19] Such proceedings, cloaked in a veil of detached recollection and analysis, admitted little affect.

Other responses to massacres of Indians were strikingly affectual. But what stands out in some of those reports is the subsequent sense of foreboding, of trouble to come and a terrible price to face somewhere downstream of a horrific act. Some Americans had a feeling that the nation would carry into subsequent decades a crushing burden placed on it by the events at Sand Creek, Wounded Knee, and elsewhere. There was affect, and there was also a sense of its stickiness, a sense that people would, for some time to come, continue feeling the emotional pains arising from complicity in mass murder.

Black Elk, speaking decades after the carnage he witnessed at Wounded Knee, lamented, "When I look back from this high hill of old age, I can still see the butchered women and children lying heaped and scattered all along the crooked gulch as plain as when I saw them with eyes still young. And I can see that something else died in the bloody mud . . . a people's dream died there."[20] For some white Americans, there was a similar feeling. The nineteenth-century writer and activist Lydia Maria Child, who passionately denounced violence against Native Americans, addressed the massacre of a band of Piegans in early 1870 (the Marias Massacre). She endeavored "to proclaim aloud that such reckless butchery," including the "indiscriminate slaughter of helpless women and innocent babies," would leave a long shadow of guilt on the nation: "The annals of our country have received an indelible stain."[21] Colonel S. F. Tappan, who served in Colorado under Chivington at the time of the Sand Creek massacre and later was appointed to lead the commission investigating it, reported the Piegan slaughter as "a massacre so atrocious as to fill the country with amazement and horror." He speculated that it might have been better to die ("better the victim than the assassin") than to have to ever after bear "the consciousness of having aided in the destruction of an entire people."[22] The *Omaha World-Herald*, which closely covered the events at Wounded Knee, deemed it a "crime against civilization" that wrought great harm to two worlds, so that "the soldiers and the Indians alike are victims."[23] The poet Elaine Goodale Eastman, a white "sister to the Sioux" and wife to a Santee Sioux man, was teaching in South Dakota at the time of Wounded Knee. Overwhelmed as wounded and dying women and children were delivered to her building in the aftermath of the massacre, she experienced "nothing short of nightmare. Our patients cried and moaned incessantly, and every night some dead were carried out. In spite of all we could do, most of the injuries proved fatal. The few survivors were heartbroken and apathetic, for nearly all their men had been killed on the spot." Considering the Christian season and her shaken faith, she reflected that "the [Christmas] tree was dragged out . . . , while the glowing cross in the stained glass window behind the altar looked down in irony."[24]

The profound affect, and the sense of loss, present in many accounts of massacres of Native Americans found one of the fullest expressions in Dee Brown's *Bury My Heart at Wounded Knee* (1970), a long-running bestseller and a book renowned for its capability to move its readers.[25] Over forty years after its publication it was still featuring in discussions of "the best literary tear jerkers" and showing up on lists such as "10 Books for a Good Cry."[26] As forecasted by nineteenth-century writers, the massacre of Indians continued to strike an emotional chord with Americans, even though those feelings went unacknowledged most of the time. But just as Thomas Jefferson wrote in the 1780s when reflecting on the long-term consequences of slavery, "Indeed I tremble for my country when I reflect that God is just: that his justice cannot sleep for ever," the white memory of violence against Native Americans would not sleep either.[27]

Religion, Ideology, and Terrorism

In making sense of Americans' experiences of trauma arising from genocidal violence—mass murder, the structural violence that weighs on communities over time, the suffering of memory—religion is a crucial frame of reference for the ideology of extermination that underwrote that violence. Such ideology, deeply rooted in monotheistic binaries of good and evil, incorporated moral categories and arguments derived from interpretation of the story of the Amalekites. That religiously inspired perspective remained embedded in much rhetoric of extermination even when the references to Amalek became less frequent. The culture of violence and its religious context no longer required explicit enunciation. The American Protestant conceptualization of genocidal warfare remained. But events such as Wounded Knee did not arise merely from ideology, as histories of the event presume. They had an emotional component as well. They were matters of affect as well as cognition. To appreciate that requires, first of all, an understanding of how scholarship on religious violence in recent decades typically has articulated it as "religious terrorism," and how that approach has skewed discussion of religious violence toward ideology at the expense of affect. It is crucially important that research on religious violence rethink its approach in a way that will bring affect forward as a component of religious violence that is equal in importance to ideology.

Religious violence is enmeshed with political and ethnic difference. It is historical and collective. Its rhetoric is a composite that incorporates political argument and the contentious images of racial and ethnic conflict with theological ultimatums. Acts of religious violence historically are appalling for their cruelty and brutality. In some instances they are enacted in complicity with the state and in others they are differentiated from it. Religious violence can be the fruit of careful planning by well-organized groups. In other cases those groups incite it but do not orchestrate its details. Such violence has a long history of multifarious modes and systems.

Scholarship addressing religious violence, which was advancing steadily in the late twentieth century, surged in the aftermath of the 9/11 attacks. It coalesced as a branch of the investigation of "the new terrorism." While absent from the 1968 *International Encyclopaedia of the Social Sciences*, the term *terrorism* emerged as the object of a broad, multidisciplinary undertaking that attended to its transnational character, its indiscriminate targeting, the horizontal structuring of terrorist organizations, and the willingness to deploy weapons of mass destruction.[28] Scholars ventured analyses aimed at abetting the prediction and frustration of terrorist acts by scrutinizing recent occurrences. For a few, that meant historical perspective was crucial. Walter Laqueur, whose *The New Terrorism* (2000) helped to set the terms for the current study of terrorism, held that the "history of terrorism remains an essential key to understanding the phenomenon."[29]

But the history of terrorism, and especially in *la longue durée*, was barely visible as a part of the new scholarship that pressed to knit together explanations for why and how terrorism had metastasized into a global threat.[30] The late twentieth-century observation that "for most commentators terrorism has no history" remained a fair assessment of scholarship even a decade after 9/11.[31] Some contended that the shock of 9/11 was a call to arms that prompted creative, ambitious industry aimed ultimately at checking terrorism, but that the attacks also provided an occasion for hurried, self-serving scholarly opportunism that skirted the trench work of much-needed historical research.[32] Some scholarship asserted that "the terrorist phenomenon has a long and varied history," and "by ignoring this history, the United States runs the risk of repeating the plethora of mistakes made by other major powers that faced similar threats in the past."[33] When a recent study asked, "What can the history of terrorism contribute?" it meant to imply that the historical study of terrorism remained underexplored.[34]

Initial scholarly hesitance to embark on the historical study of terrorism especially was visible in the reluctance to engage the specific history of religiously inspired terrorism. David Rapoport, asserting in 1984 that "before the nineteenth century, religion provided the only acceptable justifications for terror," had sketched a history of terrorism in three religious groups: the Hindu Thugs (thirteenth through nineteenth centuries), Muslim Assassins (eleventh through thirteenth centuries), and Jewish Zealots-Sicarii (first century).[35] Scholars initially were slow to follow that lead in exploring the deep history of terrorism. However, Rapoport's research, and that of a few others, contributed to the eventual willingness of investigators not only to survey the past more purposefully but to weigh the role of religion in terrorism. Some scholars then explored in greater detail motivations that they perceived as distinctively religious, differentiating them from political and ethnic motivations. They argued that the "religious imperative for terrorism is the most important characteristic of terrorist activity today," maintaining that "groups transform abstract political ideologies and objectives into a religious imperative. Violence is not merely sanctioned; it is divinely decreed."[36]

By degrees, as religion came more clearly into focus, its history was perceived as more important. Part of the reason for that change was religion's seeming accessibility: the Enlightenment had framed it as a distinct human enterprise with its own special history, and one for which there consequently was an abundant historiography.[37] That massive corpus framed religious history as an object of study within easy reach. And it prompted a reconsideration of the historical perspective. Breaking from research that cast terrorism as largely arising from contemporary political and ethnic contexts, scholars attending to religion argued for the necessity of historical study. Correctly pointing out that "the argument about 'new terrorism' is neither based on explicitly formulated criteria of 'new' or 'newness' that would enable identification of new societal phenomena" nor based on "systematic empirical-historical studies that compare various periods and terrorist campaigns," they undertook to remedy that shortcoming.[38] In fits and starts, the pertinence of historical background—not just with regard to religion but across the board—emerged as a central concern, and the history of religion specifically became a more visible theme in commentary on terrorism.

The study of religiously motivated terrorism arose in conjunction with the cultivation of scholarly interest in conservative religion. Driven partly by a series of volumes about religious fundamentalism published in the 1990s,[39] scholarship digging into fundamentalism portrayed its "strong tendency to see matters in black and white terms" and inclination to "literal interpretation" of religious texts.[40] Fundamentalist religion was "Manichean dualism," with "sharp boundaries between the saved and the sinful."[41] The "strong moral and cosmological dualism" of fundamentalism was a theological perspective enforced by a staunch authoritarian leadership.[42] As an absolutist ideology, it constructed a world "clearly divided into good and evil, light and darkness, righteousness and unrighteousness."[43] Because "the heart of fundamentalism is a binary or dualistic way of thinking,"[44] it featured an "absolutistic 'way of knowing,'" albeit one that was complex.[45]

In a fundamentalism understood as a matter of hard binaries, absolutism, and literalism, language played a crucial role. Fundamentalism, above all, was a radical discourse, a cognitive exercise that privileged language and rationality. Scholars took fundamentalism as "word-based, rational knowing" that divided the world into good and evil, us and them. It was a rigorously policed discourse that "does not allow people to improvise or develop their religious thinking." Because "words rule" in fundamentalism, it was a decidedly cognitivist style of religion: "the left brain's attempt to 'do' religion." Its "simple binary structure with black and white contrasts" posited only the in-group and the out-group. Fundamentalism, as preeminently cognitive religion, was, due to its rigidity, a religion of "impoverished cognition."[46]

As religion became a more important topic of discussion among terrorism researchers, and as fundamentalism emerged as the key paradigm for understanding the religion of terrorists, scholars settled into interpretations that foregrounded ideology. Mark Juergensmeyer boiled down talk of fundamentalist binaries, absolutism, and rational knowing to a phrase that found traction among scholars: "the idea of cosmic war." For Juergensmeyer, religion itself was language: "In my view, religion is the language of ultimate order." Religion was about doctrines and teachings, the sacred texts on which those rested, and the fact of belief in enunciated ideas. Moreover, in religious terrorism, "there is a certain logic at work," a cluster of cognitions distilled from religious scriptures and expressed in doctrine, that demonstrate the rationality of religious terrorism to its perpetrators. The religious "language of warfare" expressed "the logic of religious violence."[47] The binaries asseverated in religious ideologies of terror formed a "divine law" that justified "holy war."[48]

Some scholarship that framed religiously motivated violence as a fundamentally cognitive enterprise elaborated that interpretation in connection with group identity, albeit in a halting and partial manner. Juergensmeyer, echoing previous scholarship, proposed that "religion provides the identity that makes a community cohere."[49] Other scholars writing at the same time also reasoned in that direction: "religious terrorists embrace a total ideological vision of an all-out struggle" and "pursue this vision in uncompromising holy terms in literal battles between good and evil." They do so—and this is crucial to understanding them—because of "a perceived threat to their identity."[50] Similar interpretative conjoinings of fundamentalist ideology and social identity held, for example, that "religious fundamentalism is a pattern of reasoning that breeds radical ideologies by way of singling out certain fundamentals of a religion and elevates them to absolutes." The consequence of this process is that "these absolutes form a paradigm of the ideology that develops as a reaction to what it fears as a threat to its own identity."[51] It is important to keep in mind for now (though I will challenge this view later) that in this scholarship, such fears about identity are thought to arise immediately from the realization of material threats from *outside the group*: competing groups, liberalizing politics, shifting social customs, modernity itself. Those threats, all of which are socially and ideologically structured, are recognized, discussed, and acted on. One way in which prevailing scholarship could summarize its approach was to affirm that "social conflicts are embedded in cognitive structures" such as religion, and when social conflicts are thus "framed in religious terms," the result often is "the flames of religious hatred."[52] Specific emotions such as hatred and fear thus followed from a conscious cognitive process in the overall scheme of mental processing. But the question remained: Why did a group feel anxious about its identity in the first place? What happened that led the group to embrace absolutist ideology?

The interpretative frame for much recent study of religion and violence, then, was assembled with a sense of urgency arising from the dramatic incidents of terroristic violence that marked the late twentieth and early twenty-first centuries. Social scientists and humanities scholars began to recognize that the study of the history of terrorism should be part of their project to understand and counter terrorism. They sought more ambitiously for the keys to contemporary terrorism in the past, in the activities of groups known for their absolutism and violence. That undertaking soon focused on religion. Again, the rapidly increasing visibility of religious fundamentalism in the late twentieth century prompted that perspective. Researchers found in fundamentalism a ready model for understanding the past and present of terrorism, focusing above all on the theological categories of fundamentalism, which promoted the radical division of populations into insiders and outsiders with its hard line between the holy and unholy. Such a focus privileged ideology because it seemed that ideology could be easily observed and it appeared to offer clear rationales for and provocations to violence. At its heart, terrorism, like fundamentalist religion, was conceptualized as a matter of language and rationality. Again, cognitive aspects of terrorism were brought to the forefront of scholarly investigation, and they have remained there.

As social identity increasingly attracted interest, some scholarship attempted to define it in a way that would position it against ideology as a distinct framework for interpretation. The theory of social identity as a felt community, an idea rooted in Durkheimian sociology, began to coalesce in some corners of scholarship. That undertaking was met with pushback from researchers who were invested in strict ideological analyses. And then beyond that, some scholarship contended that a true understanding of religious terrorism must reject the claim that it be defined as a matter strictly either of ideology or of social identity. Arguing that social identity as felt community had strong ideational components, such an approach called for interpretation that braided that kind of mixed-means social identity theory with interpretation that foregrounded the power of ideology.[53] Ideology and a certain view of identity, vaguely joined, thus acquired gravity as core concepts so that theorizing about religious terrorism settled awkwardly into a fluid vocabulary about logic, community, and conflict. But, crucially, the noncognitive remained secondary, on the margins of discussion. And the idea of social identity deployed in such approaches uncritically assumed a great deal about feeling as far as its actual workings within communities.

In assessing debate about religious terrorism in recent decades it is important to bear in mind that researchers above all have endeavored to respond as concretely as possible to the crisis of religious violence exemplified by the Balkans and Rwandan genocides, the 9/11 attacks, and other tragedies. Driven by a sense of urgency, scholarship took a practical bent aimed at the production of knowledge that could be applied to the task of neutralizing the threat of religious violence before it resulted in a biological or nuclear catastrophe. Ideology seemed less messy a focus than feeling. As the theorization of terrorism and the role of religion within it has grown more sophisticated, it has become possible at this point to enlarge and redirect that project, to consider more of the emotional side of the problem, to investigate the emotionality of perpetrators—the role of emotion in identity formation and identity threat—and to address more precisely the role of religion.

The Emotional Turn

In the twenty-first century, research has begun to attend more seriously to emotion as a factor in the perpetration of violence. Organizations such as the U.S. FBI, which is charged with protecting the nation from terrorism, have explored ways in which to predict violence by reading the emotional cues of persons and groups.[54] More broadly, scholarship to an increasing extent has been manifesting the "emotional turn," a redirection of academics' attention to all things emotional, a shift that began in the late twentieth century.[55] That turn has resulted in a wealth of studies and has accelerated the theorization of emotion through the integration of research across a wide range of disciplines. It also has made clear that historical writing that does not attend directly to emotion not only leaves potentially crucial data on the table but gives short shrift to the humanity of the actors whose lives it purportedly narrates. To tell the story of a community without reference to its emotional dimensions is to tell but part of a story, to render complex lives two-dimensionally, and to risk harming the subjects whose actions constitute the narrative. At a moment in historical study when the opportunities and emerging tools for the investigation of emotion are abundantly present, the prospects for enhancing understanding of the American past, and especially the entwined histories of violence and religion, are strong.

I propose here that analysis of the ways in which religion is involved in social violence should address, alongside religious ideas, how feeling is present in such events. I foreground three facets of recent research germane to that. First, I sketch the salience of the emotional turn in recent scholarship in the humanities and sciences. My purpose in doing so is to indicate that an interdisciplinary approach to emotions studies that joins research on affect to that on cognition, while, additionally, integrating insights from a broad array of disciplines, enables appreciation for how persons and groups can be motivated to action in ways that sometimes are not perceptible to interpreters through consideration of ideas alone.[56] I likewise wish to indicate, by corollary, how analysis of religiously inspired violence—whether that be Wounded Knee or the Capitol insurrection—that neglects investigation of the emotional worlds of the perpetrators of those crimes will remain partial. It risks frustrating understanding of why such events happen for a number of reasons, including because it would miss the opportunity to fully detect crucial paradoxes wired into the emotionally rich experiences of social identity and memory that religions historically have fostered (a topic I return to in later chapters).

Second, I survey scholarly discussion about collective emotion. I note how emotional contagion shapes emotional communities and is essential to collective identity and collective intentionality. Such contagion takes place invisibly because the codes and canons of emotional practice (which is a social practice) often are hidden from actors in the very air they breathe. That is, emotional practice is a reality shaped by social and cultural forces that frequently are invisible. This is an important insight because violent groups often behave in ways that appear contrary to the claims they make regarding their beliefs and motivations. Moreover, because feeling is a key part of memory, and because social identity is built on shared memory, understanding how collective memory is constructed in affect will allow us to better see how emotion is present in group enactments of identity, including violent ones.

Third, I discuss epigenesis. I note that research on epigenesis is in its early stages but that it is converging on the finding that traits can be transmitted intergenerationally. Social groups can inherit emotional orientations. If affect arising from trauma is passed from one generation to another, that strengthens the likelihood that groups carry with them the emotional consequences of the terrible experiences of their forebears. In other words, trauma suffered by persons at Wounded Knee—whether by victims or perpetrators—is an emotional predicament that still can haunt persons in the twenty-first century—such as those who attacked the Capitol on January 6.

To begin, then, it is clear that the emotional turn has taken an assortment of directions. Of clear relevance for understanding American religious history is the nascent subfield of the history of emotions, for example, which has developed important insights about the way in which emotional life changes over time, and, equally, how the present is continuous with the past.[57] It is an area of research evidencing strong promise of clarifying why people acted in the way that they did, what motivated them, and how cultures as well as lives are shaped by collective emotional programs and performative expectations. But there is a way to enrich the approach taken by research in the history of emotions by integrating into it the insights drawn from scientific studies of emotion, and especially research that is emerging under the banner of "social neuroscience," which offers insight into how and why humans as social animals feel and behave.

Social neuroscience as a subfield coalesced in the late twentieth century as an effort to explore brain processes involved in social interactions. In attending to questions about the relation of the social to the biological, it cultivated some of the same ground as the more specialized endeavors of cognitive and emotional neuroscience, but extended those projects through its advocacy of "the doctrine of multilevel analysis."[58] The various levels of cell, tissue, organ, dyads (e.g., paired organisms such as mother/child), groups, and society all were objects of analysis in an enterprise that required "interdisciplinary expertise, comparative studies, innovative methods, and integrative conceptual analyses."[59] That interdisciplinary expertise might include, for example, neuropsychoanalytic approaches.[60]

Social neuroscience is grounded in the trust that "the causal pathway between the biological and social level is bidirectional or reciprocal." Social experiences affect biological processes just as biology influences social behavior. To map the interplay between those two realms necessitated the examination of events at levels from the biological, through the organismal, to the social. Central to social neuroscience as it has been developing is the claim that full understanding of social behavior cannot be achieved if any of the biological, cognitive, or social levels of organization are disregarded in analysis. In this developing program of research, "the nervous system cannot be considered an isolated entity" apart from social environments as "all social behavior is implemented biologically."[61] Likewise, because "the social environment affects systemic functions" of the body—such as, for example, the metabolic system, white blood cells, and immunity—social neuroscience pursues anal-

ysis of the "cumulative effects of stressful experiences on brain and body and
their interactions with each other, as well as an updated understanding of epigenetic effects on brain activity."[62]

Social neuroscience has developed to a certain extent in response to cognitive neuroscience, from which it differs in several ways. The latter has tended
to approach the brain as a machine, a kind of computer that organizes and
stores information; enables attention, reasoning, and representation; and serves
as the command center for executive function. Social neuroscience construes
the brain not as a computer but as "a mobile broadband computing device."
Such an approach—which is admittedly ambitious—draws a number of factors more closely under its research umbrella, including "communication, attachment, social perception, social recognition, impression formation, empathy, competition, cooperation, status hierarchies, imitation, norms, social
learning, conformity, contagion, social networks, and culture."[63] All of this is
to say that social neuroscience is interested in the ways that social contexts
and environmental factors "get under the skin" and equally how biology and
physiology play a reciprocal role in shaping social life.

Social neuroscience has been involved in investigating terrorism, asking
why some people become radicalized and embrace radical ideas that result in
violence. One study, for example, proceeding on the principle that such actors are otherwise "ordinary people," noted that religious fundamentalism is
often involved in political violence but that fundamentalism does not by itself necessarily lead to violence. Rather, persons develop "strong emotional
ties to narratives" that lead to their radicalization for complex reasons having
to do with brain function, bodily processes, and social environment. There is
no simple, easily defined "terrorist personality." Rather, analysis that takes a
"transdisciplinary perspective that emphasizes the multiple relationships between neural, cognitive, and social processes" and utilizes a "dynamic, recursive theoretical framework in which the connection between physiological
and psychological functioning and political expression is conceived as bidirectional" can supply more precise and consequential understandings of how
and why persons become terrorists.[64]

The agenda of social neuroscience has built on research in many areas, including the neuroscience of emotion. The scientific study of emotion made
important strides in the latter part of the twentieth century and has produced
an impressive body of new theories and syntheses in the twenty-first. The
question driving such research—"What is an emotion?"—has prompted different approaches, but among the most important has been brain research
that tracks emotional responses to environmental stimuli in intersection with
cognitive responses. The upshot of those investigations is that cognition and

feeling are closely intertwined in neural processes. The popular notion of "right brain/left brain," involving one side for feeling and the other for thinking, long has been considered by researchers a misleading mapping of brain geography. In its place have emerged theories about the extensive and *recursive* collaborations of different parts of the brain—even while some parts contribute more to emotional response and some are more directly involved in cognitive performance—in the experiencing of an emotion.

William James's writings about emotion, as part of what came to be called the James-Lange theory, prominently included analysis of the experience of fear, and that topic served for much subsequent psychological and philosophical investigation of emotion as a central case for discussion. James argued that an encounter with a bear did not result in a merely "cold and neutral state of intellectual perception," but that it prompted a physiological response— changes in heart rate, respiration, perspiration, and so forth—and that such "bodily manifestations" were "interposed between" the perception of the bear and the feeling of fear. Expanding directly on his understanding of fear, James illustrated it with reference to rage and grief: "Can one fancy the state of rage and picture no ebullition of it in the chest, no flushing of the face, no dilatation of the nostrils, no clenching of the teeth, no impulse to vigorous action, but in their stead limp muscles, calm breathing, and a placid face? The present writer, for one, certainly cannot. The rage is as completely evaporated as the sensation of its so-called manifestations, and the only thing that can possibly be supposed to take its place is some cold-blooded and dispassionate judicial sentence, confined entirely to the intellectual realm, to the effect that a certain person or persons merit chastisement for their sins." Rage, likewise, without physical manifestations would be "a feelingless cognition that certain circumstances are deplorable, and nothing more. . . . A purely disembodied human emotion is a nonentity."[65] Over a century later, James's insight remains central to emotions research, and to the argument that "emotions are not just the fuel that powers the psychological mechanism of a reasoning creature, they are parts, highly complex and messy parts, of this creature's reasoning itself."[66]

Neuroscience has contributed in major ways to the elaboration, qualification, and reinterpretation of James's thinking. It has done so in various kinds of studies. One crucial development in the twenty-first century has been the advance in mapping the neural circuits in the brain that are involved in emotion. While granting that some parts of the brain are more involved in cognition and other parts more in affect, research has shown that there is continuous communication between them. The cortex, associated with cognition and consciousness, is wired with the subcortical networks—and especially the amygdala—and the two collaborate in the experience of fear, anger, and other emotions. A large body of empirical studies has shown that a rapid-fire dialogue takes place between those two areas of the brain as the body responds to a threat. The brain, receiving somatosensory inputs from the body, takes defensive action by signaling the brainstem to stimulate action (movement, respiration, sharpened hearing, etc.), and at the same time becomes conscious of fear and draws on the working memory network, which is enhanced by an "affective charge," to comprehend the event. The zigzag collaboration of cortical and subcortical networks, and especially the anterior dorsolateral and ventromedial prefrontal cortex,[67] accordingly fashion a regulated experience that is both conscious and unconscious, cognitive and noncognitive.[68] Put another way, "Projections from the amygdala to the brainstem are involved in the expression of fear responses, and projections from the amygdala to the cortex are believed to contribute to the experience of fear and other cognitive aspects of emotional processing."[69] According to research thus far, fear, and some other emotions as well, are characterized by physiological and biological response, including *implicit* (nonconscious) processing by the amygdala,[70] together with cortical circuits involved in consciousness. Cutting-edge research now also has begun building a case for the involvement of the sensory cortex (e.g., olfaction), along with the amygdala and prefrontal cortex, as a key component of the long-term retention of memory about threats.[71] Those cortical circuits together attend to "the consequences of implicit processing by the amygdala."[72] In this way, conscious emotional experiences are "cognitively assembled by cortical circuits."[73] But "cognitions about the world are not separate from and do not cause emotion—they constitute it."[74] In simple terms, it is clear that in the experience of emotion, different parts of the neural system are enmeshed and function in concert.

One way to think about the response of the amygdala (and according to some research, the subgenual cingulate) to environmental stimuli is to consider fear as an experience of "core affect" that becomes fear when people "conceptualize their core affective state using accessible knowledge about emotion." While understanding fear as an experience "produced by the interplay of two more basic psychological ingredients: core affect and conceptual knowledge of emotion,"[75] it is important to bear in mind that "core affect" represents arousal that has not yet been cognized. That is, core affect in itself is not consciousness. But we can speak of it as free-floating feeling that can be swiftly marshaled as anger or fear based on information available to perception. The experience of emotion, then, is a perceptual act that takes place in collaboration with conceptual knowledge.[76] Fear, for example, is the "result when core affect is conceptualized using knowledge of emotion (effectively, what a person knows about the category of anger, sadness, or fear, etc.).

In an instant, conceptualization proceeds efficiently and automatically, transforming internal sensory information from the body into a psychologically meaningful state by combining it with external sensory information about the world and situation-specific knowledge of emotion learned from prior experience. The result is an intensional [*sic*] state that is *at once affective and conceptual.*[77] It is the joining of unconscious but regulated biological mechanisms with cortical processing involved in consciousness. Fear is both unconscious and conscious, at the same time. Moreover, that consciousness of fear, inasmuch as it draws on memory networks and leverages information about the world, is shaped by culture. It is "at the same time, socially constructed and biologically evident."[78] That is, there is a basis on which to understand emotion as a matter of both individual and collective experience. The "emotion categories," such as hatred, fear, and anger, "are made real through collective intentionality. To communicate to someone else that you feel angry, both of you need a shared understanding of 'Anger,' " and, importantly, "you needn't be explicitly aware of this agreement."[79]

It is worth noting as a sideline here that such an understanding of emotion, as proposed by neuroscientific research, challenges literary trauma theory. Specifically, it challenges its arguments about representation. Literary trauma theory characterized trauma as an experience that was unpresentable. It could not be spoken; subjects could not remember what had happened and had no words to describe their experiences. Trauma was perceptible only in somatic clues such as trembling, eating disorders, nightmares, flashbacks, violent behaviors, and so forth. That argument rested on a claim that feeling was separate from cognition.[80] That claim has not been borne out by scientific research (and, as mentioned previously, has been criticized by other scholars working in a number of fields). This does not mean, however, that emotional life is always about feelings of which a person is conscious. It is possible to repress feelings, including those associated with trauma. Indeed, societies, not just individuals, can repress feelings. And indeed, societies can repress feelings about trauma.

Collective Emotion

The proposal that "collective intentionality" is involved in shaping emotion leads to the possibility of "thinking of emotions as social events." As different parts of the brain collaborate to produce emotion, drawing on memory and culture in so doing, the social setting advances to the foreground of emotional life. A robber might confront one on the street and then run away, serving as a seemingly simple prompt for certain feelings such as fear and anger. But even then "emotions in social settings are ongoing, developing response systems that change over time as the interactions with other people unfold."[81] For example, in one study, Japanese and American participants, when discussing with interviewers situations in which they felt offended, evidenced different emotional responses. American participants reported becoming angry, taking the situation as an affront to their integrity and worth as an individual, while Japanese participants construed the offense as a problem arising from faulty communication, requiring reflection on how to foster harmony in future potential encounters.[82] Thus, social context conditions emotional response.

Put another way, to speak of emotion as a social event is to recognize it as a practice that is shaped, sometimes in unrecognized ways, by social life. Such "emotional practice," is guided by definitions of, assumptions about, and means of expressing feelings that are assembled in culture and history, and "though it can encompass intentional, deliberate action, it also includes, and indeed stresses, habituated behavior executed without much cognitive attention paid."[83] Emotional practice in this sense is historically conditioned conduct. In many cases, moreover, it is only tenuously related to self-awareness mediated by language. It is a performance that has more the character of ingrained habit or conditioned behavior than a consciously self-directed act. Put another way, "it differs from action in the Weberian sense of intentional, meaningful behavior, which presupposes a metaphysical subject that more or less knows what it is doing and why."[84] In Bourdieuian terms, emotional practices are socially and culturally inculcated dispositions, so ingrained as to form the *habitus*, the invisible, odorless, silent cultural air that people breathe every day. For Bourdieu, "the *habitus*—embodied history, internalized as a second nature and so forgotten as history—is the active presence of the whole past of which it is the product." In that sense, "the *habitus* is a spontaneity without consciousness or will."[85] Such a view opens opportunities to consider "affective resonance,"[86] "affective contagion,"[87] "the transmissibility of affect,"[88] and the general "circulation of affect"[89] that can take place, sometimes without persons realizing it. It also invites consideration of how societies are "affective societies" saturated with emotion that determines, sometimes in covert ways, the course of politics.[90] Much theorization of collective emotion "owes a large intellectual debt to Durkheim's (1912 [*The Elementary Forms of the Religious Life*]) account of religious ceremonies, rituals, and symbols."[91] Durkheim's notion of collective effervescence, as well as the centrality of myth and ritual in regulating emotional life, have important implications for understanding trauma, culture, and religion.

The idea that a group, institution, or nation has an "emotional climate,"[92] that there is a "social sharing of emotion"[93] that underlies "emotional communities,"[94] has acquired currency in research across the humanities and social sciences.[95] Collective emotions, understood as "the synchronous convergence in affective responding across individuals,"[96] lead to a "collective emotional orientation."[97] Through the "interweaving of memory narratives" of individuals and groups,[98] and by other means, societies create cultures of emotion. In direct engagements between persons, as mediated through institutions and discourses and by other means, an emotional culture develops that is recognizable in "long-term social and cultural practices." Emotional cultures are in no way deficient in cognitive substance. They manifest overlapping cognitive structurings and representations of emotion, and collective intentions and goals, articulated in the context of the shared knowledge of the community. All of that infuses the social sharing of emotion so that emotional culture forms in conjunction with social identity. A key part of that process is the "formation of collective memories through discourse," which functions to sustain the emotional culture over time.[99]

One way in which to discuss collective emotional orientation is to focus on how "emotion and the beliefs that evoke it are embedded in the society's collective memory."[100] That collective memory is nourished by movies, books, online formats, and public performances, among a wide range of mediating structures, and it is reinforced in educational settings and public rituals and ceremonies. Halbwachs's dictum, "It is in society that people normally acquire their memories. It is also in society that they recall, recognize, and localize their memories,"[101] speaks to some extent to the process of coalescence of collective emotion. Memory and emotion both are deeply rooted in the social, and especially in conjunction with social identity.

Collective emotion is a part of collective identity.[102] People live in social groups characterized by group-based norms and habits that shape perception and cognition, behavior and feeling. All of that has psychological consequences for group members, so that we can speak of the group itself as a psychological process.[103] When people define themselves as group entities, they identify psychologically as a group. Social identity in that sense can be articulated as "that part of an individual's self-concept which derives from his knowledge of his membership of a social group (or groups) together with the value and emotional significance attached to that membership."[104] Inasmuch as people identify with the group, they understand themselves to be interrelated parts of a whole. They define themselves as group entities. People can, as it were, "feel like a state," and group-level emotion, in certain contexts, can be more powerful than what individual members of the group experience.[105]

Crucially, social identification requires a feeling of attachment. To identify as a member of a group is to feel attached to it, and so "all identities depend on social emotions" involving attachment.[106] The group does not have a physical

body in the same way that individuals have bodies, but that does not undermine the possibilities for collective emotion.[107] Groups evolve "feeling rules"
for their members,[108] and construct a web of mechanisms that serve to regulate emotion, so that inasmuch as one identifies with a group, one's emotions
will take a patterned form in conjunction with the standards of that group. An
individual body might register feelings about matters pertaining to personal
security that are weakly schemed by social expectations: displays of emotion
in swatting a mosquito, encountering a bear, hearing a loud thunderclap, or
stubbing a toe, as well as certain experiences of relationships with other individuals. Emotions felt on behalf of a social group differ in some ways from
such experiences in that they are elicited by events having to do with one's
identity as a member of a group, and, especially, one's sense of belonging to
one group rather than another.[109]

Collective emotional culture, then, is a way of talking about how social
identity invests individuals in an emotional life structured at least in part by
mechanisms arising from the goals, motivations, ideologies, and memories
of the group.[110] The inner turnings of those mechanisms are hidden, regulating emotion in ways group members are unaware of. In Durkheimian terms,
there is unconscious obedience to the demands of the group for conformity
to shared emotional models that comprise a part of group identification. As
part of that, and in sympathy with how the biological bases of emotional response enable bodily feeling prior to language, we can "*feel* our way through
social activities," guided by habits of feeling arising from social relations, or
"emotional dispositions" as opposed to "cognitive dispositions." In the larger
view, then,[111] "feelings and emotions only arise in patterns of relationship,"
and thus "result in patterns of activity that can become dispositions—ways of
acting in particular situations that are not wholly within our conscious control and are, thus, partly involuntary," that is, unconscious.[112]

Collective emotions include those associated with collective trauma, an
experience that can be so deeply engraved on a society that it remains powerfully influential at an unconscious level for generations. Trauma has less to
do with the event that begat it than with the emotional consequences of that
trauma, which take up residence in the collective emotional life of a group.
Reflecting on the trauma of the Cultural Revolution in China, for example,
Ben Wang observed that "more a persisting condition than the violent quality of a one-time occurrence, trauma remains active as the haunting impact
of a catastrophic event."[113] As such it is because traumatic "memories have become part of communal identity and a 'felt' history" about which persons have
"a sense of collective ownership."[114] Feelings of collective trauma, like those
of individual trauma, "persist at a somatosensory level,"[115] in the sense that

while a group may not consciously recognize them, they nevertheless condition collective behavior. Those traumatic feelings "come not only from the originating event but *from the anxiety of keeping it repressed*."[116] Indeed, the event itself comes to be overlaid by repressed collective memory that, ironically, leverages and magnifies the emotional valence of the inceptive event. "It is not the past," but "rather, the emotional potency of traumatic memories," that matters.[117]

For some groups, "collective trauma becomes the epicenter of group identity."[118] It is collective trauma that constructs and binds group members into "affective communities." Trauma generates "emotional cultures" and, through its representation, constitutes bonds between individuals, binding them to the group.[119] Although "traumatic events construct political communities,"[120] so that a "pattern of identity is based not on the attractiveness of the future but on the horror of the past,"[121] some scholars also believe that groups can purposefully organize themselves in connection with "chosen traumas" that provide an emotional footing on which to build group identity.[122] "Chosen trauma," which in certain cases is a component of large-group identity, can be glimpsed, for example, in the Balkan wars of the 1990s, where it bolstered political causes by cementing bonds between persons who identified as victims of violence.[123]

Cardinally, the power of trauma to construct collective identity is located in its paradoxical capability to bond members to the group while creating anxiety about social belonging and social meaning.[124] Collective trauma felt as anxiety about social identity can be harnessed toward the "reactivation" of identity or the construction of new identity.[125] It is a severe irritant as well as a prompt to shore up or redesign the scheme of group belonging and meaning. Its pain is "acute discomfort entering into the core of the collectivity's sense of its own identity."[126] Trauma is a part of the group identity as well as a disruption of that identity.

As Native American scholars (and African American scholars, as we will see) have written in their analyses of the experience of trauma within their communities, collective trauma can be transmitted intergenerationally, a process recognized perhaps as far back as the writing of the Old Testament history of the Jews.[127] Current scholarship posits a "trans-generational collective self"[128] as a construction that can arise from memory of collective trauma transmitted by "carrier groups" within a population.[129] Collective traumas, composed of "socially-mediated attributes,"[130] can remain alive over centuries, as descendants of a traumatized group are unable to fully process "what is deposited in them."[131] Those deposits accrue interest through their rehearsal in public performances. Transmission can be fostered through the embrace of "images of the past and recollected knowledge of the past" that are "sustained by (more or less) ritual performances."[132] Such public rituals—and notably, religious rituals—are particularly effective in fostering transgenerational transmission, so that the "memory of violence, especially in its affective dimensions, may be transmitted beyond the generation of witnesses."[133] Take, for example, the ritual tears annually shed by Christians in Latin countries during Passion Week as collective remembrances of the violence done to Jesus (and so to them).[134] In general, "cultural practices contribute to the large-scale dissemination . . . of feelings," so that ritual performances, along with a wide range of other practices ranging from movies and books to art, architecture, calendar-keeping, monuments and photographs,[135] gossip, pilgrimage, and religious ceremony, remind persons not only of the event but of its "emotional consequences."[136]

There are "emotionally-laden narratives" that constitute "a shared meaning and information system transmitted across generations," which serve to inculcate feelings in groups.[137] Such cultural practices "animate the present with emotion."[138] Some transmission is effectuated cognitively, in words about the past or in images of it—even by auditory cues—or by other means that "are effective in reminding the event through the repetitive reactivation of the cognitive representation." But, again, that process is also an emotional matter. Bodies performing together, making the same movements, singing a song together, dancing or marching, amount to "collective emotional gatherings," and "this synchrony leads to an important social sharing of emotions, to the point of eliciting feelings of 'identity fusion.'"[139] When "people feel emotions on behalf of their group," they are reinforcing their bond to that group.[140] And that can occur even when group members are unaware of exactly why they feel as they do because "traumatic historical legacies may be transmitted . . . through the cultural unconscious."[141]

Epigenesis

There has been debate about whether insights derived from psychological studies of trauma are built on such a rigid foundation of disciplinary domain assumptions and methods that they cannot be joined to research conducted on a sociological or historical basis that foregrounds the group and its dynamics. Once upon a time, scholars were sure that such a vast gulf separated those two approaches that it was considered naive to imagine that they could be joined. In recent decades that confidence has been steadily eroded as interdisciplinary research has advanced impressively across several fronts and as the advantages to building bridges between research focused on the individual and research focused on the group increasingly have been in evidence.

Take, for example, the highly influential interdisciplinary study by cognitive scientist and ethnographer Edwin Hutchins, *Cognition in the Wild* (1995), a study of navigation aboard a naval vessel. Observing the techniques for navigation in a range of situations over time aboard the ship, Hutchins concluded that cognitive tasks were not achieved solely by the brain. Instead, the entire body—including the fingers for counting and pointing, for example—as well as the whole group—oftentimes with different persons assigned to different parts of the ship for different tasks—played crucial parts in the cognitive task of navigation. He concluded that cognition was not separable from culture, which meant that he rejected the exclusive emphasis on the individual, deeming it an impediment to research in cognitive science.[142] The same is true for the study of emotion.

The study of collective emotion in general has developed out of the study of emotion in individuals. That was the case for Freud, and it has remained true for much discussion of collective emotion since. But there have been shifts in perspective in recent decades, and especially as represented in the advent of a literature about the social construction of emotion (which actually began with the American pragmatists), which hit its stride in the latter part of the twentieth century in fields such as psychology, sociology, and anthropology.[143] Collective trauma, or, as it has been termed in some scholarship, *cultural trauma*, also has adopted insights from psychological studies. But it has been more inclined to a view of the ways in which trauma, as an intergenerational phenomenon, has been constituted socially. Such scholarship has explored how social bodies, social agents, and contending constituencies have constructed cultural trauma and continue to remake it over time as political contexts shift and new social forces exert influence. While there is no consensus about how cultural trauma is formed, and some scholarship has argued that "cultural traumas are historically made, not born,"[144] there is still the open question of whether "these constructions do refer to something that has its own qualities that exert some resistance in the process of construction, whether traumas, therefore, are 'nothing but' construction."[145]

Research that has advanced the effort to draw together understandings of the individual's experience of trauma with socially constructed and mediated collective trauma has foregrounded trauma's paradoxical character.[146] While an event can profoundly affect a person, directing their emotional life into pathways radically different than what had been familiar, at the same time, when persons experience trauma collectively, as for example, as a member of a Native American community brutalized by colonialism or as one of a group of slaves, the experience can be shared, contagious, and collectively familiar. And as much as persons might wish to escape the pain of that trauma, culture can hold it in memory, signaling it in various ways and perpetuating it. It is felt but also read in culture, personal but shared.

Such a view of the interrelatedness of the personal and the social is one of the core principles of social neuroscience. And one of the areas in which social neuroscience (taken to include research teams working in many fields) has explored that connection is in the transmission of genetic traits from parents to offspring and through generations. More specifically, it is the recent emergence of the study of epigenesis that has begun to change the way in which we think about the individual and the social, the body and the environment, biology and history. As the French philosopher Catherine Malabou has observed, "A new economy of inheritance emerges that situates itself at the very crossing between the biological and symbolic, thus allowing for a new concept of history to be brought to light. History would designate not only a series of past events but also a specific type of biological inheritance."[147] The focus accordingly has turned to "*cultural* inheritance, which goes along with biological evolution," and how that takes place at the genetic level.[148] Epigenesis is an "interface between the empirical and the hermeneutic." It "revives the possibility for a conversation between the empirical sciences and critical theory," and, along the way, offers support for psychoanalytic understandings of memory, including memory of trauma.[149] It is a call to include biology in the humanities,[150] one that has been getting louder as part of the surging interest in embodiment, including the scholarship that has helped to define the emotional turn.

Epigenesis refers to the dynamic interaction of genetics with the environment leading to heritable changes in gene expression.[151] While the genome remains the unaltered code for life, the expression of individual genes—how they turn on and turn off, how they transition from genotype to phenotype (i.e., to the traits observable in a person, ranging from eye color and blood type to behavioral traits)—is a matter of regulation involving biochemical processes that take place in connection with environmental stimuli. In response to environmental factors, such as pollution, diet, radiation, and stress, the phenotype can change, but not the genotype. The specific ways in which the epigenome emerges include methylation,[152] which is the attachment of a chemical group (methyl, made up of three hydrogen atoms and one carbon atom) to a DNA molecule, leaving heritable "marks" on the genome. That then disrupts the transcription process that copies DNA to RNA by blocking the proteins that attach to DNA to read the gene. Methylation typically results in repression of a gene. Depending on the gene, repression can result in adaptive or maladaptive change. Sometimes that change is observable in behavior, but epigenetic modifications also can be linked to incidence of disease and resistance to disease, an insight that has helped to drive the development of gene therapy for cancer, lupus, and diabetes.[153] Human DNA is about 80–90 percent methylated. Demethylation can also occur in response to environmental factors.

Epigenesis results in what some have called "soft" inheritance, an environmentally prompted process of gene expression the results of which can be passed from one generation to the next. Research on trauma has been an important part of the investigation of such inheritance. That research has offered important insights specifically into how experiences of trauma affect genetic expression in ways that are passed to succeeding generations. Studies propose, for example, that "epigenesis has thus become another important path for finding the biological basis for PTSD," by examining how "the interaction and relationship of DNA methylation and traumatic experiences causes the occurrence of PTSD."[154] Offering evidence that "stress related disorders, like other psychiatric disorders, are familial and heritable,"[155] researchers have argued that "there is no question that both genes and environment influence risk for depression, and recent evidence suggests that exposure to stressful life events is, itself, heritable."[156] Because "experiencing violence modifies neural and epigenetic memory," memories of violence are stored at the molecular level and can be transmitted intergenerationally.[157] The flashbacks and hyperarousal associated with PTSD are thus "manifestations of maladaptive plasticity."[158]

The "converging evidence supporting the idea that offspring are affected by parental trauma exposures occurring before their birth, and possibly even prior to conception,"[159] include twin studies, animal studies,[160] historical studies, and biological research, oftentimes in multidisciplinary approaches. Twin studies have been useful because the research design controls reduce the number of possible explanations for differences that might be detected between a pair of twins, making it easier to distinguish genetic factors involved in traits from environmental ones. Twin studies evidence heritability of PTSD in the range of 30–60 percent.[161] Rodent studies have offered "very compelling data,"[162] and include a recent study that enlarges the discussion of gene regulation to include mitochondrial DNA, which has been shown to be central to a process that epigenetically transmits stress responses over more than fifty generations.[163] A study that likewise contributed to the expansion of the field reported evidence of reversible epigenetic changes associated with behavior: bees that were subjected to environmental changes forcing them to change their roles within the hive showed reversion of subsequent DNA methylation when they were returned to their previous roles.[164]

Evidence from human studies has pointed to heritable epigenetic traits in comparatively large populations. The Dutch Famine of 1944 took place because of German blockades that prevented the transport of food into large parts of the Netherlands. Over 20,000 people died and many were permanently harmed. Children born to malnourished mothers had low birth weights. Those children, in turn, also delivered babies with low birth weights, in spite of the fact that their diet was normative as far as caloric intake. Daughters of mothers who endured the famine developed psychological disorders, including schizophrenia, at twice the rate of the general population, as well as heightened levels of diabetes and obesity and an above-average mortality rate. Research has pointed to the transmission of the trauma of near-starvation to the next generation—who were at the time in utero—through hypodemethylation (of the IGF2 gene, which is a locus for insulin-like growth factor). The 2008 study, based on analysis of blood and adult stem cells, concluded that it documented how "transient environmental conditions early in human gestation can be recorded as persistent changes in epigenetic information."[165]

A similar study of grandmothers, their daughters, and their grandchildren in Rio de Janeiro likewise was able to correlate stress suffered by the mothers with genetic changes evidenced in epigenetic patterns. Grandmothers who had experienced violence during pregnancy showed gene methylations that could be tracked to their grandchildren, which provided "support for DNA methylation as a biological mechanism involved in the transmission of stress across generations."[166] A study of Holocaust survivors likewise concluded that cytosine methylation at the FKBP5 gene evidenced "an association of preconception parental trauma with epigenetic alterations that is evident in both exposed parent and offspring," and in that way provided insight "into how severe psychophysiological trauma can have intergenerational effects."[167] Some studies have shown transmission through the male germline as well.[168] The subfield is developing rapidly in a number of directions and is aiming at an integration of insights drawn from animal studies with human data,[169] as well as understanding why some studies do not evidence transmission.[170]

The studies of the Dutch famine and of grandmaternal stress in Brazil can be understood within the context of a growing number of observational studies that have linked colonization and slavery, the Holocaust, and Vietnam War military service to intergenerational effects of stress. Studies of the aftermaths of colonialism, genocidal wars, and ethnic cleansings in the Balkans,[171] Cambodia,[172] Palestine,[173] Rwanda,[174] Australia,[175] New Zealand,[176] Armenia,[177] and among Native American and African American[178] populations have suggested that clinically observable trauma can be intergenerational. Historical studies drawing on scientific methods also are beginning to appear.[179] Epigenetic consequences of violence, and especially the experience of war, remain a major part of the study of heritable stress, with prenatal maternal trauma, as in the Democratic Republic of Congo,[180] also receiving much attention.

Major research initiatives are underway to study the ways in which phenotypes might be altered in relation to stressors, and especially by exposure to violence.[181] Discussions of racism and colonialism, in academic research as well as in lay interpretations of that research, are by degrees becoming more cognizant of the possibility that exposure to violence in the form of the trauma of slavery and subjection to imperial force can be passed through generations. The clinical studies and the epigenetic research are converging, but the case is far from closed concerning biological evidence for intergenerational transmission. It is necessary to bear in mind that as of yet we "do not know how the process of establishing and maintaining epigenetic marks might differ for historical versus ongoing trauma, or for trauma that was directly experienced in utero or in the germline."[182] In other words, we do not yet understand how punctual trauma—experience of a discrete event—might be differentiated from chronic or "insidious" trauma, an ongoing structural problem. If it is true that the experience of terrible violence can leave an epigenetic mark, it might also be the case that "systemic racism can get under our skin and into our genes."[183] Recent studies of stress transmitted from African American mothers to their children, including stress from malnourishment, points increasingly to that likelihood.

To some degree it is necessary to see epigenetic research on racism and colonialism as "a prospective and anticipatory science."[184] The dots are not yet all connected. Scientific studies have framed a mechanism of heredity that as yet is not fully understood. Historical and literary studies, however, have for some time been engaged in tracking the ways in which trauma is transmitted in culture. There is strong evidence that has been supplied by such research. But, again, there remains much to learn. Mainstream media and public discussion have been broaching translations of such research into political claims, such as for reparations,[185] but it is paramount at this moment not to magnify scientific research into historical interpretation that exceeds its reach.[186] There is strong indirect evidence (i.e., longitudinal studies, such as the Dutch famine research) for much of the argument that is made in popular media. And there is an impressive convergence across studies that approach it in different ways. But the process of discovery of direct epigenetic evidence—"direct proof" of environmentally caused changes transmitted through *multiple* generations[187]—while highly encouraging, is ongoing and still in the early stages.

At the same time, it is essential, in the shadow of the January 6 insurrection, and from within the chronic racist predicament that plagues all Americans, to explore every possible avenue to understanding how racism was and is enacted, and how the pains of racist colonialism are transmitted intergenerationally. While there is value in taking a rigorously scientific view, and in recognizing that even enthusiastic neuroscientists cautioned in 2018 that "it is not possible to attribute intergenerational effects in humans to a *single* set of biological or other determinants at this time,"[188] it is reasonable to expect that a combination of approaches, including epigenetic studies in animals and humans, observational and historical studies, and environmental research, will continue to converge, and in so doing strengthen our understanding of the transmissibility of trauma over generations. That larger project also necessitates deeper critical analysis of the role of religion in transmitting trauma. It has long been clear that Euro-Americans drew on religion to justify mass violence and genocide. It has been less clear how religion collaborates in Americans' forgetfulness about their implication in that violence, and, paradoxically, how it continues to remind them of it.

Forgetting and Remembering

Emotional Memory

A recent study concludes that analysis of "the production of memories" about the Ghost Dance and Wounded Knee Massacre evidences how "memory documents emotion."[1] It is an observation that has deep roots in academic writing, and it remains crucial to understanding not only Wounded Knee but the intersection of race, violence, and religion in American history in the long century since. The current arguments that "there is no memory save emotional memory,"[2] and that memory is "inherently relational and affective,"[3] were articulated in humanities and scientific literature in the early twentieth century. The claims that all memory is "reconstructive," that is, assembled in the moment for the purpose of responding to immediate environmental stimuli and conditions, and that such reconstruction is characterized by both "cognitive and emotional biases,"[4] making emotion "part of the content" of "memory and narrative,"[5] now are standard in scholarship. Neuroscientific studies have offered evidence for "emotional memory" in a number of areas, including research that has foregrounded the role of the amygdala "to process mnemonic events in a way that specific emotional significance can be found and reactivated";[6] those studies identified the amygdala as "a bottleneck structure that confers an affective flavour to memories, thereby enhancing the probability of their long term storage."[7] Such affective valency ensures that intensely "emotional memories are typically harder to forget."[8] That is because, as fMRI research has shown, "memory control and affect regulation engage similar brain regions": memory and emotion both are regulated through a front parietal lobe (memory) networked with medial temporal lobe components involving the anterior hippocampus and amygdala (both of which are central to emotion).[9] The neural pathways for such parallel regulation of memory and affect are thus likely equally involved in the suppression of memory and its "affective traces."[10] There is emotional memory, and then there is emotional forgetting.

The scientific consensus that memory is entwined with emotion is built on a foundation laid by Frederic Bartlett's *Remembering: A Study in Experimental and Social Psychology* (1932). Bartlett, who had set out to understand how social institutions were involved in memory (a topic that he relegated to a back burner as his experimental research advanced, but referenced periodically in writing about memory),[11] proposed that memory is never "fixed and lifeless," but rather "constructive," in that the past is not a static inventory carried in the head, or anywhere else. It is assembled as needed, in "the life of the moment," and social forces as well as personal cognitive factors and "the affective setting" frame it. People were inclined to "rationalize" in constructing memories, but "this process of rationalisation is only partially—it might be said only lazily—an intellectual process . . . the end state is primarily affective."[12] Cognitive factors weighed heavily in the construction of memory, but because "the influence of affective attitudes" was so powerful,[13] and because cultural symbols likewise exerted influence—sometimes invisibly—the construction of memory was both a personal and a social process, and both a cognitive and an emotional one.

In making such arguments, Bartlett established a framework for a number of research initiatives involving forgetting and remembering, including the study of "implicit memory," which is unconscious and unintentional (such as riding a bike, brushing one's teeth, or reaching for the delete key on a computer keyboard).[14] It is "remembering without awareness," a mental process that was important to Freud, and, increasingly, to experimental psychology, where laboratory investigations utilizing word associations, reaction times, and social behaviors find that those activities "are influenced by non-conscious primes," that is, cues.[15] Such unconscious remembering can be "readily worked into socio-historical contexts, for often memories and impulses of a social system that have not gained clear, legitimized conscious expression emerge as phenomena of the dark (e.g., crime, terrorism, mushrooming of cults, and so on)."[16]

Key elements of Bartlett's work were advanced by studies in the 1940s and 1950s. In addition to reinforcing the argument that "part and parcel of its formation and operation are the affective aspects of the individual,"[17] it became clearer that emotion influenced memory and increasingly was made apparent that memory was a matter of constant "relearning."[18] Bartlett's assertion of "the certainty that the group is a psychological unit" led him to the conclusion that "social organization gives a persistent framework into which all detailed recall must fit, and it very powerfully influences both the manner and matter of recall."[19] This was an insight that proved fundamental to an eventual line of investigation that took "a non-cognitive, social-constructionist approach to forgetting and remembering," in which feelings played a central role.[20]

Mnemonic "relearning" sometimes was grounded in the trust that "it is good to forget." Michel de Montaigne praised forgetting as the bedrock of creative thinking and central to the production of knowledge,[21] and writers long have waxed about "the virtues of forgetting" for individuals.[22] One of those virtues was identity—or more precisely, identity formed in forgetting. That is what the French anthropologist Marc Augé meant when he wrote, "Tell me what you forget and I will tell you who you are."[23] Forgetting was, in some measure, a choice that made a person who they were. Chosen amnesias could be powerful engines of identity.

Forgetting that was good for an individual could be good for a group as well. Much of that opinion has to do with forgetting collective tragedy, that is, collective trauma. In *The Odyssey*, Zeus spoke to Athena regarding the aftermath of the bloodshed that ended that story: "Let us make them forget the death of their brothers and sons, and let them be friends with each other, as in the time past, and let them have prosperity and peace in abundance."[24] History echoes that judgment. Winston Churchill, in his speech in Zurich in 1946, affirmed that "we must all turn our backs on the horrors of the past . . . there must be an act of faith in the European family and an act of oblivion against all the crimes and follies of the past."[25] The historian Tony Judt thought likewise, though in retrospect, when weighing the fruit of forgetting: "Without such collective amnesia, Europe's astonishing post-war recovery would not have been possible,"[26] because "some measure of neglect and even forgetting" is "a necessary condition for civic health," even though, in the complex workings of memory, Europe "remains forever mortgaged to that past."[27] In "a world of violence and trauma, forgetting is as elemental to human action and human life as remembering."[28] Whether in Europe or Melanesia, "forgetting gives rise to 'society.' "[29]

If we were to approach the history of collective violence "in praise of forgetting,"[30] we would not be the first to do so, and in fact would reiterate the practices of governments and nations throughout history. The record of postwar treaty making, from *The Odyssey* up to the present, illustrates the centrality of forgetting to much of that history. One starting point for that history is 403 BCE, when the murderous oligarchy in Athens was overthrown and the transitional governing body decreed that citizens swear an oath renouncing revenge, in the interest of rebuilding and stabilizing democracy. The orator Andocides recollected the amnesty: "you resolved to let bygones be bygones, in spite of the opportunity for revenge. You considered the safety of Athens of more importance than the settlement of private scores; so both sides, you decided, were to forget the past."[31] Reformation-era religious wars likewise ended in promises to forget. In medieval Europe the Latin word *absolvere* gave way to *oblivisci* and *oblivio*, and eventually *amnestia*. The Peace of Westphalia, which ended the Thirty Years' War, spelled out in 1648 that "a general and unlimited Amnesty" should be extended to all who were involved in the fighting during "the Troubles of Bohemia and Germany."[32] The Peace Treaty of Rijswijk of 1697 between the French and British was similarly direct in its declaration of forgetting, the English translation reading, "all offences, injuries, damages, which the said King of Great Britain and his subjects, or the said most Christian King and his subjects, have suffered from each other during this war, shall be forgotten."[33] The royal edicts that ended the various Wars of Religion in France (1562–1598)—witnessed by Montaigne—stipulated "the forgetting of all harms done to each other" as events that were dead and buried ("*demeureront esteintes commes mortes ensevelies et non advenue*").[34]

Such sweeping effort to command forgetting remained a core component of treaties, and the mentality undergirding it—that amnesia of some sort is good for the group—has remained fundamental to the negotiation of genocidal aftermaths. That process is complex, as we shall see, and certainly its complexity is apparent in the efforts of Native Americans and African Americans to come to terms with their historical situations, both in the distant past and in ongoing events and circumstances. When the Miniconjou Lakota leader Black Moon urged his audience to "spread a blanket over that which has passed, and forget it,"[35] he was attempting to navigate a complex process involving both forgetting and remembering. So also was Glen Coultard, a Yellowknives Dene scholar, intending to look out for the good of the community when he critically observed that "state-sanctioned approaches to reconciliation" pilot memory into seemingly safe waters "by allocating the abuses of settler colonization to the dustbin of history," and in so doing behaving as if "there is no colonial present . . . but only a colonial past." But a past may never be past, even with the help of forgetting: "In such a context, I argue that Indigenous peoples' anger and resentment represents an entirely understandable— and in Fanon's words, 'legitimate'—response to our settler-colonial present."[36]

While psychologists such as Bartlett were experimenting with forgetting in the laboratory, anthropologists such as Edward Evans-Pritchard were observing it in the field. Evans-Pritchard's classic study of social life and pastoral cattle economy in Africa is also a landmark contribution to social forgetting. In *The Nuer: A Description of the Modes of Livelihood and Political Institutions of a Nilotic People* (1940), Evans-Pritchard, who was influenced by Bartlett, investigated the "puzzle" of apparent Nuer amnesia about ancestors.[37] He analyzed why and how the Nuer "forgot" generations of their ancestry prior to the fifth preceding generation (excepting a few founding generations), thereby ensuring that those generations were no longer reckoned in the political capital of family lineage. For the Nuer, social place was defined in terms of claims to cattle. One might come to possess more cattle, and improve one's status, through marriage (though a man could not contract for a wife until a certain number of cattle, typically forty head, were available to him to set up housekeeping). But with marriages arranged with an eye to incest regulations, the recollecting of family lineages eventually would reach a point, in the small Nuer community, where a blood connection between persons in the proposed marriage was apparent, thus disallowing the marriage. Accordingly, the deliberate forgetting of generations, an ongoing process as new generations came into existence, was a practice necessary to preserving the centrality of the status-conferring cattle culture to Nuer life and to the social institutions of the group.

The central insight of Evans-Pritchard, in Mary Douglas's words, was that "institutions direct and control the memory."[38] Douglas, who was, among other things, known for her study of "how institutions think,"[39] observed that Evans-Pritchard "presented Nuer social institutions as the schematic framework of memory,"[40] and in so doing broached the concept of social amnesia in British social anthropology. The claim that the generations "are not being forgotten randomly"[41] was reinforced by subsequent studies of other societies conducted over several decades,[42] and that insight has remained central to research about the social frameworks for forgetting. The broader scholarship has grown to include studies of collective identity, nation building, international relations, race, and other topics. Such research shares the common theme of the social and institutional construction of memory.

Whether in small settings such as a British clinic,[43] in national settings in Latin America, where government machineries and media networks powerfully sway ongoing construction of memory,[44] in transformational events of *la longue durée*, or in contemporary events that briefly fascinate a broad public, such as the Strauss-Kahn scandal,[45] there are "regimes of forgetting" that route memory into grooves worn by social forces and institutions. Such "social forgetting" is an adaptive process in that it selectively screens the past in order to protect collective identity.[46] That is, regimes of forgetting function to productively interrelate the social requirement of forgetting with the necessity of conserving tradition that enables group belonging, community order, and national identity. Nations rely on forgetting. Ernest Renan's oft-cited observation that "the essence of a nation is that all individuals have many things in common, and also that they have forgotten many things" expresses how social solidarity, paradoxically, is grounded partly in amnesia.[47] That amnesia is evident in various aspects of American history, including memory of the Civil War,[48] slavery, and Native American genocide.

Is it possible to entirely forget a violent event? Does an effort to forget lead to actual forgetting? Following the 1798 Ulster rebellion (an Irish revolt against British rule), there was a "socially constructed silence," a "social forgetting," that took place among the parties involved. Such forgetting, however, did not, in effect, consign the event to oblivion. Rather, the effort to mask memory of the rebellion served, in contrast, to hold it in memory, "sustaining, rather than eliminating, social memory." Silence as a space between forgetting and remembering in that case was a part of memory, a "compulsive engagement" with the past, and an example of how social forgetting "pivots on tensions between public calls for silence and demands for recognition of private recollections." In short, memory and forgetting were entwined. In a local culture of *oublier*, people nevertheless harbored "secret feelings" (memory being entwined with emotion) that endured.[49] Similarly, in Rwanda following the genocidal violence of 1994, there remains a "memoryscape . . . shaped by forgetting as well as remembering," whereby persons on both sides chose to perform as amnesiacs, but whereby years later, the atrocities remained "open secrets, which are both known by all and knowingly not known."[50] "Social amnesia" in such a case is the process of "how an entire society can forget, repress, or dissociate itself from its discreditable past record."[51] But that record is "known and not known at the same time."[52]

Nietzsche defined "active forgetting" as an adaptive strategy that enabled individuals and groups to digest terrible experiences. Active forgetting, as a healthy defense mechanism against painful memories, concealed those memories under a blanket of amnesia. In some cases, however, "this suppression apparatus is damaged," so that "this necessarily forgetful animal in whom forgetting represents a force, a form of *strong* health, has now bred in itself an opposite faculty, a memory, with whose help forgetfulness is disconnected."[53] The result is that "a closure and a clear demarcation between . . . remembering and forgetting, is not possible."[54] Recent research bears out some of what Nietzsche had in mind, and especially with regard to the lack of closure between forgetting and remembering. Although he took an interest in collective mentalities, Nietzsche was concerned largely with the mind of the individual. And while the fit between theories of personal remembering/forgetting and theories of the same within a collective can be imprecise at points, there nevertheless are insights that translate from one to the other. At a moment when psychological theories of "distributed and extended cognition"[55] propose that "remembering does not always occur entirely inside the brain but is often distributed across heterogeneous systems combining neural, bodily, social, and technological resources," the investigation of "socially shared forgetting" can exploit memory research that aims to integrate the social with the personal.[56]

Active Forgetting and Repression

Historical research increasingly is evidencing how "national memory is interpreted and amended discursively, privileging certain stories while actively or passively forgetting others."[57] That insight, and, more precisely, the focusing on active forgetting and passive forgetting as intertwined processes, similarly has come under discussion in recent neuroscientific and psychological research. The discussion has resulted in a range of arguments about the processes of remembering and forgetting. For some, the Freudian emphasis on "the 'unity of mental life' across the conscious unconscious continuum" suggested that "repression could be *both* conscious and unconscious."[58] And some neuroscientific research in fact concludes that what has been discovered in the lab "fits exactly to the psychodynamic theories of repression as a mechanism for avoiding conscious access to conflict-related material."[59] That is, it supports key ideas in Freud's thinking and subsequent psychoanalytic theory, including the principle that repressed memories are not lost. They linger. And they can reemerge "implicitly": "It has now become clear, as clinicians had claimed, that the inaccessible materials are often available and emerge indirectly (e.g., procedurally, implicitly)."[60] Whether repression itself is deliberate or unconscious remains a topic of debate, especially for those for whom literary trauma theory remains a methodological option.[61] The majority of opinion, however, is that repressed experiences—such as traumatic ones—are repressed consciously, that they nevertheless remain accessible to memory in certain ways, and that they sometimes can influence persons in ways in which they are unaware.

Conscious perception, supported by neural processes, strongly shapes behavior. It is linked at a fundamental level with working memory. But there is something to amend in the claim that working memory is always conscious: "recent behavioral and neuroimaging evidence, however, has questioned this prevailing view by suggesting that working memory may also operate unconsciously." For example, visual cues flashed to subjects in the laboratory could be recalled accurately by subjects' "guessing" even when those subjects said they had not seen them, magnetoencephalography data in such cases evidencing that cortical circuits (i.e., neural structures that are associated with consciousness) were engaged in processing but not at the level of enabling consciousness, an indication of genuine working memory without conscious perception.[62] Such "subliminal priming"[63] with zero visibility in immediate consciousness is one way of instancing "implicit memory" (another example of which is riding a bike). Additional empirical findings in psychology "suggest that a great deal of complex cognitive behavior could take place without conscious attention."[64] Research of neural circuits involving the amygdala and cortical structures that has focused on fear—with extension to the perception of threats in general—proposes, for example, that "while attention, working memory, and their underlying circuits support consciousness, working memory can be engaged without generating conscious content."[65]

Evidence of implicit memory requires that research define forgetting—and repression—as complex processes. Sometimes people forget by making an effort to do so, and sometimes forgetting appears to come naturally. Some neuroscientific research finds that it takes more effort to forget than to remember,[66] while some philosophical and historical writing claims otherwise. Heidegger, as one of his interpreters phrased it, held that forgetting is "more primordial than remembering,"[67] and other writing has similarly proposed that "not remembering, but forgetting, is the default mode of humans and societies."[68] For now, we can note that the issues that underlie debate within research about this aspect of memory—is it "natural" to forget, do people forget willfully, or are those processes mingled—have much to do with investigating how memory can be unconscious; that is, how repressed material or material that was never fully integrated into consciousness can pilot conscious behavior yet remain inaccessible as conscious memory. Can people know and not know at the same time?

Recent research has advanced understanding of how "memory success is predicated on both successful intentional encoding and successful intentional forgetting."[69] Experiments in active forgetting, under various nomenclatures such as "intentional forgetting," "motivated forgetting," "directed forgetting," and "deliberate forgetting," collect laboratory data of subjects who, in various ways, are prompted to avoid remembering or otherwise distracted from remembering. Intentional and unintended forgetting—or conscious and unconscious forgetting—thus are tested in various experimental designs.[70] (Additional research has studied group forgetting.) Such research has focused on "the neural evidence for the role of inhibitory control processes in the voluntary interruption of mnemonic processing."[71] So, for example, a reminder, some sort of cue, is given to a person to prompt a sudden recollection of an event, a situation, a feeling, or all of those, and the person then makes an effort to chase that from awareness. Structures in the lateral prefrontal cortex and subcortical areas are involved, exercising inhibitory control over the process of memory. When there are strong emotional coefficients to the memory (as is the case with trauma), brain regions involved in affect then also are more involved. In simplest terms, the "neurocognitive model of memory suppression" attends to neural circuits that include both the cortex and the hippocampus, which "shut down episodic retrieval to control awareness" so that "people can intentionally forget recently encountered information." That process can involve, for some persons, retrieving diversionary thoughts, and other means through which "people can clearly control retrieval."[72]

Such forgetting is active and adaptive. And it can cast an "amnesiac shadow" over events occurring in time just before and after that specific memory.[73] Control mechanisms that regulate memory retrieval typically do so by systematically suppressing hippocampal function, which disrupts encoding, stabilization, and retrieval and leads to diminished retention not only of specific memories but of chronologically proximate memories.[74] In such a way, what once was considered passive forgetting—memory decay over time without active disruption—can take place as an artifact of processes that regulate specifically disrupting memories (i.e., memories that do not align with a person's emotional or learning goals). The upshot of that process is that "processes previously thought of as passive, such as memory decay[, are] revealed to be biologically regulated and active."[75] But even those "inhibited" memories "remain intact . . . without becoming accessible" to consciousness,[76] sometimes in detail and sometimes as more general recollections.[77] Inasmuch as recall is reconstruction, inhibited memories, especially in cases involving trauma, are still available to potentially "exert an unconscious effect which dramatically influences subsequent life."[78]

Such scientific research instances in one way how current scholarship on Freud's theory of repression converges on the interpretation that for Freud, repression often was a conscious process of forgetting. That understanding fits well with the large body of research on directed, or motivated, forgetting.[79] People actively choose to forget, there are neural processes involved in that choice, memories thus forgotten can be recalled in whole or in part, and these memories can influence behavior in ways of which persons are unaware. What is deliberately forgotten thus is not entirely lost. Constructive memory calls on forgotten materials in shaping conscious responses to the environment. In that sense, what is forgotten, what is in one sense unknown, is, in fact, still known.

Collective and Cultural Remembering and Forgetting

Social groups remember and forget, and sometimes they, too, find themselves guided by socially constituted implicit memory. Research on such memory has advanced on the understanding that "individual and social processes combine to influence both remembering and forgetting,"[80] and that they are "inseparable."[81] Historians, sociologists, and anthropologists, like many psychologists and the broadening enterprise of social neuroscience ("the neural system does not act in isolation from its social context"),[82] have emphasized that separating individual from social experience, in matters of memory, has no research payoff. More broadly, "the useless opposition of history vs. memory," which offers up a cluster of hard binaries that include not only individual versus social, but lay versus scientific, emotional versus cognitive, and unrepresented versus ideological, leads nowhere. It is apparent that "the whole question of 'history and/or/as memory' is simply not a very fruitful approach to cultural representations of the past. It is a dead end in memory studies."[83] Group memories are present in individual minds, and the experiences of individuals become part of the memory of the group. There are no simple mechanisms in that process and there are distinctions to be made, but there is an emerging approach to memory, individual and social, that "helps us see (sometimes functional, sometimes analogical, sometimes metaphorical) relationships between such phenomena as ancient myths and the personal recollection of recent experience, and which enables disciplines as varied as psychology, history, sociology, and literary studies to engage in a stimulating dialogue."[84]

Increasingly, scholarship is inclined to the position that "we can discern distinctive principles governing collective episodic, semantic, and procedural memories by examining the principles governing their individual analogues."[85] Those three kinds of collective memories all have their individual cognates,[86] and those resemblances are taken as points of departure for analysis in memory scholarship, on the premise that "if individuals are the ones who do the actual remembering, then how a group remembers and what a group remembers will be shaped, in part, by the nature of the individual memory. Scholars of collective memory implicitly accept this claim."[87] Personal memories are intertwined with collective memories.[88]

Collective memories refer to a range of group experiences, from the levels of the extended family and the neighborhood to those of the state and culture. Tracking the interaction between individuals and such collectives is a complicated process: "Humans acquire these memories not only via lived experience, but also via interacting, communicating, identifying, and appropriating. It is often not easy to determine where one type of memory ends and another begins."[89] Theorists have proposed an assortment of ways in which to study the interrelation of individual and collective memory, some of which stress identity, individual and collective, as a key component of both, even while holding that such identity "may or may not be explicitly articulated,"[90] and proposing that it is possible to recognize "a plurality of identities and 'memory-systems' within the individual person," as well as in collectives.[91] The *lieux de mémoire* of Pierre Nora[92]—spaces between history and memory—point beyond themselves to the likelihood of multiple sites in different modes that, in their mediative capacities, effectively dismantle the posited opposition between history and memory, and between individual memory and collective memory. This is especially important in analyzing trauma and its transmission, given that "individual and cultural trauma need to be read together."[93]

If we speak specifically of cultural memory rather than of collective memory[94]—the two are related but can be distinguished—we gain an advantage in understanding how societies remember and forget. One benefit is that the term *cultural memory* eludes some of the contentious discussion descended from Halbwachs's theory of collective memory. Halbwachs opposed memory to history and emphasized the social construction of memory—forgetting as well as remembering—above all else. Additionally, he avoided engaging biological or physiological components of memory, which actually are the bedrock of the crucial "emotional ties" of which he wrote[95] (especially in his analyses of religious collectives,[96] the gist of which Hervieu-Léger has taken up directly from Halbwachs).[97] In spite of his seeming recognition of the emotional aspect of memory, Halbwachs failed to address how memory that was felt by individuals was enmeshed with socially constructed ideas about the past.[98] His scholarship in that regard might be understood as a different approach from that of the historian of *mentalités* whom he influenced, Philippe Ariès, who affirmed an alliance between history and memory, and the suffusion of both with emotion[99] (an approach that Ariès shared with his fellow *annaliste* and early historian of emotions Marc Bloch). In short, research since Halbwachs has shown that cognitive and affectual elements of remembering and forgetting are neurally interrelated, but the Halbwachsian term *collective memory* still bears an unwanted baggage of binaries. To speak of cultural memory, on the other hand, offers opportunities for examining the collaboration of individual experience with the group in a way that does not require apologies for crossing an imagined history-memory divide.[100] It pointedly observes "the interplay of present and past in sociocultural contexts" in a manner that "is not restricted to the study of those ways of making sense of the past which are intentional and are performed through narrative."[101] It is an "approach to studying collective memory in which the individual, the collective, and the culture are treated as a single unit of analysis."[102] It is memory that "is shared outside the avenues of formal historical discourse yet is entangled with cultural products and imbued with cultural meaning."[103]

Absence, Ritual, and Religion

Memory is "fluid and changing" rather than a binary of remembering and forgetting.[104] Friedrich Nietzsche, who argued that "it is altogether impossible to live at all without forgetting," thought that remembering and forgetting were "necessary in equal measure for the health of an individual, of a people, and a culture" and ideally were related in a homeostatic fashion, a balancing between the two being most beneficial.[105] Writers on the topic of memory since Nietzsche have continued to articulate how remembering and forgetting are dialectically related, whether the framework for that is individual or group memory or an interrelated both, and whether one is looking at memory from the ground up—as do anthropologists, for example—or from the top down—as do some philosophers. A look from the ground at Congolese tribal life leads one "to speak of memory work, a dialectical notion . . . that makes it possible to think remembering and forgetting together," and to perceive "forgetful remembering."[106] One can detect, again, in the aftermath of the 1798 rebellion in Ulster, "multi-layered dialectical relationships between oblivion and remembering."[107] The view from the philosopher Paul Ricoeur's desk opens a similar vista of "the imbrication of forgetting in memory."[108] For Jan Assmann, a scholar of cultural memory, the concept is the same: "memory goes hand-in-hand with forgetting," or, more specifically, with "a process of forgetting, moments of rupture and rebirth."[109] And it may even be the case in the broader calculation of things that the process is more than dialectical, involving remembering, forgetting, and "remembering-forgetting," a kind of trialectical potentiality inherent in archives and libraries, museums and memorials, where stored materials are accessible, even if not either remembered or forgotten at a given moment.[110]

The dialectics of remembering and forgetting frame absence in a distinctive way. For Ricoeur, there is a type of forgetting that secures traces of memory rather than annihilating them. The "*oubli de reserve*," or "backup forgetting," is "a sort of forgetting kept in reserve."[111] In practical terms, such forgetting is never gone. It is an absence that is remembered, and somewhat confoundingly might become all the more powerful a memory because of its absence. Psychological research evidences that "shared memories are formed . . . as much a result of collective forgetting as collective remembering," and stresses "the importance of silences not only shaping collective memories but also individual and collective identities."[112] Anthropological research increasingly has taken a similar perspective, theorizing the "persistent non-presence" of forgetting, which "along with memory, looks as if it is on the side of permanence and retention," always active, but invisibly so.[113] What is forgotten allows other material to emerge, a process underlying "the crucial role of forgetting in the creation of social memory" and "the creation of a shared identity."[114] The forgetting of one's ancestors in a Langkawi, Malaysia, society—as was the case with the Nuer studied by Evans-Pritchard—is a positive process of social solidarity and identity maintenance, and not least because—as it is "gradual and unmarked— its effects are, in a sense, more hidden," shaping social knowledge implicitly.[115] A similar practice of disremembering the dead in another Malaysian society, where by contrast there is transparency about that practice—"forgetting is acknowledged as a collective goal"[116]—likewise functions to maintain collective identity. But in these cases, and others, the crux of the matter is the awareness of absence, whether it was a willed forgetting or an implicit process.

The 9/11 memorial at Ground Zero, "Reflecting Absence," is a plaza with two great square excavations in the ground (the outlines of the foundations of the fallen towers), surrounded on top by walls of rail height engraved with the names of those who died. Water rushes down from the inside walls of the two structures and disappears into a hole at the bottom. The memorial conjures the absence of loved ones who are not really absent, but remembered, and most powerfully so because of the unmistakable, explicit symbolization of forgetting, of names and lives seemingly draining out of the walls, out of consciousness, into a black oblivion, witnessed by the crowds who stand behind the walls. The people killed that day are absent, but they are strongly present in their absence. Such memorials can be described as "the presence of absence," and in some places, especially an absence that is *felt*, that is "marked by emotional appeals and affective investments."[117]

When we consider forgetting in connection with absence, we are thinking about the situated return of what has been forgotten. It is possible to speak of "a space of active forgetting," a counterpart to the *lieux de mémoire* of Nora, as in postcolonial Sri Lanka, where the struggle for identity among Tamil and Sinhalese communities is complex and deeply contentious, in "a space haunted by the very past that one forgets."[118] It is a space in which forgetting and remembering are joined, a "memoryscape" that is ambiguous, fluid, and shifting[119]—like Hades, where the river Lethe (the Greek spirit of forgetting) and the pool Mnemosyne (the goddess of memory) were located alongside each other. The creation of silences and absences through forgetting, paradoxically, can lend power to those things that are forgotten, holding them in memory. An absent group, such as the supposedly forgotten Armenians, can be powerfully present: "When Hitler asked, 'Who today remembers the Armenians?' the resounding answer should have been, 'We all do.' Or, at least, 'The enlightened world does.' (The irony in Hitler's question is that in fact he counted on his listeners to remember the Armenians)."[120] Deliberate forgetting can be a circular process: "It is pretty clear that just being told to 'forget it' does not quite secure forgetfulness: if anything, it increases the chance of remembering."[121] Repression is that kind of forgetfulness. Cultural memories—monotheism itself—can be repressed, and return in force.[122]

Burying memory can intensify it. One way of understanding that is to examine local practices of remembering and forgetting, especially inasmuch as they involve the actual burying or sequestering of material artifacts. Aby Warburg, in the sixty-three panels of his *Mnemosyne Atlas*,[123] a stunningly ambitious project of exhibition of art he undertook in 1924 and continued until his death in 1929, tracked the pathways by which *Pathosformeln*—emotionally charged visual tropes—faded and then emphatically recurred in Western culture, and in so doing reinvigorated and redirected memory. The spirit of that project is redolent in a growing number of studies that track memory and forgetting by attending to the cultural life of material objects. Or, more precisely, they track them through their attention to "the place of memory not in objects, but in the spaces created by rendering absent the products of memorywork."[124]

In a community in the Bismarck Archipelago in Melanesia, people make a *malanggan*, an elaborately carved or woven object that is created as part of an irregularly held mortuary rite. When the rite has finished (the artifact typically remains on the grave for a single night), the *malanggan* is destroyed or left to rot, with "no visible trace of the commemorative work that once provided the common focus for a community." Accordingly, it would appear that "not remembrance, but forgetting through the literal burying of memories thus effects the finishing of the work of the dead."[125] However, the role of such a ritual of apparent forgetting evidences that "recollection does not cease when there are no longer any traces of what is to be remembered, but draws it force from this absence."[126] Local culture, formed around a ritual in which the dead appear to be washed from memory, in fact undertakes the creation of elaborate *malanggan*, and then destroys them, because that process, "enables with its erasure, the creation of an inherently recallable image: it thus instigates a process of remembering."[127] It is the "object, which is remembered only when it has disappeared," that is embedded in memory that sustains community.[128]

Similarly, at the friary of Carmarthen Greyfriars in Wales, the medieval placement of bodies in the floor of the church exemplifies how "remembering *and* forgetting were attained through ritual activity and the use of material culture." There, memory can be seen as "as a social practice in which material culture has a central role, rather than simply a process of storage of

information. In this sense, churches and churchyards are spaces in which remembering and forgetting are 'performed' through the use of material culture
and the bodies of the dead. This performance concerned both remembering and forgetting since over time, and sometimes deliberately, the individual
person would be forgotten . . . but it also included collective remembrance of
the dead."[129] In other words, in a highly complex process that navigated between recognitions of individual and group identity, the solitary individual
was forgotten but the individual as part of a social group was remembered
as "memories were not only stored, but accreted and subsumed beneath the
floor layers and in between the steps upon which the friars walked during
their daily services."[130] Individual graves in the floor could be forgotten but
not the layout of the graves in three dimensions, because of the need to inter subsequent dead, with the result that a collective memory of the collective itself was redolent in "the spatial organisation of the church [which] was
repeatedly remembered and respected through the history of the friary."[131]

Chaco Canyon, a historic Native American site in New Mexico, is a related
case in that it illustrates the manner in which the burying of objects can rein-
force their presence. Though technically, at Chaco, certain objects—ceramics,
turquoise, wooden objects—were "stored," they were stored in a manner that
removed them entirely from presence. Artifacts were sealed behind walls,
in pilasters, and in kiva niches, hidden from the everyday life of the Pueblo
community, "secreted away rather than destroyed."[132] Secrecy, "an important
principle among contemporary Pueblos," is detectable in the "practice of secrecy" as a ritual performance "in which things that are hidden acquire value
through the acts of gathering them together and placing them in architec-
tural cavities."[133] Chaco is an example of how secrecy and hiding are part of
memory work.

In twentieth-century Rwanda, where, postgenocide, "collective identity
is . . . not only produced by remembering but by forgetting," groups invest in
a "chosen amnesia" in order to negotiate the aftermath of the violence. That
"chosen amnesia leads to a deliberate exclusion of traumatic events from discourse in order to prevent a sense of closure." Such a "remembering to forget"
at the same time leads to a situation in which persons navigate their social
roles with awareness of "hidden secrets" in the form of the memory of profound violence.[134] Such secrets themselves can be central to group identity, as
purportedly "hidden" knowledge (or what is "known but not known"). While
a group makes an effort to bury memory, at the same time, "in an apparent
paradox, the extremely disconcerting or traumatic may also be affirmed or
embraced as the foundation of identity."[135]

Forgetting is abetted by institutions and ritual practice. Regimes of forgetting[136] are constituted by "social practices"[137] of forgetting, and range in scale from the rituals of health care facilities to mass media,[138] from townships to nations. Like the social practice of remembering, such a regime is "a system-level accomplishment,"[139] in which "forgetting is an accomplishment of remembering,"[140] that "gives rise to 'society.'"[141] Institutional forgetting might be "an integral part of the organization of science,"[142] as much as a matter of addressing intrafamily frictions. Institutions play a central role in forgetting because they "direct and control the memory," overseeing "a mnemonic system that is the whole social order," and ensuring that information is "not being forgotten randomly."[143] Bartlett stressed the role of social institutions in forgetting, and that insight has been borne out in numerous studies since. In examining "practices of institutional remembering and forgetting, it is possible to see how the continuity of social life, as preserved in certain forms of social practices," is dependent on those practices.[144]

Mary Douglas placed strong emphasis on the institutional role in remembering and forgetting. In its quest for legitimacy, the institution seeks a "distinctive grounding in nature and in reason" and "then starts to control the memory of its members; it causes them to forget experiences incompatible with its righteous image. . . . It provides the categories of their thought, sets the terms for self-knowledge, and fixes identities. . . . This is Durkheim's doctrine of the sacred."[145] Institutions direct forgetting, and religious institutions especially do so.

Religious Institutions and Forgetting

For Mircea Eliade, "the true sin is forgetting."[146] Eliade accordingly foregrounded religion as a means to remembering. His emphasis on collective memory of how the world was created, how a ritual is to be performed, the religious calendar, and other aspects of religious life all were in service to his positing the "eternal return" that he saw in religion, a practiced *mentalité* that conserved tradition and relived the past—a ritual immersion of groups *in illo tempore*, the mythical time when everything began in the generative acts of the gods. His privileging of remembering was widely adopted as a framework for understanding religion, including by Hervieu-Léger, for whom religion is "a chain of memory," and whose Durkheimian emphasis on collective memory "as a regulator of individual memory" also foregrounded the specific *emotive* power of "cultural memory."[147] For Jonathan Z. Smith, who helped to carry on Eliade's vaunted history-of-religions initiative at the University of

Chicago, a crucial project was the articulation of the task of the field. About that he wrote: "I take my point of departure from the observation that each scholar of religion, in his way, is concerned with phenomena that are historical in the simple, grammatical sense of the term, that is to say, with events and expressions of the past, reconceived vividly. The scholar of religion is, therefore, concerned with dimensions of memory and remembrance."[148] These scholars, and the many who have written similarly about religion, did not deny that forgetting took place in religion, and in fact at times offered theories about how forgetting in religion was related to secularity, science, labor, and sex. But they did not propose that forgetting is fundamental to religion or that religious institutions were instrumental in fostering collective forgetting.

Forgetting is indeed fundamental to religion. Jan Assmann has built, over the course of decades, a historical argument for taking deliberate forgetting as integral to cultural memory, and for understanding the signal role that religion historically has played in that process.[149] But it arguably was Niccolò Machiavelli who made the claim more forcefully, given the politics of his milieu. He called attention to "the ways that the Christian sect has used against the pagan one: it has erased all the others, all the ceremonies of the latter and has extinguished every memory of that old theology."[150] For Machiavelli, the march of Christianity was a massive institutionally driven project of forgetting the past, of radically altering collective memory. Religion could bear the past forward or erase it. Either was as likely. For him, "religion is not just an object in the process of forgetting, it is the decisive actor; it is not religion that is forgotten, but religion (or the change of religion) engenders forgetting." He recognized "the power of religion to 'engender forgetting' implicitly and explicitly."[151]

Edward Gibbon, like Machiavelli, registered the force of Christianity in erasing religions that preceded it, as with the triumph of Christianity in the Roman Empire, which amounted to the tragic erasure of a rich pagan tradition.[152] But it was not only in the West that such forgetting occurred and still occurs. In Indonesia, conversion to Christianity served as a "technology of forgetting," as converts shifted the markings of their identities to represent their embeddedness in new communities.[153] In Bangladesh, conversion to Islam served a similar purpose, as "the very nature of the sort of conversion to 'true Islam' effected by the main instrument of Islamist Reform," a specific Islamic mission society, "entails a turning away from, a forgetting, of some of the genres of discursive self-production that have defined rural Bangladesh."[154] In medieval Iceland, conversion to Christianity was a "traumatic event" that leveraged mass forgetting in altering cultural memory.[155]

Religions foster forgetting by creating and sustaining technologies of forgetting. Whether in Bangladesh, where "Islamization or Christianization can serve as technologies of forgetting";[156] or in America, where Christian ideas and practices encoded in law have profoundly shaped a national narrative that forgets the violence of colonialism; or in the mortuary rituals of Melanesia, where the dead are ceremonially forgotten, technologies of forgetting involving texts, rituals, and patterns of everyday religious practice erode, distort, screen, and otherwise repress memory. Such religious technologies of forgetting are part of a broader inventory of instances of ritual forgetting that is evident in a wide range of social practice.

The practice of "devout forgetting" that is observable in religions can include explicit recommendations to forget.[157] Monotheism, like many other religions, values remembering. But that does not mean that forgetting is not also powerfully manifest in religious practice, and especially for groups with a mystical bent. Texts in Bratslav Hasidism "emphasize the role of forgetting as a modus operandi of the *Tsaddik*, the Hasidic mystical leader." Those "texts exemplify that forgetting is not only a cognitive and experiential phenomenon; it also has ontological, ethical, mystical, and social implications."[158] The early Muslim Andalusian mystic Ibn al-'Arabī is said to have believed that "human forgetting and human errors are necessary for the unfolding and materialization of the Divine Plan."[159] Such forgetting at times may seem accidental, but even then it can play a positive role. More important is the institutional fostering of deliberate forgetting. When church leaders promote forgetting—as in Rwanda after the genocide[160]—there is a particular dynamic at work. It is clearly evident in the deliberate forgetting advocated by Christian groups in America.

In community life, "deliberate performative practices of forgetting" are aligned alongside technologies of remembering,[161] such as, for example, what Benedict Anderson termed "print capitalism," the fostering of remembering when "capitalism and print created monoglot reading publics."[162] Communities practice a behavioral repertoire of "habits of forgetting and remembering" that guide them through collective reflection on national sacrifice and patriotic dedication to ideological goals.[163] Various groups within a society practice such a repertoire as well. Scholars frequently have discussed such habits and technologies when analyzing, for example, the predicament of migrants situated between two worlds. Immigration policies historically have functioned in such a way as to maximize the likelihood that memory of past markers of communal belonging "could be washed out through the national immigration rituals of the 'melting pot.'" The "rituals of forgetting that accompanied immigration" that fostered a change of identity were, in that moment, "not understood as a prescriptive forgetting"—although they most certainly were—but rather as a future-oriented bet on social productivity and advancement.[164] In many cases, that regime of forgetting involved religion, both as an impediment to socialization (when it was the religion of the foreigner), and therefore memory to be altered or even erased, as well as religion as an American asset that offered its own program of forgetting, which abetted the acculturation of migrants.

In writing about religious rites in some African communities, Augé commented that rites of initiation that integrate young persons into the community as adults are predicated on the trust that those rites will implement a "forgetting [of] the past, to create the conditions for a new birth."[165] That idea—that the self has to be forgotten so that a new person can be born—has been fundamental to Christianity throughout its history, and especially so in "born-again" evangelical Christianity in America. Christian rituals of forgetting are abundant, but they are joined to an ideological insistence on the necessity of emptying the self—of forgetting the self, erasing it—so that a person can be filled with God.

The Christian insistence on the cultivation of an experience of emptiness, especially in the United States and in the evangelicalism that arose there, is as old as Christianity itself. Conversion, the "new birth," was exemplified in early Christian literature in the experience of Saint Paul, and through the centuries, from Augustine to Luther, Jonathan Edwards, colonial Catholic missions, and the small army of evangelical television personalities worldwide, it has remained central to most Christian thinking about personal holiness and one's place in the world. Christian conversion is ritualized forgetting. Christian practice is an ongoing process of emptying the self. Christianity requires forgetting because remembering depends on that: the self must be emptied before it can be filled with God.[166] As the Adventist visionary Ellen Gould White advised her followers, Christians should "empty themselves of self."[167] One could not be reunited to God—one could not remember God—until one had forgotten oneself.

Christians created a world in North America that took emptiness to be a core experience of both Christian life and emergent American society. From the earliest British settlers in New England, who wrote constantly about the empty land—the "desart" of North America—to later writers who pictured the western territories similarly—as, for example, by imagining, and in fact mapping, "The Great American Desert,"[168] a Sahara-like space in the trans-Mississippi—the trope of emptiness has been crucial to white Christians' conceptions of their spirituality and to the empire that they created through westward movement. Indians were empty—empty of virtue, of grace, of knowledge. Africans who were forced to clear land, plant it, build canals, and blaze trails likewise were imagined as empty of whatever was needed to make a person moral. In other words, as they settled the continent, Christians erased its histories and cultures, which were those of the ways of life of its Indigenous inhabitants and the slaves who transformed it. White Christians applied the core theological lesson of the necessity of self-erasure to the task of taking land and making it over in the image of their European ways of life. They aimed to forget the precontact continental past and demanded that others forget it as well.

Christian institutions churned out that message in manifold ways, exploiting a vast catalog of technologies of forgetting perfected over centuries to facilitate wiping memory clean: sermons and prayers, church building, doctrinal formulations, warmongering, bodily disciplines such as fasting,[169] silence, and bleeding,[170] and doctrines such as forgiveness, which, taught John Calvin, was to "willingly banish to oblivion the remembrance of injustice."[171] The institutional power of Christianity in America since the "closing of the frontier" remains on full display, from the efforts made by the Roman Catholic leaders to erase the record of sexual abuse of children by its clergy—a particularly wishful foray at forgetting that even the formidable technologies of that organization could not, in the end, manage—to ongoing calls from revivalist ministers for persons to approach the front of the congregation and perform a self-erasure that would enable the new birth of conversion.

The Christian institutional machinery of forgetting as it gathered steam in North America included, as discussed earlier, a depiction of the opponents of white Christian ambitions as kin-like enemies. Those Amalekites, who could be identified with reference to key Old Testament texts, were to be annihilated—exterminated and forgotten. But, as the biblical text made clear, paradoxically they were to be forgotten but remembered. That is, Christians were to forget them and then take care to remember that they had forgotten them. This core paradox of the Christian engineering of forgetting in America—from the forgetting of enemies of color to the forgetting of white perpetration of genocide and other crimes—is a central component in the cycles of violence that have characterized the nation's history. Christians have made heroic efforts to forget the destruction they have wrought. But because forgetting and remembering are joined, and because sometimes the most vigorous efforts to forget result in the deepening of a sense of absence, a sense of something that was to be forgotten but is not, those efforts to forget have left the nation haunted. The ghosts do not die.

Indian Ghosts

Trauma can be "a psychic haunting" that "spreads as it enters a culture's semiotic system,"[172] shaping not just literature but patterns of everyday life as it changes the signs of things, marks events and actors, and prompts new rituals of remembering/forgetting. That "haunting transmission of trauma across generations," which involves perpetrators as well as victims,[173] can be represented in ghostlore, in the appearance of ghosts at séances or dark bedrooms, in gossip and conversation, and in religion. Ghosts are everywhere in religion, and they are vividly present in the devotions of American Christians. Whether identified as angels, devils, the spirits of dead ancestors, saints, famous figures from the past, unknown figures, or even Jesus and his mother Mary, ghosts, phantoms, spirits, specters, and other figures are lively inhabitants of the invisible/visible world they share with American Christians. They remind Christians of things they have forgotten or are in danger of forgetting. They can make their presence known at auspicious moments, but typically they appear unexpectedly, intervening dramatically in the lives of those who believe in them. They can warn and comfort, explain and obfuscate, speak of the future, and, especially, they can represent the capability of the past from which they arise to inform the present. They bear the marks of the past. They are a witness to it, and they deliver their testimony to those with whom they have contact. They might do that in language, speaking through a medium. Or they might do it simply by appearing as an Indian.

A ghost that haunts the living returns from the dead voluntarily. That return "is the symptom of a deep crisis; it is felt as a violent and threatening interruption of the present. Something that has been deemed overcome and gone appears to announce some unfinished business that needs to be addressed."[174] Americans who had plowed through the land populated by the thousands of tribes and language groups that inhabited North America, and who took on a religiously justified agenda of extermination and forgetting, of manifest destiny and Christian nationalism, were haunted by the memory of their violence against Indians. Americans tried hard, said a writer in 1876, "to forget those instances of indiscriminate massacre of disarmed Indians, which have been perpetrated by the troops of the United States government."[175] But the business of coming to terms with the massacre of Indians remained unfinished. The perpetrators, suffering from trauma, could not forget what they had done.

In 1814 Washington Irving told the story of a Sachem whose mother's grave the English had plundered and who reported to the English his dream in which his mother vowed, "I shall not rest quiet."[176] Nevertheless, Americans early on set themselves on a course to screen from memory the travail of Native Americans, practicing in each succeeding generation a forgetting that produced, in American writing of the nineteenth century, the ubiquitous expression "forgotten Indian." Forgetting the Indian meant, above all, forgetting war with the Indian. Americans had little trouble recalling bloody conflicts with European enemies in North America or even between rival American groups, such as federalists and anti-federalists, country people and seaboard cosmopolites. But Indian wars were whisked from memory, their flight abetted by contrived appraisals that there was not much there in the first place. Daniel Dorchester, the Methodist author of *Christianity in the United States*, dismissed them with a wave of the pen in 1890, boldly proclaiming, "Nor have the American people known much of the horrors of war. Compared with European conflicts, the intermittent Indian Wars, however exasperating in their frequency and decisiveness, were trivial military incidents."[177] A contemporary of Dorchester's dismissed them as relatively bloodless: "Shay's rebellion, Dorr's attempted revolution, the Whiskey War, and a dozen or so forgotten Indian wars and 'campaigns,' as they were sometimes called in the early history of the West, when there happened to be more marching than fighting, would, all combined, make an almost bloodless affair, compared with the Draft Riot in New York City in July, 1863."[178] That the author remembered Dorr's Rebellion (1841–42) in Rhode Island—which indeed was all marching and no shooting, as no one was injured and the cannon failed to fire—while forgetting the names of Indian wars was in itself eloquent testimony to forgetting.

But there were some Americans who, like Mary C. Greenleaf, a missionary to the Chickasaw Indians, warned: "Don't forget the Indians."[179] And in the broader scheme of things, the Indians did not "rest quiet." Alongside the references to the forgotten Indian were those affidavits, trailing the vines of trauma, that hedged the bet. They portrayed the Indian as "almost forgotten." And that experience of *almost* forgetting was securely interlaced with memory of war. Thus when Charles Colcock Jones was writing, on the eve of the Civil War (less than thirty years after the Indian Removal Act, which forcibly relocated Creeks and Cherokees out of his region), about Indian remains in Georgia, he chose to approach the issue with a reference to weapons: "Of all the remains that still exist, silently reminding us of the almost forgotten Indian, none are so abundant as the spear, and the arrow-heads."[180]

The almost forgetting of the Indian and the wars with Indians was a national experience. It was a collective forgetting. The ghost of the Native American was like the ghost who "understood as a medium of troubled, repressed, silenced, or forgotten past" ventured forth from "individual memory to that of the collective and shared constructions of the past."[181] That venturing forth took place in the nineteenth century among the white middle class, where "family ghosts became less important, while communal ghosts grew more significant."[182] The ghost of the Indian became a central character in a

nineteenth-century American literature that wrestled with a frightening colonial past, and especially with a record of violence against Indians that Euro-
Americans had extended and enhanced post-Revolution. As several decades of
scholarship has amply attested, the figure of the Indian, portrayed as a vanishing and defeated, but noble and natural, subject, was literarily migrated out of
the forest and plains into the pages of novels, poems, essays, and newspapers.[183]

Again, as we have seen, Native Americans proved themselves resilient.
While their numbers were in stunning decline, they nevertheless were adapting, finding pathways through the tragedies that the mad dash for land, and
its partner, the militant Christianization of the West, had caused. As much as
white Christians imagined them to be "almost forgotten," Indian communities remained a distinct presence in locations distal from the East Coast urban
centers. They negotiated their changing positions in society with a survivance
that enabled them to carve out pockets of refusal in which they fostered continuity in their cultural traditions while making concessions to the political
and economic pressures caused by white settlement and exercise of military
force. But such resilience, which would prove crucial to reconstitutions of
Native American life over many decades, was largely unknown in city parlors
and newsrooms. There, with the exception of those who were a part of the
touring Wild West shows, the Indians already were ghosts.

Just a sampling of nineteenth-century American literature that contrib-
uted to the construction of the Indian ghost would stretch from Washington
Irving's *The Sketchbook of Sir Geoffrey Crayon* and James Fenimore Cooper's
The Last of the Mohicans to an outpouring of haunted stories and essays by
Nathaniel Hawthorne, Charles Brocken Brown, Lydia Maria Child, Catha-
rine Maria Sedgwick, Henry David Thoreau, Margaret Fuller, Herman Mel-
ville, and especially Henry Wadsworth Longfellow's extraordinarily popular
The Song of Hiawatha and Francis Parkman's widely read *The Oregon Trail*.
By the early twentieth century, there seemed to be an Indian ghost haunting most towns between Pawtucket, Rhode Island, and Olympia, Washington.[184] American writing brimmed with "Native American ghosts: because
American national literature is obsessed with them."[185] Such literature spoke
of the vanishing Indians, lamenting their extinction as it literally wrote them
off, while enshrining Indian nobility and bravery, transparency and natural-
ness, grit and passion. It ventriloquized Indians, consenting to their erasure
at the same time that it mourned their passing. It canceled Indian societies
while offering white Americans a lens that focused the Indian as a model for
what they thought they could be. Such was one of the backgrounds that informed Jake Chansley's performance at the Capitol on January 6, 2021. The
"QAnon Shaman" celebrated the vanquishing of Indians at the same time that

he channeled them. Costumed to appear part human and part animal, part white American and part Indian, part patriot and part rebel, he performed as a ghost, partly remembered and partly forgotten.

Anxiety about the looming ghosts of Indians was related to another anxiety about white contact with Indians. From the earliest British settlement of the Atlantic littoral, clergy and civic leaders voiced a concern that settlers might turn into Indians. Fear of Indianization was widespread, and was of particular concern in New England, where the notion of a religiously pure holy commonwealth informed collective identity and theoretically guarded against slippage into indigeneity. Fanatical policing of its boundaries raised the stakes for any departure from that ideal. Fear of Indianization has been well documented by historians of the colonial era, who have addressed the reasons for that nervousness among New England clergy, especially.

Those seventeenth-century clergy would have been aghast at the extent to which their descendants "played Indian."[186] As much as Americans affirmed that the Indian was forgotten and that the Indian wars were trivial, not worth remembering, and not real, they could not escape the memory of Native Americans. They performed that memory in manifold ways throughout the nineteenth century, drifting in liminality between forgetting and remembering the Indian. Americans celebrating special events or national holidays, or just gathering for social occasions, called on their imaginations in dressing, whooping, hunting, feasting, and competing as they presumed Indians did.[187] They bought artifacts of Indian history and proudly displayed them in their homes, enthusiastically toured sites embodying Indian history, organized Indian study clubs, and learned Indian words. Some collected Indian skulls and bones, an epistemological gymnastic in which they sought to remember what they knew they had erased. While forgetting Indians, some Americans simultaneously were "going native."[188]

For the paradigm-setting American historian Frederick Jackson Turner, the internalization of the Indian was fundamental to American advance across the frontier.[189] It was as if "the original act of Turner's imagined American is the act of becoming Indian."[190] Turner, writing in 1893, posited a deep connection between Euro-Americans and Native Americans. That same year, the Columbian Exposition, like the Centennial Exposition of 1876, variously posed Indians on the museum stage,[191] constructing them as kin to whom Americans would forever be attached.[192] The head of an Indian ended up on the American nickel. And in 1913, ground was broken for a 165-foot-tall statue of an American Indian warrior overlooking New York harbor. The monument, which was to be taller than the Statue of Liberty, was not built, but the project conception itself ghosted New York for a century.

Indians haunted an America that had massacred them. The forgotten Indian would not go away because white Americans were attached to Indians, to a certain dream of Indians. That attachment was dysfunctional because it was rooted in repressed memory of genocidal violence. And that memory percolated in manifold ways, including through religion, and perhaps most vividly, but by no means exclusively, in the religion of Spiritualism. The American enthusiasm for Spiritualism, which began in the mid-nineteenth century and peaked at the end of that century, represented in microcosm American fluttering between the past and the present, between remembering and forgetting.[193] It is possible to identify "concerns about Indian affairs as a driving social force of Spiritualism" and track how a religious movement with perhaps millions of members across the nation made the Indian present in séances.[194] The Boston Spiritualist John Wetherbee in 1885 accordingly explained that "one of the noticeable features in the phenomena of modern Spiritualism is the prominence it gives to the departed Indian race." He was in awe of the "power of the Indian element in its departed, invisible, but still living form." Wetherbee, a rich Bostonian who sought business advice from the dead in séances, confessed that he felt badly about the white man's treatment of the Indian, and that Spiritualists were "indebted to the departed Osceolas, Black Hawks, Red Jackets, Violets, or Blueflowers of that singular aboriginal people that once covered, in their wild and natural way, this North American Continent."[195] Sometimes Indians who had witnessed massacres of their people manifested to Spiritualists.[196]

Séances were not visited solely by Indians. Figures as wide-ranging as Martin Luther, Napoleon Bonaparte, and Martha Washington delivered messages to persons in séances, in the Northeast as well as in gatherings in other parts of the country, such as in the African American Cercle Harmonique in New Orleans.[197] And not all connections with spirits were through a standard Spiritualist format—Shakers, for example, also claimed to be able to host spirits, including Indians. But in many Spiritualist séances, mediums communicated messages from the vanished-but-not-gone by giving themselves over to the spirit of a particular Indian, who informed about the past as well as circumstances of the present, and even predicted the future. Spiritualism "turned on a notion of flux, both in subjectivity and time." In a certain way, it could be about "connectedness but not identity" with a particular spirit. The authority of Spiritualism can be understood as a matter of how "Spiritualists infused their own religion with the once and future power of the (un)vanished Indian. It is precisely because Spiritualist cosmology resisted the idea of the dead as vanished that Spiritualists professed special access to Indian ghosts."[198]

Memory of the Indians, repressed in a culture that had committed generations of atrocities against them, manifested as ghosts in the embodied practice of Spiritualist religion, in which mediums and attendees registered a range of physical signs in séance—speaking, fainting, hearing things, trembling, swooning, shivering, weeping, shouting, and feeling a hand on their skin, or breath on their face—that testified to the presence of Indians who had vanished. Americans who attended the meetings reported that they could "feel the presence" of an Indian ghost.[199] But like Wetherbee, who averred, "I often feel the presence of unseen company," Americans often did not know who the company was or what it wanted.[200] Such haunting, as it expanded into many corners of the culture, influencing many things—from temperance and women's rights to constructions of gender and sexuality[201]—became "a defining aspect of national self-consciousness, particularly of white subjects."[202] In the late nineteenth century, not only in writing such as Henry James's *The Bostonians* (1886) and Pauline Hopkins's *Of One Blood* (1903), but in the federal government's estimations of the place of the Indian in America, "spiritualism served as a tool for analyzing and contesting national identity in postbellum America."[203] The Indian ghost in séance typically was wise and patient, but a monster nonetheless, because it exemplified the undead.[204] It represented the predicament of a group of living white people who, it might be said, "are unable to integrate the trauma into their cultural identity and, at the same time, they can never let go of what has happened. It becomes a monster that haunts them unceasingly."[205]

5

Anxiety, Erasure, and Affect

Not all Americans were Spiritualists, and not all Americans were Christians. But Spiritualism, with its mass appeal in the nineteenth century, and the centrality of the Indian ghost within it, bespeaks the predicament of Americans who sought to exterminate Indians. Christianity, while not commanding the obedience of every American, nevertheless dominated the national culture. Protestant Christianity was interwoven at every cultural level into family, politics, education, government, war, and empire. Its intellectual frameworks and collective performances remain a central part of how the majority of Americans understand themselves and their place in the world. Many Americans identify as believers in Christian ideas and, while the number who indicate that Christianity is "very important" in their lives has been declining in the early part of the twenty-first century, the power of Christianity to influence American life is still strongly evidenced. The uncivil behaviors of those who think that Christianity has lost a step in America in recent years—a notion unceasingly stoked by conservative politicians and media entertainers—is an indication of just how deeply embedded Christian religious sensibilities are in the United States.

Christian Erasure of the Past

The born-again ritual trope, which is the calling card of evangelicals, is a representation of a *mentalité*, a way of swimming in a *habitus* that is continuously informing of the importance of emptying the self, of forgetting the self and forgetting much else, too. Americans are in the habit of converting.[1] They convert from one denomination to another, they convert from a life they judge as spoiled to one that is full of promise, and they convert a sense of failure or error into oblivion. They convert memory into amnesia—although in a complex process involving brain and society, remembering never fully yields to forgetting.

In the twenty-first century multiverse of electronic social media and internet marketing, the web is awash in Christian exhortations to forget. Literally millions of religious websites, web-posted sermon texts, and Christian social media commentaries urge Christians to follow the advice of Saint Paul to "forget the past." They direct readers to the Pauline Letter to the Philippians, 3:13–14. The core of that text, which is relentlessly cited as a guidepost to living a Christian life, reads, in the King James Version, "but this one thing I do, forgetting those things that are behind, and reaching forth unto those things that are before." It is proffered as a route of escape from guilt, as a stone of wisdom to hold onto "to help you let go of past mistakes."[2] Although occasionally Christian writers appeal to it in the course of urging forgiveness of those who have offended someone, its meaning for contemporary Christians clearly is vested in its tendering of consolation for failure and its reassuring theme that forgetting the past is sound Christian practice.

The American Christian message to forget the past is given both shorthand and elaborated phrasings by its interpreters, which in the internet era is everyone. Those interpretations appear, as well, to be shaped by the therapeutic and self-help emphases that are so pronounced in American culture, and especially on the democratic internet, where lay articulations of causation, mental health, conspiracy, and reality are deeply rooted. It is the touchstone for discussions about "How can I forget my past sin and stop myself from being guilty?" and "How to get over guilt,"[3] as much as it is for the tip to "Forget the past and God will bring better things."[4] Such recommendations from online Christian writers dovetail with a certain kind of psychological discourse, as instanced by the magazine *Psychology Today*, where one likewise can read about "How to Forgive Yourself and Move on from the Past."[5] The popularity of Philippians 3 has something to do with its resonance with the signals sent by what appear to be credentialed mental health authorities, although the theological presuppositions of popular readings of Philippians 3:13–14 differentiates it from the discussion of forgetting in publication venues that are not explicitly Christian (but may be imbricated with Christian metaphysics and ethics nonetheless). Relatedly, there are those discussions of the topic by Christian seminary faculty, such as a Yale theologian's Christian take on *The End of Memory*,[6] and the academic-authored articles for religious magazines and journals that offer commentary that reinforces the Pauline message by interlinking it with other biblical verses, from both the Old Testament and the New Testament (e.g., Isaiah 43:18, "Forget the former things, do not dwell on the past").[7] Popular expressions of such cross-texting about the message of forgetting also are available in virtual space, as, for example, the Everyday Servant site article, "Top 13 Bible Verses—Forget the Past," which joins Philippians 3:13–14 to a dozen Old and New Testament texts.[8]

The explicitly Christian encouragements to follow the lead of Saint Paul are everywhere adapted on Christian-inflected websites such as the Pinterest site Forgetting the Past, which offers the "12 Best Forgetting the Past Ideas."[9] They also can be found on vending sites such as Spreadshirt, which sells a "Forget the Past, Christian Motivation" travel mug.[10] Christian bookstores advertise online a cornucopia of books, poetry, images, clothing, calendars (again indicating the complexity of forgetting), stationery, and greeting cards. But understanding that "all Christians are commanded in the Bible to forget the past" includes appreciating that "this command is not just for Christians who've had a traumatic experience."[11] Because, simply, "you may regret the past,"[12] embracing biblical guidelines to forgetting "when we want to forget a bad experience"[13] is recommended as a way to "putting the past behind you."[14] In some online Christian theology, forgetting is joined to a view of forgiveness that offers a salve to regret for one's failures, because "the slate is wiped clean and you get a fresh start."[15] Oftentimes, forgetting is treated as an act of will, and one that, because it is commanded in the Bible, is natural, moral, and productive of spiritual growth.

Christian publications in some instances temper the call to encompassing, willed forgetting with interpretation of Philippians 3:13–14 that ambiguates forgetting: "We cannot interpret these words to mean that for Paul the past counts for nothing," so that "he doesn't forget the past entirely." That understanding might also underlie the placement of the words, "Forget the past, forgive yourself, begin again," on the cover of a "portable Christian journal."[16] The message might seem to be at odds with the ostensible purpose of a journal, which is to remember the past—to contrive attachments to the past, to make memory of it—but in fact, a journal dedicated to forgetting might bespeak on its own terms a Christian experience of the complexities and ambiguities of forgetting and remembering. Nevertheless, "there are times to forget" in wholesale fashion, because some memories—and here we begin to ironically and subtextually reengage the matter of race and forgetting—are "dangerously enslaving."[17]

While advocacy for such Christian forgetting is everywhere on the web, it is not a new development in the history of American Christianity. A century ago, a minister from Chapel Hill, North Carolina, began his exposition of Philippians 3 with the observation, "A great many sermons have been preached from this text."[18] The popularity of the text can be documented more than a century before that, in sermons, books, and articles of the early republic. Taken together, and viewed alongside examples of the strong contemporary focus on Philippians 3:13–14, such literature frames a view of Protestant Christianity as one that has, for the entire history of the United States, urged on the nation the performance of forgetting.

Christian publications as well as those that were not explicitly Christian emphasized that the capability to forget was a crucial asset to human survival and happiness, and one that persons should practice diligently. "What a blessed thing it is that we can forget!" gushed the *Christian Index* in 1885 in commenting on "the art of forgetting."[19] That specifically Christian forgetting in almost all cases was conceptualized as a matter of forgetting the self. A standard articulation of that belief explained: "Our salvation lies in forgetting ourselves."[20] The message sometimes was broadened to take note of the social context, as in, "to forget self and remember others."[21] But typically the case was presented for "self-forgetting" as a "principle," and one that was even better than self-sacrifice: "Its rule is, forget yourself in the service of God . . . serve God and forget yourself, says self-forgetting." Following the established Christian understanding of emptying oneself in order to be filled with God, the author emphasized that "self-forgetting" was joined to the faith "which fill's men's souls."[22] Given the context of Protestant theology—and even after allowing for that as a broad spectrum of thinking—it was common to think of "the grace of forgetting" as a virtue, because "whatever virtue is cultivated in a Christian spirit becomes a grace. Therefore forgetting is a grace." In fact, forgetting was more than a virtue that the devout might practice. There was actually "a moral obligation of forgetfulness."[23]

Some published Christian commentary on forgetfulness aimed at disarming persons of ill will they bore toward others who had harmed them. It recognized that "the art of forgetting is a difficult one, a necessary art, a noble triumph of mind and heart." Recognizing the power of will, such messaging urged persons "to habitually refuse to think about the injuries that we have suffered, further than is absolutely necessary for our own protection." Exemplifying the trust that Christians had in that process, it reiterated with regard to such hurts, "Let them be driven out of mind; constantly, regularly, habitually expelled from our thinking." Such a view was predicated not only on the notion that persons could will memory into oblivion, but also, crucially, that the process of accomplishing that rested on the formation of a "constantly, regularly, habitually" practiced behavior. Forgetting indeed was an art, but it required regulation because if not engaged continuously, the forgotten contents might rise from their submerged depths. Forgetting was a habit, and necessarily so.[24] The payoff to such behavior, however, was significant, because forgetting slights from others was liberatory: "It is the remembering of them that makes the burden, when forgetting would give freedom of soul."[25]

While some authors advised—sometimes in the context of a discussion of "forgive and forget"—that forgetting was useful in getting past the wrongs done to a person by others, the majority of writers focused on the importance of forgetting personal failure. The therapeutic culture of the late twentieth and early twenty-first centuries, which brought to maturity the idea, incubated in the nineteenth century, that personal growth required forgetting one's errors, is on broad display in American Christian writing from the early nineteenth century onward. Framed within a theology of emptiness/fullness, saturated with notions about selfishness and self-sacrifice, and inflected with trust in the redemptive power of the blood of Christ, Protestant discussion of forgetting "failures of the past" proffered the same advice. Protestant thinking in this regard had a vaguely legal aspect to it, as represented in the reported counsel of New Yorker Rev. Henry Belden, who stated simply that "he had a right to forget them, for the blood covered them."[26] That right was reinforced when it was restated as a duty, as was often the case. Discussing "the art of forgetting," the *Christian Observer* asserted that "there is a real duty to forget the failures of the past, the mistakes we have made, the blunders we have committed, and the follies that have marred our lives."[27] Couched in a more Pauline phrasing, the message was that "the 'forgetting of those things which are behind' is a necessary condition of successfully 'reaching forth unto those things which are before.'"[28]

What is striking in the American literary record of Protestant thinking about Philippians 3:13–14 is that from the beginning it showed signs of nuance. In 1810, the *Vermont Evangelical Magazine* published an article titled, "On Forgetting Those Things Which Are Behind." It emphasized that Paul "lost the remembrance of what was past," but not completely: "But when the apostle speaks of his 'forgetting those things that were behind,' he is not to be understood to mean, that he literally forgot, or had utterly lost all manner of rememberance of his former services and acquisitions." Rather, Paul placed the past behind him in a way—and here I volunteer my understanding of the article by offering a contemporary example—in which the driver of a car sometimes cannot remember parts of the trip, how they got from here to there, while nevertheless sensing that they registered the trip in memory. For Paul, "The forgetfulness he meant, was similar to that of which a person has the experience, who is eager in running a race. He has not the remembrance of the ground he has passed over so much upon his mind, as to induce him to lessen his speed."[29]

   That interpretation was reiterated in other journals and magazine articles.
The Brooklyn Presbyterian pastor Samuel T. Spears, writing about memory in
1861, chose Francis Bacon and Samuel Taylor Coleridge to ventriloquize the
opinion "that nothing in one's antecedent history is ever irrevocably forgotten." And Spears added, for good measure, an appeal to philosophical logic:
"Whether the opinion be true or false, it is not possible to prove the negative
of this view, since the argument would imply the memory of the very thing
alleged to be forgotten and would therefore be self-contradictory."[30] More
pointed was a discussion in *The Western Messenger Devoted to Religion, Life,
and Literature*, which began by challenging the pagan Greeks: "The Greeks
thought it essential to the happiness of the departed, that they should forget
the woes of this life. . . . What folly in this idea, and what ignorance of our
spiritual nature." Christian sensibilities were different: "We would not forget
therefore, if we could. But it is not ours to choose. We cannot forget. Our experience often shews us, that we still remember what we *supposed we had forgotten*."[31] A similar claim, constructed with a different angle on the Greeks,
discussed "the wise man of old, who prayed for the power of forgetting, probably wished to be able to exercise this act partially, and at his will. The waters
of Lethe are too often sadly capricious in their current, and while they sub-
merge much we would willingly remember, leave untouched much we would
readily forget." Memory was complicated, and "volumes might be written on
its vagaries."[32] Christians frequently applauded the practice of forgetting and
urged its application to experiences that were upsetting or, as we have just
seen, "traumatic." But they also were thoughtful about the possibility of the
"*oubli de reserve*," memory held in backup forgetting, even if it was thought
to be forgotten.
   Christian discourse about forgetting, finally, was infused with an awareness of the psychological aspects of experience, and especially so with regard to events that signaled a failure or inadequacy. When Christian writers
recommended forgetting the missteps one had made in life, they were not
speaking merely about not reimaging an event in the mind. They meant to
say that the psychological consequences of such events were targets of forgetting. One was required to forget the feeling of failure as much as the act itself.
Shortly before the Wounded Knee Massacre, a Christian magazine writer advised that "it is a great waste of strength to make one's faults and blunders and
sin impedimenta in the onward march. There is no virtue in continually be-
moaning the past. . . . Leave behind depressing memories of failure and defeat."[33] That view was present in much other writing. Brooklyn Baptist minister Wayland Hoyt encouraged Christians to forget the "darker side," asserting

that "the art of forgetting is sometimes as valuable as the art of remembering. A good 'forgettery' is as serviceable as a good memory. The past is to be
cherished, but not all of the past. . . . Our mistakes we should forget." He continued: "Our discontents we should forget . . . our growling with murmur-
ing," the "sullenness" that arises from attachment to memories of mistakes.
The answer was in "the forgetting of the darker" in favor of remembering the
brighter.[34] When, during the Civil War, the *New York Evangelist* commented
on northerners who, "in their effort to forget slavery," had simply been content to look the other way in order to avoid war, it was appealing to a vast
body of Christian writing that had recommended forgetting of all sorts of
things, and had framed the process as a Christian virtue, a moral imperative,
and a matter of psychological health.[35]

Alongside the theological and doctrinal arguments for forgetting, Christians practiced rituals that fostered it. The various Christian churches that
received immigrants in the late nineteenth and early twentieth centuries—
cultivating in those immigrant communities a forgetfulness about their past
lives and religious habits—had been drilling slaves in rituals of forgetting for
generations. Slavers and slaveholders had invented an assortment of ways
in which to inculcate in slaves forgetfulness about African local cultures, as,
for example, forcing drugged slaves at the former African port of Ouidah to
continuously circle "trees of forgetting" to drive memory from them. On the
American plantations, there were various rituals that even more pointedly
bred a religious forgetting that has been termed the "African spiritual holocaust,"[36] a term that while overreaching and underestimating African American resilience, nonetheless captures something of the determination of white
Christians to erase African religion in the slave communities. The Catholic
port programs directed by the St. Vincent de Paul Society and the Charitable
Irish Society that aimed at remaking the faith of migrants at times could be
functionally "punitive" in their efforts to teach forgetting: prayer language,
bodily disposition, and behavior around religious authorities, among other
things, had to be ritually implanted in the lives of those disembarking the
ships. The process was sometimes forceful.[37] In many cases, such as through
the program in Charleston, those efforts were highly effective in a short period of time.[38]

Among the ways in which Christians in America practiced ritual forgetting, one of the most recognizable was the segregation of church graveyards.
The refusal of churches to allow African American interments was a tactic of
forgetting Black Christians whom they had enslaved, or, in the case of free
Blacks, relegated to a life in mean and menial circumstances. About the time
of the construction of the first Dutch Reformed Church in New York in 1641, a

separate graveyard for Blacks was established at a distance from the church.[39] The Anglican Trinity Church in Manhattan likewise asserted its own policy in 1696, the year the church was erected: "No Negro shall be buried in Trinity Churchyard."[40] The "Negroes Buriel Ground" uncovered in Manhattan three centuries later held the remains of 15,000 to 20,000 people, most of whom died as slaves.[41] Such a proscription was common in the United States regardless of region. In most places, "white and black people were segregated in death, as they were in life."[42] There were exceptions. In Baltimore, for example, two Catholic graveyards and one white Methodist church graveyard permitted burial of African Americans.[43] In some places, a few Blacks who had been accorded special status were given churchyard burials. Such was the case in St. John, U.S. Virgin Islands, where baptized, literate Black Moravian missionary teachers were allowed church burial (but all other Blacks were excluded).[44] And in some other places, such as Narragansett, Blacks were interred in the churchyard but in a remote section of the yard, symbolizing as much or more of an alienation of slaves from Christian time (that is, to be held in Christian memory) as the "slave spatial alienation [that] continued after their death."[45] Blacks were churchgoing members of congregations throughout the nation, but ultimately whites wished to forget them (and with that, to forget their own treatment of Blacks), and religion assisted them by constructing silences about the lives Blacks had lived. In Philadelphia, "despite their participation in churches as congregants, marriage and baptism recipients, and preachers, they were *not* buried in the corresponding churchyards."[46]

Given that the mandate to construct a burial ground was a prerequisite to constructing a church building, the rules governing burial space were a singular expression of the orientation of the churches to issues of memory and forgetting. The fact that race was such a central factor in devising those rules and restrictions regarding burial illustrates just how much whites were religiously invested in forgetting Blacks. Like another Christian ritual of forgetting—the segregated seating within the house of worship, an issue that contributed substantially to the founding of the African Methodist Episcopal Church in Philadelphia and the African Methodist Episcopal Zion Church in New York—the alienation of Black space served always to obscure Black lives. Ironically, that effort at obscuration begat an enlarged collective African American presence in memory: "Because white northerners excluded Black corpses from their burial grounds the graveyard became the first truly African-American institution in the Northern colonies, and perhaps in mainland North America."[47]

The encouragement of forgetting by the churches can be glimpsed in the theologies and rituals of American Christianities. It is also present in the

institutional management of religion, the ways in which the powerful leadership structures of religious institutions set the courses for communities as
a whole. In the Roman Catholic Church in America (and elsewhere), the silence of the church about clergy sexual abuse illustrates the institutional role
in managing forgetting. The reports of sexual abuse of children and adults by
Catholic clergy that began to appear in media in the late twentieth century became a catastrophe for Catholic leadership in the twenty-first century, in the
wake of the revelations about the Archdiocese of Boston, and, as reporters elsewhere pursued the theme, revelations in other cities and towns nationwide. It
became clear that church officials, in responding to instances of internally reported abuse, had silenced the matter and relocated the perpetrator to a community where he was free to abuse others. The financial and reputational damage to the institution was enormous, as dioceses went bankrupt, Catholics fled
the denomination, and church officials played defense while in freefall. The
standard tactic they employed was to command clergy and any other church
employees—and whomever else they believed they could influence, from reporters to mayors and district attorneys—to keep silent about the matter.

Recently, "alongside analyses of mnemonic narratives, speech, and representations," memory researchers "have seen a growing scholarly interest
in silences, omissions, and exclusions." In particular, "scholars of collective
memory have been able to examine official representations of the past in the
aim of noting those topics that were left out and silenced. These silences have
become the first indication that specific topics have stood a chance of being
permanently sidelined, forgotten, or denied altogether." The church's silence
about sex abuse is one of those "silences aimed at forgetting."[48] It was an institutionally driven program grounded in the enforcement of a "code of silence."
The Massachusetts attorney general asserted that the clergy "chose to protect
the image and reputation of the institution rather than the safety and well being of the children entrusted to their care. They acted with a misguided de-
votion to secrecy. And they failed to break their code of silence" even when
confronted with overwhelming evidence of wrongdoing.[49]

The institutional "template of silence"[50]—the "sacred silence" of denial[51]—
that the church deployed to address cases of sexual abuse was grounded in the
historical practice of the "oath of silence" within the Catholic Church.[52] The
Catholic theologian Hans Küng, a longtime critic of the Vatican who himself
had been officially silenced as a Catholic teacher for his theological dissents,
spelled out the central role of silence in the church's approach to sexual abuse:
"There is no denying the fact that the worldwide system of covering up cases
of sexual crimes committed by clerics was engineered by the Roman Congregation for the Doctrine of the Faith under Cardinal Ratzinger (1981–2005).

During the reign of Pope John Paul II, that Congregation had already taken charge of all such cases under oath of strictest silence. . . . Cases of abuse were sealed under the 'secretum pontificium', the violation of which could entail grave ecclesiastical penalties."[53]

That kind of institutional control was itself an extension of a larger approach to conflict that church leadership had practiced intermittently for centuries. While sometimes eager for war—the Catholic spiritual inducements for Crusades soldiers and the church's involvements in the devastating Thirty Years' War come to mind—the Vatican historically was just as willing to preach forgetting, and practice silence. That orientation had been well in evidence throughout the twentieth century, not only with regard to the Holocaust—about which the wartime pope, Pius XII, was notoriously silent[54]—but in connection with enduring frictions between Christians and Muslims, which Pope Paul VI dismissed in 1965: "Since in the course of centuries not a few quarrels and hostilities have arisen between Christians and Moslems, this sacred synod urges all to forget the past."[55] Silence was a Catholic institutional technology of forgetting. Its practice in the abuse crisis bespeaks not only the Catholic institutional reliance on silence, and forgetting more broadly, but the constitution of all Christian organizations in America that have similar institutional programs for amnesia.

Forgetting as a behavior promoted by Christian organizations and theologies in America defines a practice that overflows its specifically religious contexts. To be invested in Christianity, as many Americans are, is to be invested in the virtue—in the moral necessity, or expediency—of forgetting. Forgetting is a habit, as many Christian writers said, and that habit encompasses religious activity and experiences but equally extends not only to matters of race and sexuality, but to gender, class, and ethnicity. To be a Christian in American is not only to feel emptiness—to cultivate emptiness to some degree—but, in association with that, to forget. Remembering, and being spiritually "filled," also matter. But remembering is always braided with forgetting, just as emptiness is braided with fullness in Christian reasoning about affective spiritual experiences. Christians who are in the habit of forgetting as part of religious practice can enlarge the scope of their forgetting to include slavery and the genocidal campaign against Native Americans.

Feeling Forgetting

Forgetting has a cognitive dimension. More importantly, forgetting is a feeling. That feeling was well known to Americans at the end of the nineteenth century. Men and women reported it in their correspondences, characters in works of fiction stumbled through episodes of it, and magazines speculated about it. Newspapers regularly ran stories in which men, women, and children had a feeling of forgetting. Those stories might simply portray "the air of a man who was forgetting something" but could not remember what it was, or students who thought they had forgotten something when they turned in their exams. Newspapers often made references to the feeling of forgetting when it involved serious matters, even if they sometimes did so with a smirk. A Washington, DC, man traveling on his honeymoon, after packing a wagonload of trunks and suitcases, told the porter, "I feel sure I am leaving something behind, and yet I can't think of what it is." It was, in fact, his wife. In Minneapolis, a woman left a dinner party at a friend's house, sans her baby. "She knew she was forgetting something when she left, but could not think of what it was." A mother in Fort Worth who likewise forgot a small child, in that instance on a railroad car, echoed that refrain: "I knew I was forgetting something but I couldn't think what it was." People who experienced a feeling of forgetting could experience an accompanying fear, so that, for example, "the victim starts from sleep in the dead of night with the fear upon her of forgetting something." In 1881, a man left a baby on a train in Massachusetts, confessing later that "he knew he was forgetting something but couldn't think what it was." When a Chicago paper reported the incident, it ran a notice next to the column announcing that "Tom Nast, the caricaturist of *Harper's Weekly*, is on his way to the Black Hills, where he owns a mine." Nast, the talented but anti-Semitic, anti-Mormon, virulently anti-Catholic illustrator, was off to visit a mine that likely was part of the treaty-breaking white rush to the Black Hills that began in the mid-1870s when gold was discovered there. That gold rush set in motion the events that would end in the Wounded Knee Massacre. Did Thomas Nast have a feeling of forgetting about the Indians?[56]

Philosophers have investigated the feeling of forgetting under the category of metacognition. They have suggested that the feeling of forgetting is a feeling about a past that is both present (to consciousness) and absent. The feeling of forgetting is an epistemic feeling, meaning that it is a feeling about knowing. Sometimes called a "noetic feeling" or a "metacognitive feeling,"[57] it is the feeling, for example, of leaving home while experiencing a nagging worry that something has been left undone, or becoming aware, looking at one's watch, that there was something one was supposed to be doing, but one cannot remember what that was. It is, more precisely, a feeling of *not knowing* something,[58] not being able to pin down something that flits in memory from shadow to shadow, barely glimpsed as it repeatedly slips just out of frame. Related to the tip-of-the-tongue experience, the feeling of forgetting can take many different forms.[59]

Another related descriptor for such feelings is "epistemic feelings,"[60] or E-feelings, which also include, for example, feelings of knowing, not knowing, confidence, error, certainty, doubt, and familiarity. Epistemic feelings signal to a person something about their mind.[61] They are "bodily feelings that have acquired the function of indicating cognitive conditions."[62] Although it is an area of rising interest for philosophers, the investigation of epistemic feelings is not entirely new. The mid-nineteenth-century London philosopher Alexander Bain posited a category of "emotions of the intellect" that included discussion of "the emotion of similarity, or the feeling excited by a flash of identification between things never regarded as like before," and "the feeling of inconsistency," which was said to "operate on the mind as a painful jar."[63] Epistemic feelings typically are described as "embodied appraisals,"[64] which are tuned to the internal situation. The feeling of forgetting is a metacognitive feeling, an epistemic feeling that is part of an implicit mechanism that invisibly audits cognition and delivers its reports as feelings.[65] As one of several such feelings, it "embodies signals that have been recruited to represent internal processes."[66]

Studies of the feeling of forgetting have maintained, for example, that the "experience seems puzzling because it indicates that something, to which the subject does not have access, is missing. It indicates that something is lacking, that there is a gap; and at the same time, it indicates it in a very specific way: only a specific object would relieve the subject from this feeling. So, it is of interest to understand how this kind of feeling is produced and how it can point to an absent object, an object of which the subject is unaware."[67] The experience, oddly, is one of feeling, yet it is a "conceptual experience" as well.[68] E-feelings appear to have a cortical substrate.[69]

We might speak more specifically of a gap between the feeling that one has forgotten something and the absence of recognition of an object that has been forgotten. For example, with the tip-of-the-tongue experience, as William James wrote, "there is a gap therein; but no mere gap. It is a gap that is intensely active. A sort of a wraith of the name is in it, beckoning us in a given direction." We can recognize immediately what the wrong words are, as "the gap of one word does not feel like the gap of another, all empty of content."[70] For James, there was "a gap we cannot yet fill with a definite picture, word, or phrase, but which . . . influences us in an intensely active and determinate psychic way. Whatever may be the images and phrases that pass before us, we feel their relation to this aching gap."[71]

Metacognitive feelings, which are complex and multifaceted, can evidence both that gap and the leap across it. Such feelings are mediatory in the sense that they "serve to interface between implicit-unconscious-automatic processes on the one hand, and explicit-conscious-controlled processes on the other." It is their "double-sided nature" that enables them to facilitate communication between two layers of consciousness.[72] In that sense, a metacognitive feeling is "a conscious summary representation of a variety of unconscious processes."[73]

Metacognitive feelings are triggered by "somatic cues."[74] For example, a person may feel spatially disoriented without being able to express it propositionally. That emotional element is often experienced as anxiety, but it can also include feelings of helplessness or confusion, and the feeling of unfamiliarity. Such feelings are "non-metarepresentational." That is, again, the experience of such feelings does not require that a subject frame the experience propositionally.[75] They are *metacognitive* in the sense that they are "first-order representations which happen to be about internal rather than external states. They are first-order yet self-directed, as opposed to world-directed."[76] Felt uncertainty, as a "contentless mnemonic cue," is such a metacognitive feeling.[77] It might also be understood as a sort of heuristic, a "shortcut" in cognitive processing, a process that consists in the fact that it just "feels right." As "sheer noetic feeling," metacognitive feelings "play a causal role in affecting behavior."[78] The findings of philosophical investigations of such feelings dovetail substantially with evidence regarding the neural *interconnections* between cortical and subcortical brain structures that are primary factors in, respectively, cognition and feeling.[79]

A person need not have in their mental inventory concepts such as certainty or uncertainty "in order to undergo E-feelings such as feeling certain or feeling uncertain."[80] Young children can have such feelings, for example. But at the same time, the explicit concept of forgetting is one that is supplied by culture. It is "acquired in the social practice of interaction."[81] Thus, the feeling of forgetting has a "Janus-faced character."[82] It belongs to the class of epistemic feelings, which "both precede and follow behaviour."[83] Its causal antecedent is a mental event, an implicit "unconscious referential process" that determines action.[84] But at the same time it is constituted as an effect, a conceptual experience arising from behavior shaped by language and culture: "I am forgetting something."

The topic of metacognition and epistemic feelings is a complicated one, especially because it has been explored energetically by both psychologists and philosophers, and their language about it—rooted in the discipline-specific categories that they invoke—does not always overlap. In short, the feeling of forgetting is comprised of interwoven conscious and unconscious elements, which are neither exclusively a cause or an effect. The feeling of forgetting thus has an "indistinct, spreading, blurred quality" that situates it on the "fringe of consciousness."[85]

That understanding is not too far off from what memory researchers call "fuzzy-trace theory," an approach to memory that utilizes an evocative terminology to make points similar to those of philosophers and psychologists who study metacognition and E-feelings. Research on fuzzy-trace theory has the additional advantage of addressing forgetting. Broached also as "gist trace" theory, it refers exactly to what those words suggest: people recognize and remember the gist of an experience even when they seem to have forgotten it. The gist trace, or fuzzy trace, remains in memory even when persons make attempts to forget the experience. The "forgotten" material lives on in memory, as a sort of "general representation" rather than a particular one that could be represented propositionally, that is, via "verbatim" memory.[86] Fuzzy-trace theory does not substantially address the emotional aspect of memory. It is more concerned with the apparent survival in memory of very "general" representations—even though they can be nonverbatim—of an experience. But at the same time, some research in this area has evidenced that "blurred memories"—that is, "fuzzy" memories, "which cannot be verbalized and defined"—can be known "by their affective content."[87] Fuzzy-trace theory has developed as a kind of intuitionism, and has been relied on to understand decision making in fields such as law, medicine, and public health.[88]

Another way in which to think about epistemic feelings is to see them as similar to intuitions. Intuitions can be defined as "rapid and nonconscious thinking processes that work on the basis of heuristics and are independent of working memory and cognitive ability."[89] In connection with that definition, it is helpful to think of intuitions themselves as feelings.[90] It is argued that in making many daily-life judgments, "people prefer to work with gist-based or fuzzy representations and find working with verbatim representations difficult." Intuition is itself a kind of shortcut process that is embraced as an alternative. Does a person feel that they are right? That they know something? That something is familiar? That they are forgetting something? That they know someone's name but will not be able to recall it? Those are judgments in which intuition plays a central role, which is to inform about whether a cognitive process is working well. A feeling of forgetting is a feeling about memory not working well, "but the cues that give rise to that feeling are not likely accessible." Intuition is an affect heuristic that works to inform judgment below the level of personal awareness. In other words, "emotional experiences are inextricably integrated with the cognitive processes that give rise to intuitive judgements" in a way not apparent to a person.[91]

Such feelings are important to religion. William James proposed that noetic feelings were essentially feelings about what was "real" as opposed to what was claimed as "knowledge," observing that "the feeling of reality may be something more like a sensation than an intellectual operation so-called."[92] Religion values noetic feelings, "the fuzzy, non-verbal qualia of feelings,"[93] as judgments about what is real, for their capability to signal a depth of reality that reaches beyond what seem to be everyday "real-life" experiences. When researchers observe that "religious, spiritual, and mystical experiences (RSMEs) are often described as having a noetic quality,"[94] they are concerned above all with personal reports of what feels real. For American Christianities, which were an important source for James's research and much subsequent research on noetic feeling and the real, there is a strong inclination to value noetic feelings (intuition, E-feelings, metacognitive judgments) as guides to what is real.

American Christianities promote such feelings. Christians foster the construction of selves in which those feelings loom large, so that they reach not only into the religious aspects of a life—influencing ritual behavior and confession of belief—but into the rest of life, including politics, race, and health, where feelings about conspiracies, critical race studies, and vaccinations can serve as touchstones for determining the real. And that can lead to staking out positions in cases where there is strong countervailing evidence: "When a person experiences this noetic feeling—even if it is unjustified in the opinion of the world—he or she may tend to believe in the truth of the conclusion drawn. The feeling may presage the person's subjective belief, even, in some cases, when that belief flies in the face of what is objectively accepted as being true."[95] Even more importantly, noetic feelings can come into play when "individuals may feel tensions that they cannot cognitively understand and hence cognitively resolve." In such instances, consciousness can take shape based more on affective feelings rather than knowledge.[96]

In summary, E-feelings, such as the feeling of forgetting, bridge the conscious and unconscious, feeling and cognition. They are affective-cognitive experiences that recognize absence at the same time that they affirm presence. They are powerful and can determine behavior. They are a kind of intuition. And they evidence one way in which culture and subjective experience of internal states (a "feeling" of forgetting, or knowing, or familiarity) collaborate. It is important to bear in mind, regarding that aspect of E-feelings, that culture helps make emotion. Psychological research has indicated that "emotion categories," such as hatred, fear, and anger, "are made real through collective intentionality. To communicate to someone else that you feel angry, both of you need a shared understanding of 'anger,'" even though "you needn't be explicitly aware of this agreement." An epistemic emotion of "forgetting," while not the same as anger, also requires a collective intentionality to imbue the feeling of forgetting with conceptual meaning, even though there is no known object of forgetting and the mental monitoring that takes place and reports as a feeling is unconscious.[97] It is likely that "on the one hand, metacognitive feelings are influenced and shaped by nonanalytic heuristics that operate implicitly and automatically to produce a sheer metacognitive feeling." Yet alongside that process, such feeling "becomes part of the conscious, explicit mode of operation and it can serve as the basis for controlled action."[98]

Contemplating the paradoxical character of the feeling of forgetting is productive because it reveals how feelings can be constituted by unconscious and conscious elements at the same time, and that the body, in its monitoring of mental activity, has implicit modes of operation that result in feeling while at the same time those feelings are shaped by cognitions. This means that the *habitus*, which is a product of culture, and which shapes feeling in ways unseen (as discussed in chapter 3, "Emotion"), is only a partial source for the practice of emotion. Feeling can also arise as a collaboration of the *habitus* with a distinct bodily phenomenology that broadcasts its own signals, experienced, for example, as the feeling of forgetting. For individuals, that means that the messages about feeling constructed in culture, with reference to an emotionology,[99] are sometimes oddly braided with an intentionality and indeed, an emotive quality and valence that arise independent of them. That matters here, because when we look at trauma, we try to see how something can be felt but not always explicitly represented and how a certain feeling can remain in memory seemingly apart from cultural regulations that might otherwise chase it, invalidating or proscribing it. Pondering the paradoxical feeling of forgetting in connection with trauma is a way of avoiding becoming imprisoned in rigid conceptualizations when we ask, "How can we be aware of something that is unknown to us, and, how can we forget and remember at the same time?"

The feeling of forgetting in individuals can frustrate attempts to forget the past, and especially events that persons do not wish to remember. Emotionally charged events that people experience in negative ways can be durable and stubborn in memory, "loitering even when asked to leave."[100] The feeling of forgetting reports on the memory of those events. Memory communicated by the feeling of forgetting may be memory of trauma.

Uncertainty and Anxiety

Freud, as we have seen, was an important thinker for trauma theory scholars in the latter part of the twentieth century. An important supplement to his analyses of trauma and memory was his writing about the uncanny. Freud wrote of the uncanny (*unheimlich*) in 1919 as that which "arouses dread and horror."[101] It was a special form of the terrifying that took its power from repressed memory. It was "that class of the frightening which leads back to what is known of old and long familiar."[102] For Freud, first of all, "what is involved is an actual repression of some content of thought and a return of this repressed content."[103] It is "in reality nothing new or alien, but something which is familiar and old-established in the mind and which has become alienated from it only through the process of repression."[104] Consulting dictionaries and other etymological reference collections, Freud attempted to develop a thumbnail inventory of the kinds of fears that are associated with the uncanny. It is a long list and includes such fears as castration, a severed head or hand, dolls, the return of the dead, being buried alive, demons, the evil eye, the haunted house, and a sense of being in a womb. The uncanny sets a person adrift between a sense of the familiar and unfamiliar, a feeling of knowing something and not knowing it.

For Freud, the fear that a person feels when experiencing the uncanny arises from a sense of familiarity coupled with unfamiliarity, a sense of being present to the object and at the same time alienated from it, of comprehending yet not comprehending, knowing and not knowing. It is the paradoxical experience of "the other within, that which is 'there' in the house but cannot be comprehended by it or integrated into it."[105] The uncanny is both an epistemological predicament and a matter of strong feeling. Thomas Hobbes, who believed that fear made the world go around, prompting war and peace, and both engendering civil society and preserving it, identified fear of the unknown as the primary fear that propelled culture. If, for Hobbes, "our most primal fear is of the unknown,"[106] the uncanny, for Freud, is, relatedly, "precisely the fear of not knowing,"[107] coupled with a sense that one somehow does, in fact, know. It is an epistemic emotion, a feeling about not knowing.[108] It is a "preconceptual latency."[109] The uncanny, as a "dialectic between reminiscence and forgetting," a category of "frightening experiences that cannot be put into words," makes what is known unknown even as it signals remembrance.[110] As such, it aligns is some ways with the feeling of forgetting, and is an intense experience that "lies somewhere between anxiety and terror."[111] It is what Julia Kristeva termed "a fluid haze, an elusive clamminess."[112] It might also be referred to more generally as a deep, powerful anxiety, arising from a certain kind of uncertainty, namely, a sense of being caught in liminality between knowing and not knowing, between past and present.

If we circle back for a moment to the discussion of trauma, we can identify an aspect of literary trauma theory that was essential to that theory and that still remains useful for understanding how people and groups experience aftermaths of trauma. For Caruth, literature is essentially a project that is "interested in the complex relation between knowing and not knowing. . . . the specific point at which knowing and not knowing intersect."[113] That point of intersection is the complex joining of feeling and cognition in the form of a certain category of experience. That experience has been the focus of research on metacognition. More pointedly, metacognition research has proposed that E-feelings have evolved in connection with uncertainty and that "we can define metacognition as a means to cope with the uncertainty of the mind." The play between forgetting and remembering, the challenges of fully registering events in the mind, the presence of contradictory data in reasoning processes: such complications left persons uncertain, half-knowing, half–not knowing, so that "feeling-based metacognition evolved to help the subject cope with mental uncertainty. . . . to allow subjects to cope with uncertainty about the contents of their own memories."[114]

The uncertainty that is present in the feeling of forgetting is a kind of anxiety. It is anxiety along the lines of what Freud described as the uncanny. It is anxiety arising from experience of the predicament of simultaneously knowing and not knowing. It is not fear per se, or dread. Rather it is more of a feeling of the uncanny, of things being out of sorts. It is about a memory that is fuzzy or hazy, that cannot be accurately recalled, that is absent at the same time that it is present.[115] Freud's claim regarding a traumatic moment, that "anxiety is not aroused as a signal but is generated anew for a fresh reason,"[116] might be equally phrased as an emphasis on "anxiety as an experience that can be generated anew at any time without any obvious referent."[117] It can arise as a result of "unconscious mental processes that have a signal function of anticipating danger,"[118] but because they are unconscious processes, the subject is caught between knowing and not knowing that there is a potential threat, or what the nature of the threat might be. In framing that understanding more pointedly, one might say that such anxiety can, in some instances, manifest similarly to a panic attack, arriving without a signal to the conscious subject, but with very heavy affective baggage. Giving no warning and in absence of a referent, the experience is profoundly upsetting and disorienting. Panic attacks often arise from "internally-generated cues, such as certain bodily sensations," but subjects can be unaware (that is, not consciously aware) of those cues.[119] Panic attacks can be "suddenly occurring episodes" of powerful affect "experienced without the warning of signal anxiety that permits psychological preparation or defensive maneuvering."[120] Clinicians, in fact, have linked panic attacks directly to the experience of uncertainty.[121] And researchers have found panic attacks to be a part of the aftermath of trauma, and associated with anxiety.[122]

The power of a panic attack, like the anxiety of both knowing and not knowing, can render the experience quintessentially "real." For the psycho- analytically minded Lacan, "anxiety is precisely the meeting point where you will find" a joining together of many of his ideas, to such an extent that one observer has asserted that "there is only one affect that interests Lacan: anxi- ety."[123] And for Lacan, anxiety had to do with what was "real,"[124] and especially so because of its seeming emergence out of nothing. Anxiety experienced without a warning, without any signal beforehand to indicate a threat, was a profoundly "real" experience. Such a view is comparable to the philosophical position, mentioned previously, that noetic feelings—which are so important in religion—can be experienced as pointers to what is "real."

In foregrounding the experience of uncertainty and its relation to anxiety I have emphasized how it is the predicament specifically of simultaneously knowing and not knowing that is crucial. I have proposed that affect and cognition are interwoven in the experience. Rather than splitting emotion from cognition, as literary trauma theory tended to do, I have endeavored to sketch active collaboration between feeling and thinking, conscious and un- conscious, that enables an appreciation for the experience of uncertainty as one of braided knowing and not knowing. That approach, with regard to the broader field of emotions research, draws on the theory of core affect.

Core affect theory recently has coalesced as an alternative to basic emo- tions theory (BET), which was developed by Silvan Tompkins and Paul Ek- man beginning in the 1960s. BET considered emotions—fear, anger, surprise, and a few others considered "basic"—as natural kinds. That is, such emotions were thought to be hardwired in the human brain, recurring in behavior be- cause of their evolved biological and social functions. Over several decades, BET proponents built out the theory to account for more complex emotions as combinations of basic emotions, but the central claim that such emotions are natural kinds has remained foundational to BET.

Core affect theory, which has been constructed and popularized by James A. Russell, Lisa Feldman Barrett, and others, rejects the claim that discrete emo- tions categories (fear, anger, etc.) reference natural kinds that are hardwired in humans. It offers instead a view of core affects as gauges that inform a per- son about the nature of their interactions with their environment. Those af- fects are not understood as fear, anger, and so forth but, rather, as feelings of different valences (along a spectrum of pleasant/unpleasant) and activa- tion/arousal (along a spectrum of greater or lesser). As such, "core affect is characterized as the constant stream of transient alterations in an organ- ism's neurophysiological state that represents its immediate relationship to the flow of changing events."[125] Core affect "is available to consciousness,"[126] but it also "can exist and influence behavior without being labeled or inter-preted, and can therefore function unconsciously."[127] It "can be experienced as 'free-floating' mood"[128] and as "objectless."[129] Persons can be entirely un-aware of the causes of their core feelings, as experiments having to do with smell (pheromones), vision, and other perceptual events have shown.[130] Stud-ies evidence how "some of these causes are beyond one's ability to detect consciously, such as ionization in the air and ultrasound. A key to under-standing core affect is that people have no direct access to these causal con-nections and limited ability to track this complex causal story. Instead, a per-son makes attributions and interpretations of core affect. Sometimes the cause is obvious, but at other times, one can undergo a change in core affect without knowing why."[131]

According to core affect theory, emotions that in lay discourse are termed fear, anger, and so forth, then, are constructed on the fly out of various com-ponents that include core affect but also include cognitive factors, such as situational information and conceptual knowledge of emotions. Each emo-tional episode is made anew based on context, perception, bodily responses, and other factors, in a complex cultural, biological, and neurological process that involves a great many circuits, loops, and "prior knowledge and experi-ence,"[132] which are "not specific to emotion,"[133] and that adjust to each other as circumstances unfold. That process, inasmuch as it might begin because of core affect prompted by events of which the subject was unaware, neverthe-less, as it developed, took a clear direction involving an object: "Most of an emotional episode's components are intentional in the philosophical sense of being directed at something."[134] There is, in the process of construction, in-tentionality, even if core affect initially was only a matter of valence or acti-vation, and even if that was unconscious.[135] Psychological constructionism hypothesizes that "people automatically and effortlessly categorize the ebb and flow of core affective changes using some kind of meaning-making pro-cess.... So that the experience of an emotion will pop out as a separate event in ongoing core affect." Accordingly, "people automatically divide ongoing changes in core affect into meaningful and distinct experiences."[136] Activa-tion becomes emotion, but not because an object of which the subject was conscious triggered a hardwired emotion (such as joy). Rather it was because a construction involving culture, cognition, affect, intention, and conscious and unconscious elements fashioned the appropriate emotion as the event unfolded.

The core affect most important for understanding the particular after-maths of trauma that I am concerned with is high activation/high unpleas-antness; in other words, a feeling of unpleasantness alongside a feeling of high

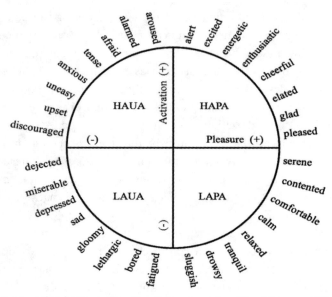

Some feelings and their locations within the affective circumplex. Abbreviations are: HAUA = high-activation unpleasant affect, partly summarized as anxiety; HAPA = high-activation pleasant affect, partly summarized as enthusiasm; LAUA = low-activation unpleasant affect, partly summarized as depression; LAPA = low-activation pleasant affect, partly summarized as comfort. Peter Warr, Uta K. Bindl, Sharon K. Parker, and Ilke Inceoglu, "Four-Quadrant Investigation of Job-Related Affects and Behaviours," *European Journal of Work and Organisational Psychology* 23, no. 3 (May 4, 2014). Reprinted with permission of Taylor & Francis Ltd., http://www.tandfonline.com.

arousal. If we picture core affect as a circumplex, with axes of activation and valence, that particular combination would be located in the upper left quadrant of the figure above.[137]

High-activation unpleasant affect can be characterized as anxiety. How that affect will be translated into fear, anger, or some other emotion has to do with the person's material and cultural situation, as well as the circuitry in their brain, and the changing circumstances of the event. The point is that anxiety is one way of talking about a particular configuration of core affect. Tenseness or uneasiness might be other ways to speak of it. But anxiety is an expedient way to express it. given its place in discussions about trauma and repression. In context, as the event unfolds, for a certain person in a certain culture speaking a certain language, the emotion that arises from a core affect experience of anxiety will be variously named. As the psychological constructionist Russell explains, "For example, Tahitian includes 'mehameha,' which refers to the uncanny anxious feeling one has in the presence of a ghost."[138] In New York, one might say "fear."

The emotions theory of core affect offers some clarification for how an experience of uncertainty can lead to anxiety. Research indicates that "uncertainty is experienced subjectively as anxiety,"[139] and "anxiety primes an implicit goal of uncertainty reduction."[140] A person might experience an environmental stimulus, possibly in an unconscious way, of uncertainty. Perhaps that stimulus is seeing a billboard with the image of an Indian on it, or, for a certain white person, the experience of sharing a subway car with an African American. Either of those experiences might prompt a sense of knowing but not knowing, an uncertainty. A core affect of anxiety can beget a constructive project focused on managing an experience of uncertainty, and it can result in intentional behavior toward an object. If the constructive process leads to the emotion of fear, that behavior then might include actions that defend against a perceived threat. The process leads "from uncertainty to anxiety,"[141] and then to an emotion and possible behavioral adjustments. In neural research, "many studies have historically demonstrated that uncertainty as a common feature in threat context may elicit fear and anxiety."[142]

Thus, for example, imagine a white male living in Maryland, who is a descendant culturally and perhaps biologically from slaveowners, and who carries with him traces of perpetrator trauma. Intergenerational transmission of an anxiety epigene might be involved, but it might not. He sees a Black Lives Matter banner on the lawn of a multiethnic Christian church. He returns with spray paint and defaces it. He likewise defaces subsequent replacement banners. We might imagine that the sight of the banner caused a core affect of high unpleasantness/activation. He cannot consciously access memory of complicity in slavery or Jim Crow, but he experiences uncertainty. He has a feeling of forgetting about white treatment of Indians and/or Blacks. His anxiety grows, and in a process involving both cognition and affect, he frames an understanding of what he is experiencing that motivates him to engage in intentional, object-oriented behavior: the destruction of the banner. But if asked why he vandalized property, would he be able to explain it, or was the process opaque to him?

If the vandal's experience was similar to that of an actual perpetrator who was caught in 2021, the answer likely would be no: the process was opaque. The *Washington Post* reported that Jim Nix, who staked out the site in order to catch the perpetrator at the Colesville Presbyterian church in Silver Spring, Maryland,

> sped to the church and found himself face to face with the sprayer: a terrified 60-something White man whose face trembled behind his glasses. For months, Nix had envisioned his adversary as a "rebellious kid or an old,

nasty-looking dude." But the man quivering before him "could have been a church deacon—glasses, tucked-in, buttoned shirt," he says. "It wasn't some down-on-his-luck lowlife trying to piss other people off. It was my uncle or older brother." When Nix shouted, "Dude, why . . . are you messing with the sign?" the shivering man replied, "It makes me uncomfortable." Uncomfortable? Nix, who had been "ready to throw [the guy] in the middle of the road," was stunned.

Uncomfortable. Of course the perpetrator's word disarmed Nix. Like me, Nix assumed that consuming rage or contempt was fueling the sign tamperer's actions. And while such feelings probably contributed to this mild-looking man's behavior, it was discomfort that he expressed.[143]

How does affect that we might characterize as anxiety, which persons can feel for reasons that are not clear to them, translate into intentional acts? More specifically, how does a feeling of discomfort or unpleasantness, a core affect, lead to vandalism or other violence? Answering that question requires recognition of the role of culture, and ideology in particular, in the construction of emotion. The construction of emotion is a process that interweaves many factors, one of which involves culturally grounded definitions of emotion and cultural standards for the expression and concealment of emotion. Ideology regarding place, class, gender, race, ethnicity, authority, religion, and other factors also is involved. In that regard, the emotional constructionist approach of psychologists is similar to the way anthropologists, as well as some scholars in sociology and history, view emotions. As has been pointed out, the emotional constructionist approach "is in perfect agreement with the constructionism that a good number of anthropologists have adopted to make sense of their fieldwork on emotions." Accordingly, "there is a convergence between a social science fundamentally dependent on hermeneutics, that is, the work of interpretation, on the one hand, and on the other, an experimental science that, on the contrary, relies on 'objective' measures."[144] That convergence has been recognized by a few psychologists, but the general unwillingness of researchers in that discipline to venture into interdisciplinarity in researching emotion has prompted one psychologist to characterize their reticence as "a scandal."[145]

World Defense, Fear, and Violence

Uncertainty arising from repressed collective trauma can be felt as the anxiety of being caught between forgetting and remembering, a disorienting position that undermines social identity, diminishes a sense of belonging, and sometimes prompts people to take desperate measures to recover meaning

and purpose as a group. People and groups are motivated to reduce such uncertainty, and the higher the level of uncertainty, the more motivated they
are to reduce it.[146] "Felt uncertainty" is a "powerful self-integrity threat,"[147]
which thrives on lack of closure and a concomitant sense of collective invalid-
ity.[148] In uncertainty-identity theory, the person or group experiencing such
a threat adopts defense mechanisms, creating a "worldview defense" in order
to manage the uncertainty and restore a sense of group identity.[149] Because
"uncertainty is highly anxiety provoking and stressful—it makes us impotent
and unable to predict and control our world," persons experiencing that uncertainty will sometimes resort to highly ambitious, even extreme measures,
to set things in a right order again. That effort to compensate includes ag-
gressively positioning the group vis-à-vis others in an effort to clarify group
identity. In some cases, the "uncertainty-related self-integrity threat" leads
to "intergroup bias and worldview defense effects" associated with violence
and terrorism.[150] It is possible to speak of "the context of uncertainty typical of most genocides,"[151] and how a "collective angst" underlies intergroup
violence that culminates in genocide.[152] And, equally, it is possible to view
colonial and postcolonial settings as hothouses of "epistemic uncertainties"
and "epistemic anxieties."[153] The collective campaign to resolve uncertainty is
driven by a complex of psychological processes that, "under certain circumstances, produce extremism out of uncertainty—transforming feelings of uncertainty about who we are into . . . violence."[154] Religion plays a role in many
such instances, as groups turn radically intolerant and construct theological
platforms for holy war.[155]

Anxiety about identity arising from uncertainty is an anxiety about what
is felt as "forgotten," as in the feeling of forgetting: something known but not
known. A perpetrator group, shaped in its collective feeling and thinking by
what it has repressed, feels the consequences of that process as an anxiety
about what that group is. The perpetrator group is uncertain of its identity. It
is uncertain because it has become lost in the haze between remembering and
forgetting. It is out of place. Emotionally fraught, the group endeavors to restore identity. It does so in many cases through defensive maneuvers that can
take extreme forms, as the group embraces absolutist ideologies and leverages
those ideologies in ways that advance its self-defense.

None of this is to say that victim groups do not experience trauma as a
challenge to social identity. All traumatized groups that experience anxiety
arising from repression can be uncertain about group identity, and that will
inform a range of behaviors by both victim and perpetrator groups. Both
groups are haunted; both are anxious. But I am concerned with how perpetrator groups repeat their crimes, carrying out what a historian of the Third

Reich has termed "serial genocides," in which a perpetrator group is poised to aggress again.[156] Such serial genocides include the Crusades as a religiously legitimated, centuries-long sequence of expeditions to destroy Muslims; the 500-year campaign of Europeans to exterminate Native Americans, also ordained by religion; and the even longer Christian war against Jews that culminated in the Holocaust. Likewise, recent genocides in Africa, the Balkans, and Cambodia were ongoing campaigns by perpetrator groups whose denials, and repression of memory of events, were the signs of what was yet to come: "Denial is the final stage that lasts throughout and always follows genocide. It is among the surest indicators of further genocidal massacres. The perpetrators of genocide dig up the mass graves, burn the bodies, try to cover up the evidence and intimidate the witnesses. They deny that they committed any crimes, and often blame what happened on the victims."[157] Like serial killers who find release and relief from the anxiety of identity problems by committing another homicide,[158] a group experiencing trauma can manifest problems with identity that also lead in a general way to violence, but it often arrives at genocide by a different pathway than the actions of individual serial killers.

A group can experience a collective feeling of forgetting. It feels the presence of something but cannot recall exactly what that is. It is not that the keys have been left on the desk as the door closes, but, rather, that an atrocity has been installed as a ghost in memory. Such a collective epistemic emotion, arising in connection with repressed memory that is present as a ghost that haunts the group, is so powerful that it disrupts group identity and underwrites a social program of defense that leans into ideologies that cast the world in absolutist terms. A collective feeling of forgetting—as the uncanny, or a profound anxiety—by such process sets the table for perpetrator groups to embrace extremist ideas and embark on a path toward violence. Uncertainty, and especially a group's uncertainty about its identity, leads to the embrace of radical ideologies that scheme the world in absolutist terms. In such renderings, which are ruled by hard binaries, where absolute good and absolute evil are at war and the boundary between us and them is uncrossable, violence incubates.

Fear and Hatred

Scholars often rest their understandings of religious/political violence on invocations of fear and hatred as its causes. Fear, anger, resentment, and hatred all play roles in collective violence.[159] Fear and hatred, however, can be understood as "secondary emotional reactions . . . defensive coping strategies."[160]

Hate and fear typically are present in some measure (although sometimes less than might be predicted)[161] in violence between groups. But if we are to speak of hatred, we should recognize that hatred is not the root cause of violence. Rather, it arises from affect, which in turn can be prompted by signals of which a person is unaware, including prompts from the environment that spark "forgotten" memories of previous acts of violence.[162] With regard to fear, we can distinguish fear of an actual opponent—another religious group, or ethnic community, for example—from a different kind of fear: the fear that is constructed out of affect and cognitions, sparked by a stimulus of some sort—an image, a line of prose, a sound—which *then leads* a person or group to embrace extreme ideologies that encourage hatred or anger and prescribe violence as seemingly defensive action. One psychoanalytically framed shorthand way of talking about this process is to say that "the fear of the unknown can become intolerable to contain internally," at which point "it is unconsciously projected onto the presumed source of the threat to one's safety."[163] Another such shorthand is to think about fear of the unknown as a specific emotion constructed of anxiety arising from repressed trauma and felt in such a way as to disrupt social identity with uncertainty. That uncertainty can lead to an embrace of ideology that constructs other groups as threats. If the anxiety is particularly severe, the ideology will be more chiseled and inelastic and the possibility of violence more likely.

Fear, anger, resentment, and hatred all play their roles in collective violence.[164] Such feelings, to a certain extent, can be transmitted through society and across generations as a "collective fear orientation" that moves through a group.[165] International relations research has shown that emotions associated with trauma find representation in media images and historical narratives and that they are crucial in affecting collective identity and political affiliation as they move through a collective in sometimes tenebrous and unpredictable ways.[166] Thus framed, it is possible to see fear "less as 'fear of X' and more as an unsettling anxiety whose opacity permits latitude and flexibility in how 'X' is imagined," which animates a process leading to violence. When we conceptually steer away from rigid definitions of emotion and toward more open-ended, constructionist understandings, we can envision fear, hatred, and anger as related emotions, what might be termed "mixed emotions," that rise or fall, collaborate, overlap, and alter each other in the emotional practice of groups.[167] Emotional life, as Catherine Lutz argued in her ethnography of the people of Ifaluk, can be constituted by clusters of emotions in which each of the several components (e.g., *fago* as compassion/love/sadness) are variously foregrounded and backgrounded depending on social context.[168] The anxiety arising from repression of memory of trauma can supply the affective force for the experience of the emotions of fear, hatred, anger, and resentment that cluster around it and are variously clarified as social and cultural circumstances help to shape their construction.

Anxiety that prompts a group to question its identity can lead to different kinds of emotions (i.e., hatred, anger, or fear), depending on a group's shifting ideological engagements. If the ideology is extreme, the process can result in violence, but whether particular emotions such as fear or hate play a role will be determined by circumstances that are immediate and local, not by a dynamic inbuilt to the process itself. Thus, the proposal that we move "beyond fear and hatred in international conflict"[169] in analyzing motivations to violence is a step in the right direction. The same is true for understanding violence in the United States such as Native American genocide and the legacies of colonialism that negatively impact persons of color.

Feelings such as fear and hatred can recur in a group, as can the feeling of forgetting. Collective emotion is part of collective identity.[170] And the violence that they inspire can recur as well. Scholars refer to mass religious and political violence as occurring in connection with "cycles of hatred."[171] Studies of genocide often posit "cycles of violence" and "cycles of killings."[172] Those who study transgenerational trauma emphasize the idea of "the repetition of cycles of destructiveness."[173] In almost all those cases, the primary concern has been with how those who suffer trauma as a result of violent encounters with another group carry the memory of their suffering forward into subsequent encounters with that group. Scholarship, with attention to groups defined as victims, in that way focuses on how the trauma of such groups incites in them reactionary anger or hatred that results in further violence. In other words, victim groups retaliate against those who have oppressed them because of the powerful memory of trauma that they bear.

I am interested in a different cycle of violence, namely, how killing begets killing, how and why perpetrator groups continue to enact violence against those whom they already have battled. When some Poles who had engaged in the mass killing of Jews in Poland returned to their localities after the war, they renewed their murderous anti-Semitic campaigns. They did not do so in retaliation for previous violence against them, but for other, more complex psychological reasons having to do with identity and self-legitimation.[174] The massacre at My Lai during the Vietnam War escalated quickly once soldiers had begun killing civilians, and U.S. soldiers who took part in Vietnam War operations such as Operation Speedy Express and the killings in the Central Highlands by the infamous Tiger Force likewise engaged more readily in killings of civilians, sometimes in large numbers, once they had participated in such an atrocity.[175] Experimental studies since Stanley Milgram have evidenced some of the dynamics of increases in aggression among persons,[176] emphasizing that perpetrators continue to kill once they reach a "point of no return," whereupon killing "perpetuates itself."[177] There is such a thing as a cycle of violence in which smaller acts of killing lead to larger ones and new episodes of killing follow, after a time and in sometimes unpredictable ways, from previous ones. One understanding of that cycle is that "perpetuation of killing may be motivated in part by efforts to cope with the psychological threat engendered by prior killing."[178] Killing constitutes a psychological problem for perpetrator groups, posing a threat to their self-understanding, and prompting them to engage in extreme behavior as they struggle to come to terms with their deeds.[179] Perpetrator groups are haunted by a past that can drive them to further killing, and to killing that is more spectacular an enactment of their aggressiveness than previous instances. "Killing appears to perpetuate itself even in the absence of retaliation." Moreover, "this effect should arise particularly when a killer perceives similarity to the victims."[180]

Perpetrators' relationships to victims are a problem of dysfunctional attachment. Parties remain attached, but in a destructive way. That attachment, sometimes through hate, at other times through anger, "maintains the status quo" in the sense that it keeps one person or group in relationship with another.[181] In interpersonal relations, "almost invariably, the function of hate, as opposed to apathy, for example, is to keep the person only partially distant. They may be pushed away, reviled, or even attacked, but they are psychologically kept close by the client."[182] Indeed, perpetrators are "'attached' to their victims; they are obsessed with them."[183] By remaining attached to the object of hatred, and reinforcing that attachment periodically in enactments of aggression against it, a perpetrator group maintains possession of a primary ingredient for the process by which it copes with pain from previous trauma, even as it creates new trauma.

I have been focusing on collective perpetrator anxiety as an instance of the epistemic feeling of forgetting in that it manifests knowing and not knowing at the same time. It is a very serious and consequential instance of the feeling of forgetting. It is not identical to fear, but it can lead to fear. Most of the time, when scholars talk about collective hatred, anger, and fear, they refer to emotions directed at other groups. That is, fear is a fear of another group and hatred of another group. Those emotions certainly are central to the emotional practice of religiously inspired and legitimated violence, and other kinds of collective violence. And they are central to the power of the state, which is constantly "rewriting trauma into linear narratives" (some of which involve fear and hate of other states) that both define the feelings of the group and obscure the memory of the events underlying the trauma.[184] There is a cognitive element to that kind of hatred and fear, to emotions that are formed as collective emotions in keeping with the emotionology of the culture. That is, collective emotions are formed as feelings become more deeply embedded in emotional cultures and more interwoven with media, performance, group narratives, and everyday behaviors. Emotions such as hatred, anger, and "fear can be institutionalized within organizations and in patterns of action and reaction between groups including states."[185] To say that "fearful emotions can be understood as a possible practice of the state,"[186] is to talk about ideology together with emotion. That is an important part of understanding religious violence. Ideology is always present, shaping collective feeling in different ways, depending on the historical and cultural setting and the force of present events. In order to understand how that happens, however, it is necessary to look closely at those settings and events, and bear in mind that neither fear nor hate arises as full-blown emotion purely from ideologically framed binaries.

Race, Religion, and Nation

Braided Traumas

Americans are a forgetful people. They steer memory away from recollection of disturbing political and social events. They endeavor to forget traumas, and especially those involving race and religiously legitimated violence.[1] A large percentage of the American population in January 2022 did not want to remember the Capitol insurrection of a year before,[2] which was marked by religious and racial rhetoric and Christian and Confederate symbology. Some dismissed the insurrection as a minor episode, a media-inflated nonevent, or an event that was in reality different from what it seemed (i.e., a false flag operation). Within two weeks of the insurrection, Republican leaders were urging amnesia on Americans. Senator John Cornyn stated, "I think we ought to encourage people to move on rather than to live in the past." Senator Thom Tillis told Americans that "I'm really more focused on moving ahead." Senator Marco Rubio agreed: "I just think we need to move forward."[3] Like the Christian leaders and advisers whose message regarding Philippians 3:13–14 was to focus on "putting the past behind you"[4] because "all Christians are commanded in the Bible to forget the past,"[5] Republicans insisted that the public good was best served if Americans forgot about the insurrection—and the racial and religious bigotry that went with it. In other words, they should do what many Americans had always done.

The statements of these politicians following the Capitol insurrection made sense to many Americans because American Christianities (although some more than others) foster a culture of forgetting. That culture is an emotional one, a way of experiencing the world that blends ideas and emotions, affect and memory, feelings of which persons are aware with feelings that are active and motivating but are outside awareness. What is remembered is felt, and what is forgotten sometimes is felt as well. How can we write about such things, forgotten but remembered, felt but hidden just below the horizon of consciousness? And in societies where identity and memory are constituted in collective emotionalities, how do the forgotten memories of one group stand in relation to those of another? How are the repressed memories of perpetrators of violence related to the memories—some plain, some hidden—of those who have suffered that violence? An initial step toward answering those questions is to appreciate how the memory and feeling of one group can overlap with—be conjoined with—that of another group. We must be careful in how we characterize that relationship, and especially so as we try to name the common experience, the content of what is shared between two groups. But what is shared can be constituent of national identity, even given the rifts and fissures of society. According to one perspective, we can recognize that forgetting is an important part of the construction and maintenance of national identity. But we also can recognize that repressed memory, emotionally coded, haunts Americans in a way that is understandable largely as living paradox, even as it produces real effects—violent effects—in the everyday world of Americans.

Ralph Ellison, remarking on forgetting as an element of national character in 1964, observed: "Perhaps more than any other people, Americans have been locked in a deadly struggle with time, with history. We've fled the past and trained ourselves to suppress, if not forget, troublesome details of the national memory."[6] Toni Morrison stated that view more pointedly thirty years later: "We live in a land where the past is always erased, and America is the innocent future in which immigrants can come and start over, where the slate is clean. The past is absent or it's romanticized. This culture doesn't encourage dwelling on, let along coming to terms with, the past."[7] A large part of that coming to terms has to do with race. Many Americans would just as soon forget that there is a long history of racial violence, and ongoing racial strife, in America. James Baldwin, discussing Americans' efforts to erase, specifically, the memory of slavery and its violent aftermath, noted that that there is "the past we deny . . . which lends to interracial cocktail parties their rattling, genteel, nervously smiling air. . . . Whenever the Negro face appears a tension is created, the tension of a silence filled with things unutterable. It is a sentimental error, therefore, to believe that the past is dead. It means nothing to say that it is all forgotten."[8] That is to say that the past haunts, said Richard Wright, asserting that "if America has forgotten her past, then let her look into the mirror of our consciousness and she will see the living past living in the present."[9] That act of looking, whether Americans are aware of it or not, takes place every day: "In the American context, race, memory, and forgetting are central. Their uneasy relationship infects the everydayness of our life

in common, our identity, and our moral fabric. Its attendant injuries and injustices are also a part of that memory, present and so woven into what we are
as a political community that they work among us even if not always at the
forefront of our consciousness."[10]

American political community is shaped by what Americans have tried to
forget, and by what they want to forget. The call by Republicans to forget the
insurrection immediately after it had occurred was driven by the assumption
that any lasting focus on it would further damage the national standing of
the party. There was enduring trepidation about investigating what had happened, and a powerful impulse to bury and forget the event. Just as the ghost
in Toni Morrison's *Beloved* was "the figure for a certain anxiety about the very
idea of race,"[11] so also "Republican anxiety about a commission focused on
January 6 and the Trump conspiracy theories"[12] was a ghostly haunting. It was
not just a matter of dreadful video that flickered daily on cable news shows,
but the looming specter of violent events of a more distant past that whites
had tried to forget, but could not. For Republicans, America remained an ex-
ceptional nation for which events such as the insurrection were mere speed-
bumps on a highway, mapped by God, leading to a glorious destiny. That exceptionalism required "an enforced psychic amnesia that can return only as a
type of repetitive national haunting—a type of negative or absent presence."[13]

Previously in this book I discussed how Native Americans have been
haunted by the colonial past (and by its traces in the colonial present). One
way that Native American writers characterized that haunting is as the recurring, in individual and communal life, of trauma, as represented by the symptoms of PTSD. Native Americans have explored a range of means by which to
address the suffering caused by that PTSD, and they have continuously theorized its causes, its manifestations over successive generations, and its intersection with the difficulties faced by other minority populations in America.
Some Native American commentary additionally has attended to the ways
in which white Americans are implicated as perpetrators in that suffering
but also the extent to which whites and Indians are dysfunctionally attached
to each other in a morbid dance, in which they "were somehow destined to
be each other's victims in unique and profound ways."[14] Whites have reaped
their own suffering from their violent subjugation of Indians, to whom they
remain attached, oftentimes perversely, in a way dramatically performed by
January 6 rioter Jake Chansley, the horned "QAnon Shaman."

Scholars in recent decades have written extensively about trauma transmitted from one generation to the next. They have also examined how white
trauma is enmeshed with the trauma of persons of color. The racially engendered sufferings of whites and nonwhites in America "are in fact implicated

by one another."[15] That is not the case only in America, but elsewhere as well. In South Africa, for example, the long history of racial strife under colonialism and the structural violence begot by apartheid have damaged both Black and white communities, traumatizing both, and, while the traumas are different in some ways, "this white trauma . . . is nevertheless unavoidably entangled with black trauma."[16] Such understandings of entanglement in Africa reiterate a concept central to Fanon's writing, and those who have drawn from it, such as Mbembe and Sarah Nuttall.[17] Such interpretation relies on the principle that "widespread trauma as it becomes understood, processed, and articulated eventually conditions an entire culture, affecting everyone who is addressed and interpellated by it; as they become disseminated, trauma's effects can become entrenched as part of a shared cultural system."[18]

African American scholars have discussed the nature of white trauma in conjunction with the racial melancholy experienced by African Americans. In order to appreciate how that argument about melancholy is made, it is necessary first to understand its psychoanalytical framework. Drawing on Freud,[19] and especially on Judith Butler's interpretation of Freud,[20] as well as the interpretations of her protégés, David Eng and Anne Anlin Cheng,[21] Black literary scholars have described the complexities of African American identity, feeling, and struggle with reference to an experience of melancholy that is transmitted intergenerationally.[22] Freud had argued that the process of mourning involved eventual separation from the lost love object. In mourning, a person might in various ways memorialize what was lost and remember it in that way. Such was the process of letting go. But in some cases, the grieving of a loss persisted indefinitely, as the subject failed to relinquish the object. The subject instead attempted to psychically incorporate the object in order to remain engaged with it. That strategy led to psychic friction between ego and internalized object, which resulted in ongoing self-reproach as the internalized object, in a process involving the superego, became the voice of criticism of the ego, beating it down into emptiness. The melancholic, who resisted remembering the loss and repressed awareness of the internalized object, experienced a deepening emptiness as the ego withered, fracturing identity.[23] In Kristeva's phrasing, the melancholic senses that they are "afflicted with a fundamental flaw," an "unnamable" wound, that forms them as "incomplete, empty."[24]

Recent scholarship about race in America, in its departure from writings about melancholy several decades ago, has argued that the melancholic is not entirely successful in forgetting the past, and that for all the energy spent on repressing memory, glimmers of it remain. In other words, "the melancholic is always already suspended within the boundary between mourning and melancholy, knowing and not knowing the object or ideal is lost."[25] That insight has informed a view of racial melancholy in America that rejects the claim that melancholy is necessarily a pathological condition.[26] It proposes instead that it is a mood or affectual status that, while often like despair, can precipitate hope as well. It should not be entirely distinguished from mourning, because the work of grief that moves toward resolution, it is argued, goes on even while melancholy situates a subject in ambivalence. It is an understanding of melancholy that redirects theory in such a way as "to defuse the melancholic's self-aggression" and harness feeling to the project of partial remembering.[27]

In other words, recent interpretation has sought to ambiguate the (early) Freudian distinction between melancholy and mourning, and suggest instead an experience of ambivalence that stresses the "irresolution of melancholy,"[28] alongside memory that is engaged by mourning.[29] It is a way of speaking about the grief experienced by Black Americans, Asian Americans, Native Americans, and American Latinx communities as a continuous prompt to reject historical integrations of losses into a narrative that conceals past and present harms. It is a grief that recognizes the social conditions of its genesis, and urges rejection of a status quo in which injustices and violence remain as component parts of racial minorities' social experience. It "names a way of remembering and being opened up by the often unacknowledged forms of violence and cruelty that social arrangements produce and rely on." It does so even as it underwrites, as melancholy often has been thought to do, "a kind of vulnerability that threatens coherent identities and narratives."[30] It is about memory on the edge where knowing and unknowing swirl, which can lead to "resistant subjects created out of losses."[31] For African Americans, in its typical form, it is a "melancholic knowing and unknowing of slavery,"[32] which situates Blacks in ambiguity regarding identity and social place while equivalently grounding identity in memory of loss that inspires resistance. That process is described paradoxically as one in which "the ego is ironically sustained by its own emptiness, filled to the brim with losses that cannot be known."[33] The melancholic "has ambivalent feelings of love and hate for the other,"[34] both driven to put the other out of mind, but, attached to it, refusing to give it up. In such a way, for African Americans, it is possible to speak of a "hope made possible by melancholy."[35]

What remains, then, haunts. Loss is both remembered and forgotten. Melancholy, as a "mode of unknowingness,"[36] is a matter of "the ubiquity of hidden affect that defies conscious recognition" and "works through cultural practice to reconstitute itself across time and social space as it shapes and forecloses identification possibilities."[37] That "hidden affect" is the foundational experience of "transgenerational haunting," in which "people are actually marked by unknown wounds, living the unknown transgenerational reconstituted melancholy."[38] While "haunting constitutes the work of melancholia,"[39] the means by which that haunting is effected are not easily detected. One proposal has been that "rituals of melancholy" in Black communities— including musical performances such as jazz, certain religious exercises, a way of speaking, and other rituals—convey something of the traumatic experience from generation to generation. Such rituals may include "cryptic conversations," and other practices that "place the past and present in dialogue."[40] They are cryptic precisely because "they transmit and reconstitute disavowed social loss and hidden affect discreetly." They often are joined to religious practice, and, in one scholar's view, have something sacred about them generally.[41]

Returning to the matter of the braided traumas of whites and Blacks in view of this conception of melancholia, one might speak of "the true cultural codependency that mechanizes performances of racial grief for both white and nonwhite performers and spectators." The "hidden affect" that looms in Black experience is not an aspect of that experience alone, "but a marker of our own cultural codependency" that is "transmitted not just through performance, but through the social reflections and interpretations of that performance" as they take place through "performative exchange," which involves the "collective exchanges of grief" between whites and Blacks.[42]

Whites and Blacks grieving together are attached to each other, and in general that attachment is dysfunctional. Such dysfunctional attachment is characterized by simultaneous feelings of love and hate for the other,[43] what Kristeva pointedly called "identification with the loved-hated other . . . which demeans me and of which I desire to rid myself." Indeed, the fact of "oppressive slavery bound two peoples together in a bitter antagonism while creating an organic relationship so complex and ambivalent that neither could express the simplest human feelings without reference to the other."[44] For some scholars who have reflected on that attachment, the racial predicament of whites is a form of melancholy similar to what Blacks experience. That is, it is said to be essentially a melancholy shared with Blacks.

But what haunts whites, with regard to their exchanges with Blacks? What is their loss? In scholarship focusing on melancholia, the situation of whites is described in a number of ways, but several interpretations stand out. One argument is that whites mourn the loss of an ideal. Another proposes that whites are melancholic as beneficiaries of whiteness. A third view, which is closely related to the second, is that whites mourn their loss of civility, their humanity.

Freud specifically named "loss of an ideal" as a starting point for the emergence of the feeling of melancholy in a person. Mourning "is regularly the reaction to the loss of a loved person, or to the loss of some abstraction which has taken the place of one, such as one's country, liberty, or an ideal, and so on."[45] Scholars drawing on Freud accordingly have described white melancholy as a feeling about the loss of the ideal of equality, alongside an incapacity to consciously recognize that loss because memories of the events underlying it—such as slavery and Native American genocide—have been repressed. That repression is abetted by "discourses of American exceptionalism and democratic myths of liberty, individualism, and inclusion" that "force a misremembering" of past instances when those ideals were betrayed.[46] Accordingly, "it is not difficult to conceive of dominant white identity in America as melancholic."[47] It is not difficult to see that "the history of American national idealism has always been caught in this melancholic bind" between professions of inclusion and acts of exclusion. It can be asserted, moreover, that "American melancholia is particularly acute because America is *founded* on the very idea of freedom and liberty whose betrayals have been repeatedly covered over."[48]

A second and related argument, developed in scholarship about South African apartheid but applied to the American scene, is that whites are melancholic because they are the beneficiaries of whiteness. Whiteness is power, money, health, rewarding work, economic security, and freedom. But whites are unwilling to admit that fact. They do not acknowledge that their social status is their whiteness. Whites experience discomfort about their status even as they deny its reality. They experience a sense of personal diminishment because of their unearned status at the same time that they endeavor to bury knowledge of it. In this view of white melancholia, then, it is an artifact of whites grappling with their sense of undeserved privilege.[49] Scholars taking that approach assert that white struggle then typically involves the formation of feelings of shame and guilt.

There is a third way of approaching the matter of white melancholia that does not draw exclusively on Freud, or on literary theory generated entirely out of psychoanalytic axioms. It begins, again, with the observation of "racial melancholia initiated through the recognition that one is the involuntary beneficiary of whiteness." But it is less about emotions of shame and guilt, and less explicitly about a general sense of white privilege. Rather, "it is the recognition that under the mantle of whiteness there is the perpetration of violence, terror, and the infliction of psychological damage. It is with horror that we come to own the destructiveness that is a part of whiteness."[50] This approach to understanding white trauma focuses on the acts of destruction perpetrated by whites and white efforts to forget them. In simpler terms, it is about "whites haunted by their own barbarism."[51]

Whites and Blacks alike carry burdens caused by the trauma of slavery and the harms arising from the systematic enforcement of inequality post-slavery. To speak of "the trauma of slavery injected into slaveholder children," and the transmission of that trauma to succeeding generations, is to recognize, first of all, that "for children, whether slave or free, the savagery of radicalized battle, whether overt or covert, constituted the traumatic arena in which they lived out their childhoods." For whites, those early-formed "slaveholder psyches were transmitted from generation to generation"[52] through such cultural formations as the Lost Cause, which "relied on two kinds of repression—the burying of traumatic or unacceptable experiences in the unconscious and the silencing of dissident voices and competing social memories."[53] What comes to the fore in an exploration of the connections among affect, repression, and white power is a view of "attempts of the perpetrators to deny knowledge of themselves as violent aggressors, morally destitute, even barbaric." Whites in America "have worked hard to repress and discredit that history," and that effort has "deepened the trauma rather than opened avenues of accountability and healing."[54] Crucially, white racial trauma has led whites to "reproduce the very violence that was the source of their own dis-ease."[55] American history with regard to whites is "a history of traumatic recurrence" of the violence of slavery and postslavery.[56]

A central feature of white racial trauma concerns the understanding that "white people carry with them memories and experiences that tell them something is desperately wrong."[57] It is both a collective and an individual experience. When we speak of white racial trauma, "the trauma in question is slavery, not as an institution or even experience, but as a collective memory, a form of remembrance that grounded identity-formation of a people."[58] That collective trauma is the consequence of the enslavement of Africans and Native Americans, and includes genocidal violence against Native Americans, and exclusionary and destructive campaigns against Asian American, Hispanic American, and other minority communities. Additionally, however, it is important to recognize that cultural trauma should not be separated from personal experience. As I have argued previously in this book, research ranging from emotional constructionism to social neuroscience, anthropological studies, and genomic research urges us to acknowledge the fact that collective experience and individual experience are interwoven. While collective forgetting occurs, and collective trauma is felt, those occurrences, as much as they are manifest in institutions and cultural media, are also experiences of individual Americans.

White racial trauma recurs in enactments of violence toward nonwhites (and in some cases against other whites who are perceived as aligned with those minorities). Repression and denial lead to "historical repetitions" that "have a compulsive, even post-traumatic dimension when patterns or templates from the past are regenerated."[59] When the "trauma of perpetrators goes largely suppressed and denied," that failure leads to a "time trap of endless trauma hurriedly cleansed, erased and avenged," amounting to "a 'negative circularity,' as it revolves around the already happened and yet to happen again."[60] The individual collaborates with social institutions in refusing accountability. For some scholars, "society's refusal to understand or interrogate [a] perpetrator's traumatisation is the result of the refusal for that very society to accept responsibility for putting that perpetrator into a position" where violence against others was presented as a matter of citizenship.[61] It is also a position where violence is socially authorized again and again.

As I have noted previously, I am concerned with how perpetrator groups repeat their crimes; how "serial genocides,"[62] such as the long, violent war against Native Americans, take place; and how violent episodes such as the religio-political insurrection of January 6 arise from deliberate forgetting. I note in the previous chapter that scholars refer to mass religious and political violence as occurring in connection with "cycles of hatred."[63] Studies of genocide often posit "cycles of violence" and "cycles of killings,"[64] and, with regard to transgenerational trauma, the idea of "the repetition of cycles of destructiveness."[65] Most of that research has to do with the experience of persons and groups characterized as victims. When we turn our attention to perpetrator trauma, we see a distinct but related cycle of violence, namely, that killing begets killing. Serial perpetrator violence is an attachment problem, among other things. It can take place when an other perceived as "close by" or otherwise connected as "kin"—like the Jews' perception of Amalekites in the Old Testament narrative—serves as a focus for the hatred and anger of the perpetrator group. In turn, that act of violence, repressed in memory, can fuel a new cycle of violence.

Such is the pattern observed by some scholars in the case of mob violence against African Americans, where lynching has been read as a performance of attachment to the victim—whose role is that of sacrificial object—even as it functions as a kind of expiation of the sins of racism, or, in other words, and with a Christian inflection, a process of forgetting (racism) and forgiving (themselves). Lynching rituals, "infused with religious meaning," served as "expiation for Southern racial sins," as "rituals of repentance and retribution," and, especially, as rituals of forgetting, serving as an occasion meant to bury memory of racial sins.[66] By such a ritual, the execution by hanging of thirty-eight Dakotas at Mankato, Minnesota—the largest mass execution in U.S. history and one carried out after five-minute trials in some cases—in late 1862 was both a white performance of self-absolution and a gesture of a renewed effort to forget genocide.

Beyond Basic Emotions

In arguing that ideology alone is not the prompt to violence for perpetrator groups, and that feelings and repressed memory can be involved at the most fundamental level, I mean to say that persons do not embrace an extreme ideology and then naturally feel fear, anger, and hatred. Again, hate and anger do not spring fully formed from such exposure. A young, white, American male does not read propaganda on a neo-Nazi website and then suddenly feel hate. There is much background involved that shapes the affective response.

What in the past have been termed "basic emotions" such as fear and hate are more complicated in their development from environmental stimuli than basic emotions theory had proposed. Emotions are constructed of bits and pieces, in a process involving body, mind, and culture. For this reason, I reject aspects of much recent writing about religious terrorism because it rests on a direct correlation between ideology and a specific emotion (i.e., hate, sometimes morphing into anger). Some people are exposed to extremist ideology and do not experience hate. Some people experience, eventually, other emotions. People read ideology in different ways. Why one group turns violent and another does not is a matter involving their social and cultural backgrounds. And sometimes those backgrounds are hard to see.

Additionally, I am less inclined than many other scholars to subscribe to a theory of melancholy, as has been deployed in literary studies and some historical writing. Researchers who have adopted Freudian ideas and psychoanalytic theory more broadly (as I do, but qualifiedly) often have leveraged those theories to great advantage in making sense of the experiences of Americans with regard to race. And in some cases that research is nuanced and reflexive in a way that begins to recognize the limits of "melancholy theory." However, melancholy is not a distinct natural kind emotion that can be transmitted whole from one generation to another and, like hate and anger, it is not a feeling that emerges initially as a finished product of encounter with the external world. It might be possible to begin describing it as something like anxiety, but there are hurdles to jump in doing that—hurdles put up by constructionist theory and by the neuroscientific and psychological research on which it is based. In some ways, melancholia as a central theme of literary interpretation involving trauma, and in many cases race, retains some of the features of trauma theory as it was practiced in the last century. It has co-alesced partially as a critical remaking of trauma theory that can appear to have avoided some of the problems of trauma theory—for example, by steer-ing away from the latter's fixation on the epistemics of representation and by taking more seriously the complexities of cultures of communication and the possibilities for polyvalencies and fluidities in emotional life. Insights such as the potentiality of melancholia to manifest as both hope and despondency are crucial not only to understanding racial trauma, but to appreciating the broader cultural dynamics of forgetting and memorialization.

But how melancholia, as a feeling, itself serves as motivation remains un-clear. So also does the process of how melancholia, as specific affect, is trans-mitted in culture. I find *melancholia* to be a useful term for understanding some of the otherwise hidden machinery of culture and history, and espe-cially for the history of racism in America. But as theory, it remains apart from and uninformed by scientific and social scientific research from which it might benefit. And, as such, it leaves the gaps in interpretation wider than they might otherwise be with regard to issues involving memory and the re-lationship between emotion and ideology. Jermaine Singleton's valuable study of Black melancholia, for example, ends up confessing, "The ritually main-tained and propagated melancholy this project uncovers through a close read-ing of American and African American literatures and cultures has left us in a lurch between biologism and social construction."[67]

I propose that one way in which to bridge that "lurch" between under-standing the biological aspects of a feeling and its ideological aspects is to take an emotional constructionist approach that identifies core affect, rather than an emotion, as a starting point. That core affect follows from a stimu-lus that can be conscious or unconscious. It might be a bear encountered in the woods. Or it might be an unconscious engagement with a memory about race. Triggered by something in the environment—perhaps by some-thing that signals race—it produces affect characterized by high activation as well as unpleasantness.

In the extremely rapid process of the construction of an emotion from that initial experience, cognition plays a crucial role. That means ideas mat-ter to the construction of an emotion. And that means ideology matters—ideology as carried forward in culture by all the usual cultural vehicles of communication, ranging from electronic media and print cultures and me-morials, music, and other material culture to national government projects, neighborhood collaborations, and circulating gossip. But what kinds of ideas are persons drawn to that transpose a repressed memory and core affect into violence?

Repressed memory about race—which might be triggered by any number of stimuli in the environment—is an experience of knowing/unknowing. It is a feeling of forgetting with a decidedly dark side. It is an experience of the uncanny, an uncertainty. It leads to a core affect that, as it develops in a complex process of emotional construction, we might call anxiety. In that process, as cognition and consciousness play their roles, ideas contribute to shaping the emotional experience. That experience, as it forms, can lead to what I have discussed, following social psychology, as worldview defense—as defense of identity that is threatened by uncertainty. And such a defense, which rests on reconfirming group belonging, can draw on extremist, binarist ideologies that divide the world into opposing groups in existential conflict. In such a way repressed memory, emergent as a feeling of forgetting about past violence against racial others, can lead to hatred and anger as the emotion fully forms, and those emotions in turn can find expression in violence. Such violence finds its target in a group to which the anxious group is dysfunctionally attached. Violence, such as the expiative and seemingly redemptive drama of a lynching, then, is a tactic deployed to kill memory—that is, to act to repress it—even as it confirms and sustains the status quo of racial antipathy, thus guaranteeing a new cycle of violence.

But hate and anger are not emotions predetermined by the stimulus provided by a repressed memory of racial trouble. Because of the widespread accessibility of extremist ideologies—in recent decades in the United States, fabrications such as QAnon, replacement theory, American Identitarianism, and other alt-right improvisations—the construction of an emotion stimulated by repressed racial memory can take a direction toward violence by accepting such ideas as necessary for a worldview/identity defense. Other ideological systems are present in culture, however, and, depending on context and timing, they also can provide ideas to a worldview defense that need not include hate and anger as end products. Much has to do with context. Just as Black melancholia may result in hope or despair, depending on the situation, so also white racial anxiety may end in emotions other than those that can lead to violence.

In America, religion has a primary role in all of this. I have written elsewhere about the centrality of the feeling of emptiness in American Christianity, and how American Christianities vigorously and unceasingly exhort persons to feel emptiness—to empty themselves of self.[68] American Christianities, and especially evangelical Protestantism, encourage experiences of uncertainty. Personal identity, group identity, a sense of belonging to a group, a sense of location—such experiences always have a tenuous, volatile quality in persons and groups that endeavor to ritually strip themselves of identity. White Protestant evangelicals who seek to kill off the old self so that there can be a new self—and who pursue without rest the lifelong impossible mission of killing off that old self—historically have been drawn to ideologies that picture the world as a battle between forces of good and forces of evil, between the saved and the damned. White evangelicals often are drawn exactly to those ideologies that, when accessed in support of worldview defense (a necessity when persons and groups feel emptied of identity), are likely to offer ideas that lead to destructive emotions, and to violence. Given the further complication that so much of evangelical history is southern history, and that undigested complicity in slavery and its violent aftermaths in the South profoundly haunt Americans who live there—as well as Americans in other parts of the country who take their religious bearings from southern evangelicalism—it is not difficult to recognize the enmeshment of white racial violence with evangelicalism.[69] As one historian recently observed: "Racism is a feature, not a bug, of American evangelicalism."[70]

But it is not only white evangelicals who have been responsible for violence against minority racial groups. White Americans, and some other Americans as well, who, from the colonial period through the nineteenth centuries campaigned violently against Indians, were from others of the various branches of American Christianity, and included Catholics and Mormons, and members of various Christian sects, as well as a broader field of Protestants. And the trauma arising from the perpetration of genocide against Native Americans by all these American Christians is deeply embedded and intractable in terms of its imprisonment in repressed memory. Reinforced by white culpability in slavery—again, Catholics and mainline Protestant groups were involved in that as well—what remains deep in American memory about Native American genocide is the starting point for understanding the mingled symbology of Christianity and racism, the crosses and the Confederate flags, the Christian banners and the anti-Semitic T-shirts, that broadcasted the insurrectionists' thoughts and feelings as they assailed the Capitol on January 6, 2021.

In addition to American Christian insistence on emptiness, which can induce dangerous consequences for worldview defense, Christianity urges forgetting on its membership. Whether it is to forgive and forget others, or to forget one's own failures and "move ahead" so as not to "dwell in the past," the Christian promotion of forgetting conditions American Christians to repress memory of painful events. Christianity is a central factor in Americans' willingness to screen from memory past sins, among which genocide is the most mortal.

Christianity also collaborates with the construction of hatred and anger out of the provocation caused by repressed memory because of its ideological justification for mass violence. The reasoning of eighteenth- and nineteenth-century military leaders, clergy, soldiers, and their civilian supporters that Indians, as Amalekites, the ill-fated tribe of people exterminated by the ancient Jews, deserved extermination became an ideological platform for violence, built deep into the nation's psyche, that endures. It is an extremist ideology, offering exactly the kind of hard binaries that international studies experts in the current day recognize as ideological prompts to terrorism. It is a starkly Manichean figuration of the world, and, while few today actually refer to the Amalekites, the reasoning that structured that story was long ago absorbed into American thinking about conflict. Its influence can be perceived across the board in U.S. international relations and domestic policy, from the legitimation of nuclear war against Japan to the torture of suspected terrorists under the George W. Bush administration and Donald Trump's willingness—and his followers' eagerness—to torch democracy in the interest of Christian white supremacy and religious rule.

Because the dynamic underlying serial racial violence in America has so often operated invisibly (repression has done its work well in that sense) and because of the complicity of Christianity in that violence (a Christianity that has a politically unassailable public image in America and that at the same time encourages forgetting), Americans have made painfully slow progress in coming to terms with past racial sins.

National Identity

The historian Robert Wiebe, in describing *The Search for Order, 1877–1920* (1967), characterized those decades, during which the Wounded Knee Massacre among others took place, as an American "revolution in identity."[71] As "island communities" transitioned into an urban, industrial, and bureaucratic American nationalism, Americans came to think of themselves differently, as a modern collective that productively navigated a rational, ordered society. Spiritualists imagined themselves part of that march, steadfastly insisting that their discovery of life behind the veil was a scientific breakthrough, and they broadcasted that conceit in publications such as *Fact*. Even the members of Mary Baker Eddy's fledgling community, the Church of Christ, Scientist (founded 1879), while denying the reality of disease, the body, the world, and the material universe, demanded recognition of their faith as a scientific one. In the case of both those religious emergences, and like many other late nineteenth-century social and cultural movements, what the left hand gave, the right hand took away. Science was tenuously paired with wildly imaginative unscientific cosmologies, professions of human equality with Jim Crow racism, and women's rights with a patriarchal and muscular Christianity. All were ingredients of an identity crisis, in a string of crises narrated in writings stretching from Benjamin Tompson's poetic telling of *New England's Crisis* (1676)[72] to the present.[73]

Historians half a century after Wiebe have learned to see complexities and contradictions in the period. They are less interested in a consensus narrative marking out the process of coalescence of a rationalized and nomothetic social order and more interested in narrating how lingering cultural confounds and newly forming social ontologies disrupted it. More specifically, it has become clearer that when Americans felt the presence of Indians, they were collaborating in a disruptive cascade. If the "practice of representing the Indians as ghosts works both to establish American nationhood and to call it into question,"[74] the crisis of national identity in the latter part of the nineteenth century was, to some extent, germinated from a profound anxiety about white relations with Native Americans that reached back into the seventeenth century. The crisis of identity that eventuated in the massacre at Wounded Knee in 1890 emerged from an abiding anxiety that Americans felt as a mysterious presence, a nameless attachment, and a feeling of forgetting. It arose especially from the repressed trauma of perpetration of Indian massacres.

It can be said that America "is obsessed with an originary sin against Native peoples" and that the nation feels "compelled to return to it again and again." White Americans historically have engaged Native Americans "as internal entities whose oppression must be repressed, but must not be given up."[75] In the late nineteenth century, as immigrants flooded the ports of American cities, vastly complicating the vision of what it meant to be an American, American fascination with Indians increasingly came to the forefront of national consciousness.[76] But it is the memory of violence against Indians that is at the bottom of the crisis of identity in the late nineteenth century. It is what Sarah Rivett, writing about Anglo-American literary forays at defining what it meant to be an American, has described precisely as "the trauma of loss that resulted from colonial and early national violence and policy toward indigenous populations."[77] The repressed trauma of violence against Native Americans that haunted the nation was felt as the anxiety of uncertainty about national identity. Caught between forgetting that violence and remembering it, and unmoored in an uncanny, liminal space that destabilized collective identity, Americans historically struggled to frame ideology to address that predicament.

Uncertainty about identity, which is a threat to the integrity of the collective, leads, for some collectives or subsets of collectives, to actions aimed at "transforming feelings of uncertainty about who we are into . . . violence."[78] America historically has been, as Carroll Smith-Rosenberg terms it, *This Violent Empire*,[79] in which violence has recurred regularly and especially was in evidence during the nineteenth century. Scholars have argued that American violence is a problem arising from a crisis of collective identity. Americans are an "uncertain people," and from that uncertainty flows violence: "Out of the uncertainty of our sense of national belonging, out of the contradictions that destabilize our national discourses and compromise our embrace of our Declaration of Independence, comes our penchant for violence, our need to punish the Others." It was precisely "the instability of Americans' national sense of self," the "unstable national identity never quite at peace with itself," that led to violence. Underlying that violence was an "anxiety."[80]

The "delicate psychological and ideological balance"[81] of American national identity remained an unstable one in part because Americans experienced the feeling of forgetting. The ideological statements that defined enemies and deployed justifications for their extermination arose in the wake of an epistemic feeling that informed of something that lurked below consciousness. Uncertainties about identity were rooted in that collective emotional experience, in the anxiety that accompanied the feeling of forgetting. The ideologies that Americans fashioned and refashioned in the interest of shoring up identity were of various sorts. Some were trained on market economics, others on political process, and others still on gender and sexuality. Those that focused on race took as their point of departure a trust that the character of a person—or of a people—marked them as either a member of the in-group, or a dangerous outsider.

American racist discourse always has orbited around the topic of character. From colonial times, Americans organized their thinking about social groups partly on assumptions about their character and temperament. In 1720, Robert Hale entered in his Harvard commonplace book: "The English are melancholick, the French are rash and unsteady, the Germans are phlegmatic and martial, the Spaniards are jealous, proud, and lustful, and the Italians are grave and revengeful."[82] That way of thinking included as object the Native American, whose character was the topic of a great many essays, poems, and novels over several centuries. While Jonathan Edwards and other missions-minded Christians wrote that Native Americans could develop

"Christian virtue," Americans questioned the Indian capacity, specifically, to learn the practice of "republican virtue," which emerged in the eighteenth century as a signifier of white Americanness. It did not matter that republican virtue was not easily defined beyond a sense of civic duty and a small inventory of behaviors that included opposition to corruption, moral leadership, defense of rights (especially property rights), and sacrifice for the collective. What mattered, in the dialogics of identity construction, was that Indians were the opposite of all that.

Religiously justified serial violence against Native Americans, sparked by a feeling of forgetting about repressed trauma, advanced under the banner of an ideology that centered on the depravity of Indian character. That judgment was the estimation of a great many treatises and essays authored by Americans, stretching over generations, about the "traits of the Indian character." An American history textbook in 1881 condensed those writings into a concise code: "In short, the study of Indian character is the study of the unregenerate human heart." The book went on to explain that failure as the reason Native American civilizations had become stuck between two elementary stages of development, the "Upper Grade of Savagery" and the "Middle Grade of Barbarism."[83] The predicament of Native Americans most commonly was clarified in lists of their moral failures, literary constructions remarkable in themselves for their length and their assertiveness. Besides having "no definite ideas of property or human rights," a common complaint leveled by advocates for republican virtue, they were "ruthless and revengeful, narrowminded and brutal, dissolute, lazy, selfish, gluttonous, polygamous, and lustful."[84] Christian missions organizers looked at them and saw "the grossest and most immoral character," including "night vigils, which in some cases close in orgies."[85]

Christian missionaries and their supporters, however, needed a raison d'être for their own activities. Accordingly they also saw in Native Americans signs that they could be "tamed" into persons of good character. In *Traits of the Indian Character* (1836), the western land speculator George Turner allowed that Indians were treacherous but hospitable, fickle but generous, sneaky but brave, and possibly capable of Christian virtue given the right guidance.[86] Other writers specifically pressed the case that the ideology of republican virtue, founded in a Christian morality, was applicable to Indians. And in the great nineteenth-century missionizing of Indians west of the Mississippi, a growing enthusiasm for the progress of the Indian inspired strong language about their looming redemption. "As Christianity has wrought itself into human history," it was becoming clear in 1887 that "now, as never before, the whole world of men are the associates and the recognized kin of every man."[87]

Indians becoming closer "kin" meant that they were becoming Christian. That was the message floated on top of the declamations about Indian immorality, about the unregenerate Indian heart and the disgusting behavior. Because of the labors of missionaries, "their wild habits have become in a great measure subdued by the restraining influences of Christianity, and they themselves transformed into industrious cultivators of the soil."[88] At the end of the century, it was progress among the Sioux that especially occupied the imaginations of white American Christians. "The most conspicuous change, however, has been wrought among the Dakotas, the dread Sioux of old."[89] A report from the front lines boasted "a good degree of success," given that "the religion of the Dakotas, in their heathen state, is demon-worship."[90] A month before the Wounded Knee Massacre, a Presbyterian writer exulted over the conversion of the Dakotas, explaining that "success is crowning the efforts of these missionaries of a pure faith" and surmising that "what is true of the Dakotas is true, also, of the other Indian tribes in the United States."[91] But the full import of the celebrations of Indian conversions was not lost on those who had written them. The Missionary Education Movement of the United States and Canada published an overview after the turn of the century that confessed, "The story of the Church's enterprise in giving the native American race the Christian gospel should be more fascinating and worthy of close study than the history of Indian warfare, romantic frontier struggles, and bloody massacres."[92] And that was regardless of whether Americans still felt the trauma of those massacres.

In 1890, thinking about Native Americans had been in crisis for a long time, at some moments more so than others. Massacres of Indians had taken place throughout the nineteenth century, and a harsh rhetoric foregrounding Native American inferiorities circulated widely. At the same time, Americans imagined that Indians were becoming closer kin to them. Some Americans, playing Indian, to an increasing extent migrated Indians across an ideological boundary distinguishing them from whites. They brought Indians closer. But that attachment remained dysfunctional—the Indian was judged far from redeemed, or tamed—and propinquity abetted the targeting of Indians as cultural intruders as much as it seemingly bridged a divide. White perpetrators remained attached to victims, and that attachment directed their reenactments of violence. In terms offered by one historian, "Native and European Americans alike experienced the erosion of differences as chaotic, 'bewildering,' and deeply threatening." Thus, in the end, "racist violence (rhetorical as well as literal) emerges, in part, at least, out of frustration with the repeated erosion of difference."[93]

Jake Chansley's performance of his identification with Indians on January 6, 2021, while the banners proclaiming Christian liberty waved on the steps of the Capitol, was a dramatization of the enduring power of buried racial trauma. Close to Indians, dressed as if he were kin, but yet distanced from them, as a white who benefits by the harm done to Indians, he sought confirmation of his Americanness in his attack on the Capitol. For him that Americanness was defined as his "rights." His religion, steeped in evangelical idioms, framed the experience for him as nothing less than a nation being "reborn." And in that violent rebirth, he signaled his subsequent renewed forgetting about Indians, about the genocidal white campaign against them, by removing his horned headdress to pray these words:

> Thank you, Heavenly Father, for gracing us with this opportunity . . . [takes off hat] . . . to stand up for our God-given unalienable rights. . . . Thank you for allowing the United States of America to be reborn. Thank you for allowing us to get rid of the communists, the globalists and the traitors within our government. We love you and we thank you, in Christ's holy name we pray![94]

The Feeling of Forgetting

The violence at the Capitol on January 6, 2021, exemplified the entanglements of religion and race in America. The banners, flags, signs, songs, dress, props, and words of the insurrectionists joined political grievance to a claim of religious righteousness. The mob assembled in Washington, DC, after a preparatory period of internet racist exuberance, as represented in preinsurrection social media postings such as, "It's time for the day of the rope. White revolution is the only solution."[1] Gathered around the Capitol, the insurrectionists prayed and sang Christian hymns before the television cameras. They pressed forward with shouts expressing their certainty that their cause was God's cause. They waved Confederate stars-and-bars flags, one of the most potent symbols of racism in America, as they fought past the police. During the subsequent criminal trials, it became ever clearer that many of the insurrectionists had records of membership in racist organizations and long social media trails of vicious rhetoric directed at racial minorities. But such a conjoining of white racial grievance and extremist Christian dominionism was nothing new. It was an enactment of a definitive social dysfunction that has plagued America since its colonial beginnings, and that has precipitated a long history of violent incidents, from wars and massacres to lynchings, bombings, and assaults. It bespeaks an American anxiety, an uncertainty about identity, manifest as the serial enactment of rituals of violence performed in the interest of emphatically marking boundaries in an effort to shore up collective identity.

The Capitol riot was the most recent episode in a centuries-long series of dramatic national reenactments of violence involving religion and race. It was a reenactment because the circumstances that framed it have been present in many other outbreaks of violence in American history. While the insurrection took place in a twenty-first-century context of political rhetoric, corporate power, social and economic predicament, and media influence, it was an event graphing a new point in the continuous series of incidences that preceded it. The insurrection was a religio-racial drama framed by emotionally rich memory of catastrophic white violence toward Native Americans, African Americans, and other minority groups. That memory percolates below the level of awareness for many American whites, who vocally insist that they have no social privilege arising from their whiteness and no accountability for slavery or genocide, Jim Crow or internment. They have sought to consign those events to oblivion, which is to say that they have repressed the memory of those events.

But as much as persons try to forget the past, they often cannot. In fact, the effort to forget sometimes more securely installs in memory the experience of events, together with the feelings that partly constitute them. Such memory festers just out of conscious awareness, but given the right prompt from the environment—a disorienting sight, a chilling turn of phrase, a disturbing social experience—it makes its way, typically unrecognized, into behavior. Stimuli from the environment prompt an affectual response that very rapidly can build to an emotion such as hate or anger as the phenomenological experience of bodily excitation is processed together with cognitions. These emotions, once formed, can manifest in acts of violence. And this violence can be followed, serially, by other acts of violence, whether over a short or a long period of time. There are serial killers haunted by their crimes who, in proceeding from one murder to the next, leave a trail stretching weeks or perhaps decades into the past. And there are violent American communities whose trails are generations long. An effort to forget does not guarantee escape from the past. The attempt to bury memory of the perpetration of violence can haunt for generations. The feeling of forgetting remains.

White America is haunted by the ghosts of those whom they sought to exterminate. Genocidal campaigns against Native Americans, the enslavement and destruction of African American bodies, the efforts to erase other minorities—as in the internment of Japanese Americans—remain in American memory. On occasion, we glimpse those ghosts. The spectral Indians who became one of the centerpieces of Spiritualism, the headstones in Black-only cemeteries, and the avatar presented by Jake Chansley on January 6, 2021, all conjure memory of white violence. But such conjuring typically delivers heat, not light. White Americans, who are so practiced in forgetting, often cannot see what is right before their eyes.

Americans have a habit of forgetting that is similar to what is found in other cultures around the world. Forgetting is universal. What differs from place to place is what a people choose to forget and how they go about forgetting it.

In America, Christianity has played a central role in personal and collective forgetting. Indeed, it has fostered forgetting throughout its history. It has, of course, also promoted remembering, and many Christians understand their faith as a call to remember doctrines, calendars, rituals, and community. But in America, the Christian call to forget is loud, and especially so in an evangelical Protestantism that unceasingly demands that the old self be forgotten and the new self lived. The past, they say, quoting the apostle Paul, is to be put behind. One's own failures, especially, are to be forgotten.

Forgetful evangelicalism, which took deep root in the South before spreading to other parts of the country, carries with it a specific agenda of forgetting. Southern-made evangelicalism above all has sought to forget its past involvements in racial violence, and it has done so even as it periodically has reinforced its commitments to white supremacy, as if white supremacy bears no animus toward nonwhites, and bears no intent to subordinate those other groups. Evangelical conjoining of white supremacy with religion—in the present as well as in the past—is well documented by scholars, and especially in recent decades. But memory, built from feeling as much as from cognition and often hidden from consciousness, resists even the most piously undertaken Christian exercises to forget. White memory of perpetration of violence against nonwhite groups is a hidden trauma, and like many traumas that are repressed, it remains an active influence on the way groups think and behave. The past is felt. The feeling of forgetting haunts. It will not lie down. Christians' attempts to forget their history of violence might seem to deliver some short-term relief from accountability. But such energy exerted in trying to erase the past and rinse from white consciousness any accountability in fact can feed the beast rather than obliviate it. Consequently, at times, forgetting seems to demand a sacrifice to do its work of concealment—a lynching, a massacre, an attempt to kill democracy.

White trauma is conjoined with the trauma of Native Americans and African Americans. Native Americans have been resilient, as have African Americans. But both groups suffer the pain of a colonial present as well as the memory of what has happened in the past. Both are traumatized and have lived their entire histories of encounter with colonizing whites in North America as expeditions undertaken to come to terms with their trauma, which, in spite of their adaptations and resistance, continues to harm them as social groups in the United States. To say that their trauma is mingled with white trauma is to recognize that the circumstances of white trauma have been different—whites have been the perpetrators—but both whites and nonwhites have been damaged and remain damaged by the violence perpetrated by whites. Their histories are so intimately coupled that whites and the groups they have harmed remain dysfunctionally attached to each other. They see each other as kin—distant kin, perhaps, but as groups deeply connected to each other, whose fates at times seem tragically joined, and whose attachment is always a matter of friction, not union. White violence against Native Americans and African Americans mirrors the violence that occurs between dysfunctional human couples, where the very fact of the felt closeness to the other person can feed the rage between them.

Monotheistic religions, which took root in the soil of Manichean distinctions between good and evil, truth and falsehood, and us and them, fostered the construction and maintenance of sharply drawn boundaries between ingroup and out-groups. That mentality was on display during a rally by Trump supporters on the Ellipse on the eve of the Capitol attack. Trump adviser Roger Stone, who the previous year had declared, "I was reborn as a Christian,"[2] exhorted the excited crowd: "This is nothing less than an epic struggle for the future of this country between dark and light, between the godly and the godless, between good and evil."[3] Such extremist rhetoric is characteristic of dysfunctional social relationships. But it also belies the complexity of seemingly absolutist ways of imagining the world.

Communities steeped in the Manichean categories that shaped monotheism are inclined to refuse compromise with the other even when an attachment to the other—as in the case of the Jews and Amalekites—is evident. Indeed, it is precisely the attachment, which is dysfunctional, that intensifies the anxiety about social boundary violations. It is the dysfunctional attachment that exacerbates violence. Native Americans and African Americans who demonstrated some acceptance of Christianity were potentially more dangerous than unconverted whites because white Christians imagined them as capable of surreptitiously passing through the gates that separated them from white society as a whole. Whites who imagined that Indians were blending their own rituals with Christian ideas and symbolism, as was the case just prior to the Wounded Knee Massacre, were alarmed. For them, the Ghost Dance scrambled categories of "like us" and "not like us," and that caused deep uncertainty among whites about what it meant to be a white Christian American. It further destabilized white identity and triggered worldview defense reactions that included anger and violence.

The insurrectionists at the Capitol proclaimed themselves patriots. They imagined themselves answering the call of a president to keep America safe from evil. They imagined a world turning upside down, in which Blacks were reaping a range of privileges and whites were not being respected. They sensed a world in-the-making in which nonbelievers and heretics were supplanting an American Christian destiny with a secular state that would dictate evil social policy, and in which a once-robust white population would inexorably be degraded and eventually replaced by persons of color. Those who stormed the Capitol bore the legacy of white trauma, repressed over generations with the help of Christian machinery that abetted forgetting. Their agenda also was informed by a reading of Christian tradition that legitimated violence against groups to which they were dysfunctionally attached. The "day of the rope" demanded by internet agitators was intended to be an exercise in stabilizing white Christian identity. It was intended to be an occasion of renewed Christian commitment to forgetting the racial sins of the nation, to burying them in memory again, until the next time.

Acknowledgments

As I was working on this book, I reaped the benefit and advantage of critical discussions of some of its arguments in meetings with colleagues who were in residence or visiting participants in several university lecture and colloquium settings. Such gatherings are the lifeblood of humanities scholarship, and the intellectual engagements among colleagues in such settings are invaluable. The generosity of scholars on display on these occasions is one of the finest things about academia. So I thank those who invited me as well as those in attendance who tried on, encouraged, and criticized my ideas. I am grateful especially to Paul Heck and Richard Schweder at Georgetown; Bernard McGinn and Alan Thomas at the University of Chicago; Axel Schäfer and Anthea Butler at the Obama Institute of the University of Mainz; Thomas Marks, William Reddy, and Monique Scheer at Yale; Ayyaz Gull and Ali Daud Ul Rehman at the University of Lahore; Christian von Scheve, Meike Haken, Nur Yasemin Ural, and Hubert Knoblauch at the Free University of Berlin; Georges Tamer, Muetaz A. Al-Khatib, Allan Mittleman, and Marianne Heimbach-Steins at the University of Erlangen; and Courtney Bender and Josef Sorett at Columbia.

Jan Plamper read an early version and offered excellent criticisms that helped me both to broaden and refine the argument. The anonymous readers for the University of Chicago Press provided careful, detailed readings of the manuscript and advised edits that improved the book in many ways. I am deeply grateful to all these colleagues for their thoughtfulness, encouragement, and candor. Any missteps that remain of course are my own.

I also thank colleagues at Florida State University who sat with me to think about various themes addressed in the book and who offered leads for my research. Martin Kavka was a great help in thinking about trauma; Greg Hajcak and Alexandria Meyer on neuroscience; Thomas Joiner and Jon Maner on epigenesis; and David Kirby and Mark Pietralunga on the Capitol insurrection. I thank my research assistant extraordinaire, Devin Burns, both for digging out sources and for her discussion of them.

I began parts of this project on full-time research courtesy of a fellowship from the American Council of Learned Societies. I finished it while enjoying the support and conversation of researchers I collaborated with while an Antibigotry Convening Fellow at the Center for Antiracist Research at Boston University. I thank Ibram X. Kendi and Caitlin Glass for inviting me in, and for making possible the illuminating conversations with other fellows.

It has been a pleasure working with Kyle Wagner at the Press. He listened. Carefully. I likewise thank Kristin Rawlings and Elizabeth Ellingboe at the Press for their roles in moving the project along. Nicole Balant did such a truly outstanding job copyediting the manuscript that I consider her a collaborator. Paul Anthony and Will Perez did an excellent job proofreading, and Derek Gottlieb made a great index. I thank as well Alan Thomas and Tim Mennel at the Press for their long-term support and intellectual partnership.

Notes

Introduction

1. Compass Church of Salinas/Marina, "How To Erase Bad Memories: Philippians 3:13–14," Life Group Discussions October #2, 1, accessed December 12, 2021, https://irp-cdn.multiscreen site.com/6c0a5854/files/uploaded/Memory%20Sermons.pdf. "People want happy memories but they keep bringing up the past. They aren't willing to pay the price of breaking the habit of being HISTORICAL" (2).

2. "Perhaps the most neglected doctrine of theology is the forgetfulness of God" (Brian L. Barbour, "The Forgetfulness of God," Center for Christian Ethics at Baylor University, 2001, 52, https://www.baylor.edu/ifl/christianreflection/ForgivenessarticleHarbour.pdf).

3. A full discussion of this is in John Corrigan, *Emptiness: Feeling Christian in America* (Chicago: University of Chicago Press, 2015).

4. The best starting point for understanding the American Christian campaign to remember and recover an imagined evangelical Christian past is in Michael J. McVicar, *Christian Reconstruction: R. J. Rushdoony and American Religious Conservatism* (Chapel Hill: University of North Carolina Press, 2015). Concise overviews of current Christian thinking about remembering and recovering the past, in the context of Christian nationalism, are Andrew L. Whitehead and Samuel L. Perry, *Taking America Back for God: Christian Nationalism in the United States* (New York: Oxford University Press, 2020); and Philip S. Gorski and Samuel L. Perry, *The Flag and the Cross: White Christian Nationalism and the Threat to American Democracy* (New York: Oxford University Press, 2022). On the merging of whiteness and religion, see Kate E. Temoney, "Anatomizing White Rage: 'Race Is My Religion!' and 'White Genocide,'" in *The Religion of White Rage: Religious Fervor, White Workers, and the Myth of Black Racial Progress*, ed. Stephen C. Finley, Biko Mandela Gray, and Lori Latrice Martin (Edinburgh: Edinburgh University Press, 2020), 149–65.

Chapter One

1. Congressional inquiry testimony of Sgt. Harry Dunn regarding words spoken to a fellow police officer confronted by rioters, July 27, 2021, reported by Brandi Buchman and Jack Rogers, "Insurrection Probe Opens with Harrowing Police Testimony," *Courthouse News Service*, July 27, 2021, https://www.courthousenews.com/committee-kicks-off-probe-of-jan-6-insurrection/.

2. Michelle Boorstein, "A Horn-Wearing 'Shaman.' A Cowboy Evangelist. For Some the Capitol Attack Was a Kind of Christian Revolt," *Washington Post*, July 6, 2021, https://www.washingtonpost.com/religion/2021/07/06/capitol-insurrection-trump-christian-nationalism-shaman/.

3. Ibid.

4. Rachel Weiner and Spencer S. Hsu, "Virginia 'Bible Study' Group Was Cover for Violent Militia Plans, Prosecutors Say," *Washington Post*, July 6, 2021, https://www.washingtonpost.com/local/legal-issues/capitol-riot-bible-study-group-militia/2021/07/06/e5e6cd26-de82-11eb-ae31-6b7c5c34f0d6_story.html.

5. Chansley is sometimes identified as Jake Angeli.

6. Joseph Pierce (Cherokee), "The Capitol Rioter Dressed Up as a Native American Is Part of a Long Cultural History of 'Playing Indian.' We Ignore It at Our Peril," *artnet news*, January 18, 2021, https://news.artnet.com/opinion/native-capitol-rioter-1937684.

7. Philip Joseph Deloria (Standing Rock Sioux), *Playing Indian* (New Haven: Yale University Press, 1998), 191.

8. Sarah Nelson, "Indiana Woman Becomes First Person Sentenced in Capitol Riots, Will Not Serve Time," *Indianapolis Star*, June 23, 2020, https://www.indystar.com/story/news/crime/2021/06/23/capitol-riot-sees-1st-sentence-given-indianas-anna-morgan-lloyd/5309991001/.

9. Sidney Howard, "Gone with the Wind, Final Shooting Script, January 24, 1939," 254, accessed March 6, 2021, https://www.dailyscript.com/scripts/Gone_With_the_Wind.pdf.

10. Jennifer Graber, *The Gods of Indian Country: Religion and the Struggle for the American West* (New York: Oxford University Press, 2018), 14.

11. Paul Gilroy, *Postcolonial Melancholia* (New York: Columbia University Press, 2005), 88.

12. "The Indian Council: Character of the Assembly," *New York Times*, June 17, 1871, 5.

13. Ned Blackhawk, *Violence over the Land: Indians and Empires in the Early American West* (Cambridge, MA: Harvard University Press, 2006), 202, 203.

14. Black Moon (Miniconjou Lakota), quoted in "Document 2.23. From: Volume 26 (1897–98): The Sioux and Their Apostles," in *Lakotas, Black Robes, and Holy Women: German Reports from the Indian Missions in South Dakota, 1886–1900*, ed. Karl Marcus Kreis, trans. Corinna Dally-Starna (Lincoln: University of Nebraska Press, 2000), 257.

15. "George Washington to Major General John Sullivan," May 31, 1779, Founders Online, National Archives, https://founders.archives.gov/documents/Washington/03-20-02-0661.

16. Black Moon (Miniconjou Lakota), quoted in "Document 2.23," 258.

17. Patrick Wolfe, "Settler Colonialism and the Elimination of the Native," *Journal of Genocide Research* 8 (2006): 387.

18. Ibid.

19. Chris Mato Nunpa (Wahpetunwan Dakota), "Dakota Commemorative March: Thoughts and Reactions," in *In the Footsteps of Our Ancestors: The Dakota Commemorative Marches of the 21st Century*, ed. Waziyatawin Angela Wilson (St. Paul, MN: Living Justice Press, 2006), 69.

20. Tiffany Hale (Afro-Cherokee), "Hostiles and Friendlies: Memory, U.S. Institutions, and the 1890 Ghost Dance" (PhD dissertation, Yale University, 2017), 26-6, 17.

21. Vine Deloria Jr. (Standing Rock Sioux), *Custer Died for Your Sins: An Indian Manifesto* (New York: Macmillan, 1969); and Deloria, *God Is Red: A Native View of Religion* (New York: Grosset and Dunlap, 1973). A careful analysis of Deloria's thinking about Christianity and colonialism, with additional insights into the broader academic emergence of Indian intellectual life in the twentieth century, is in David Martinez (Akimel O'odham/Hia Ced O'odham), *Life of the*

Indigenous Mind: Vine Deloria and the Birth of the Red Power Movement (Lincoln: University of Nebraska Press, 2019).

22. Jeffrey Ostler, *Surviving Genocide: Native Nations and the United States from the American Revolution to Bleeding Kansas* (New Haven: Yale University Press, 2019), 122.

23. Cited in Jeffrey Ostler, *The Plains Sioux and U.S. Colonialism from Lewis and Clark to Wounded Knee* (Cambridge: Cambridge University Press, 2004), 193.

24. Katherine A. Grandjean, "The Long Wake of the Pequot War," *Early American Studies* 9 (2011): 410. See also Albert A. Cave, *The Pequot War* (Amherst: University of Massachusetts Press, 1996).

25. Jill Lepore, *The Name of War: King Philip's War and the Origins of American Identity* (New York: Alfred A. Knopf, 1998); Lisa Brooks, *Our Beloved Kin: A New History of King Philip's War* (New Haven: Yale University Press, 2018); and Christine M. Delucia, *Memory Lands: King Philip's War and the Place of Violence in the Northeast* (New Haven: Yale University Press, 2018).

26. Delucia, *Memory Lands*, 23.

27. Quoted in Alden T. Vaughan, "Frontier Banditti and the Indians: The Paxton Boys' Legacy, 1763–1775," *Pennsylvania History: A Journal of Mid-Atlantic Studies* 51 (1984): 4.

28. Ostler, *Surviving Genocide*. Ostler writes: "The United States did not make outright genocide its first option for elimination," but "U.S. officials developed a policy that 'wars of extermination' against resisting Indians were not only necessary but ethical and legal" (4). See also Ostler, "Genocide and American Indian History," *Oxford Research Encyclopedia of American History*, ed. Lynn Dumenil (New York: Oxford University Press, 2015), https://oxfordre.com /americanhistory/view/10.1093/acrefore/9780199329175.001.0001/acrefore-9780199329175-e-3. He evidences the Native American belief that whites planned to exterminate them in " 'To Extirpate the Indians': An Indigenous Consciousness of Genocide in the Ohio Valley and Lower Great Lakes, 1750s–1810," *William and Mary Quarterly* 72 (2015): 587–622. See also Brendan C. Lindsay, *Murder State: California's Native American Genocide* (Lincoln: University of Nebraska Press, 2012). James Daschuk stresses the roles of starvation and disease in *Clearing the Plains: Disease, Politics of Starvations, and the Loss of Indigenous Life* (Regina, CAN: University of Regina Press, 2013). R. Paul Eli explains how the First Sioux War led to the Wounded Knee Massacre in *Blue Water Creek and the First Sioux War, 1854–1856* (Norman: University of Oklahoma Press, 2011).

29. Ostler, *Surviving Genocide*, 4.

30. "Notes and Documents: John M. Chivington, 1860: The First Colorado Regiment by Col. John M. Chivington," *New Mexico Historical Review* 33 (1958): 145.

31. Jennifer Graber, "Religion and Racial Violence in the Nineteenth Century," *Oxford Handbook of Religion and Race in American History*, ed. Paul Harvey and Kathryn Gin Lum (New York: Oxford University Press, 2018), https://www.oxfordhandbooks.com/view/10.1093 /oxfordhb/9780190221171.001.0001/oxfordhb-9780190221171-e-24?print=pdf.

32. Harry S. Stout, "Review Essay: Religion, War, and the Meaning of America," *Religion and American Culture: A Journal of Interpretation* 19 (2009): 284.

33. A full discussion of the colonial deployment of the Amalek story to justify violence against Native Americans is in John Corrigan, "New Israel, New Amalek: Biblical Exhortations to Religious Violence," in *From Jeremiad to Jihad: Religion, Violence, and America*, ed. John D. Carlson and Jonathan H. Ebel (Berkeley: University of California Press, 2012), 111–25; and Corrigan, "Amalek and the Rhetoric of Extermination," in *The First Prejudice: Religious Tolerance and Intolerance in Early America*, ed. Chris Beneke and Christopher S. Grenda (Philadelphia: University of Pennsylvania Press, 2011), 55–74.

34. "A Declaration . . . wherein the grounds and justice of the ensuing war are opened and cleared," in Ebenezer Hazard, ed., *Historical Collections; Consisting of State Papers, and Other Authentic Documents; Intended as Materials for an History of the United States of America*, vol. 2 (Philadelphia: T. Dobson, 1794), 50.

35. All citations are from the King James version, *The Holy Bible, conteyning the Old Testament, and the New* (London: Robert Barker, 1611). Centuries of exegetes both clerical and lay have tried their hand at interpreting the seemingly mixed message of Deuteronomy 25:19. I am not aware of any seventeenth-century American theological writings that directly address how the Jews were to both forget and remember. One possible interpretation for New Englanders is that Jews were to remember what God ordered them to do, while erasing the name and memory of the Amalekites, but even that reading calls for a braiding of memory with erasure of memory.

36. Roberto Cubelli, "A New Taxonomy of Memory and Forgetting," in *Forgetting*, ed. Sergio Della Sala (London: Routledge, 2010), 44.

37. Jan Assmann, *The Price of Monotheism*, trans. Robert Savage (Stanford: Stanford University Press, 2010); and Jan Assmann, *Moses the Egyptian: The Memory of Egypt in Western Monotheism* (Cambridge, MA: Harvard University Press, 1997).

38. Paul Gilroy, *After Empire: Melancholia or Convivial Culture?* (London: Routledge, 2004), 137.

39. Some early Spanish and English missionaries to the Americas constructed Indians as lapsed Christians, claiming that they had been the recipients of the gospel in an earlier age but had drifted from it over the centuries. They thus were both prepared to re-receive the gospel (a God-given *praeparatio evangelica* among Native Americans) and a danger, because of their partial, but perverse, religious kinship with Christians. The residuals of that idea contributed to a Christian sense of mission on the western frontier.

40. See Corrigan, "New Israel, New Amalek"; and Corrigan, "Amalek and the Rhetoric of Extermination."

41. Cited by Frederick D. Huntington in *Celebration of the Two Hundredth Anniversary of the Settlement of Hadley, Massachusetts* (Northampton; n.p., 1859), 31.

42. Cotton Mather, *A Discourse Delivered unto Some Part of the Forces Engaged in a Just War of New England* (Boston: n.p., 1689), title page, 37, 28.

43. Thomas Symmes, *Historical Memoirs of the Late Fight at Piggwacket, with a Sermon Occasion'd by the Fall of the Brave Capt John Lovewell* (Boston: n.p., 1725), i (also paginated as "Front Matter 1").

44. "History, as Expounded by the Supreme Court," *Putnam's Monthly Magazine of American Literature, Science, and Art* 9 (1857): 543; George Bancroft, *History of the United States*, vol. 3 of 10 vols. (Boston: n.p., 1837–74), 408; and F. A. Walker, "The Indian Question" *North American Review* 116 (1873): 330.

45. The clergyman William Hubbard, who commented in detail on the violence, drew on that in constructing "an identity for the English settlers in New England as a unified and traumatized people" (Matthew H. Edney and Susan Cimburek, "Telling the Traumatic Truth: William Hubbard's 'Narrative' of King Philip's War and His 'Map of New-England,'" *William and Mary Quarterly* 61 [2004]: 344).

46. Captain John Mason, "Brief History of the Pequot War," in *History of the Pequot War*, ed. Charles Orr (Cleveland, OH: Helman-Taylor, 1897), 44–45.

47. Bernard Bailyn, *The Barbarous Years of North America: The Conflict of Civilizations, 1600–1675* (New York: Alfred A. Knopf, 2012), 443–48.

NOTES TO PAGES 22–23

48. Thomas Shepard, *The Autobiography of Thomas Shepard* (Boston: Pierce and Parker, 1832), 62.

49. Captain John Underhill, "Newes from America," in *History of the Pequot War*, 81.

50. Underhill, "Newes from America," 84.

51. Edward Eggleston, *Century Illustrated Magazine* 26 (1883): 717; and *The Living Age* 111 (1871): 462.

52. Cited in Gray H. Whaley, *Oregon and the Collapse of the Illahee: U.S. Empire and the Transformation of an Indigenous World, 1792–1859* (Chapel Hill: University of North Carolina Press, 2010), 90.

53. Corrigan, "New Israel, New Amalek"; and Corrigan, "Amalek and the Rhetoric of Extermination."

54. Cotton Mather, *Optanda* (Boston: n.p., 1692), 79.

55. John Gottlieb Ernestus Heckewelder, *A Narrative of the Mission of the United Brethren to the Delaware and Mohegan Indians* (Philadelphia: M'Carty and Davis, 1820), 68.

56. As already noted, the notion that Indians were descendants of the Lost Tribes of Israel circulated widely in colonial America and remained in effect during the nineteenth century. The idea was an important component in the construction of a sense of attachment that colonists and later Americans felt for Indians. At the same time, as a marker of kinship, it rendered more consequential and dangerous the conflicts between Indians and Euro-Americans.

57. Heckewelder, *A Narrative of the Mission*, 86.

58. *Pennsylvania Gazette*, July 17, 1766. Quoted in Vaughan, "Frontier Banditti," 15.

59. Quoted in Mark Puls, *Henry Knox: Visionary General of the American Revolution* (New York: Palgrave, 2008), 207; "Henry Knox to Lucy Flucker Knox, New York, NY, Saturday, 7 September 1776," in Phillip Hamilton, *The Revolutionary War Lives and Letters of Lucy and Henry Knox* (Baltimore: Johns Hopkins University Press, 2017), 59. The reference to Philistines was to "Savages" Knox was fighting on Long Island in 1776.

60. Discussed in Ostler, "'To Extirpate the Indians,'" 621.

61. Quoted in Michael Fellman, *Citizen Sherman: A Life of William Tecumseh Sherman* (New York: Random House, 1995), 264.

62. This is a criticism leveled by *The Friend: A Religious and Literary Journal*, July 15, 1876, 382.

63. "Memorandum by Sir Jeffrey Amherst, 4 May 1763," in Henry Bouquet, *The Papers of Col. Henry Bouquet*, ed. Sylvester H. Stevens and Donald K. Kent (Harrisburg: Pennsylvania Historical Commission, Department of Historical Instruction, 1940), 161.

64. Richard Slotkin, *Regeneration through Violence: The Mythology of the American Frontier, 1600–1860* (Norman: University of Oklahoma Press, 1973), 77.

65. William Hubbard, *A Narrative of the Troubles with the Indians in New England* (Boston: John Foster, 1677), 19.

66. Ostler, *Surviving Genocide*; and Ostler, "Genocide and American Indian History." See the pointed discussion by Steven T. Katz in "Pequots and the Question of Genocide," *New England Quarterly* 68 (1995): 641–49.

67. D. H. Lawrence, *The Cambridge Edition of the Works of D. H. Lawrence*, ed. Ezra Greenspan, Lindeth Vasey, and John Worthen (Cambridge: Cambridge University Press, 2003), 43.

68. In characterizing dysfunctional attachment among social groups as a condition arising in part from trauma, I extrapolate from a large body of psychological literature that addresses the attachment problems of individuals. Some of the earliest research is in John Bowlby,

Attachment and Loss: Vol. 1: Attachment (New York: Basic Books, 1969); Bowlby, *Attachment and Loss: Vol. 3: Loss, Sadness and Depression* (New York: Basic Books, 1980); and Bowlby, "Attachment Theory and Its Therapeutic Implications," in *Adolescent Psychiatry: Developmental and Clinical Studies*, ed. S. C. Feinstein and P. Giovacchini, vol. 6 (Chicago: University of Chicago Press, 1978), 5–23; Victoria A. Fitton, "Attachment Theory: History, Research, and Practice" *Psychoanalytic Social Work* 19 (2012): 121–43. A suggestive, more recent study is Daniel K. Lapsley, Nicole M. Varshney, and Matthew C. Aalsma, "Pathological Attachment and Attachment Style in Late Adolescence" *Journal of Adolescence* 23 (2000): 137–55.

69. I discuss haunting later on but note here in this discussion of colonialism that some arguments about the appearance of Indian ghosts to whites risk reinscribing colonial presuppositions on Native American communities. See Emilie Cameron, "Indigenous Spectralities and the Politics of Colonial Ghost Stories," *Cultural Geographies* 15 (2008): 383–93.

70. United Nations General Assembly, "Declaration on the Granting of Independence to Colonial Countries and Peoples," Resolution 1514, 1960, https://legal.un.org/avl/ha/dicc/dicc.html.

71. Waziyatawin Angela Wilson (Upper Sioux Community), "Manipi Hena Owas'in Wikunkiksuyapi (We Remember All Those Who Walked)," in *In the Footsteps of Our Ancestors: The Dakota Commemorative Marches of the 21st Century*, ed. Waziyatawin Angela Wilson (St. Paul, MN: Living Justice Press, 2006), 9.

72. David Treuer (Ojibwe), *The Heartbeat of Wounded Knee: Native America from 1890 to the Present* (New York: Corsair, 2019), 451, 452. Treuer points out that while Americans imagined the massacre as "the final blow, a full stop" to colonial brutality, the Indians survived.

73. Brian Ward, "Selling Off Wounded Knee," *Socialist Worker*, May 15, 2013, https://social istworker.org/2013/05/15/selling-off-wounded-knee.

74. Vincent Schilling (Akwesasne Mohawk), "Wounded Knee Sold? Tim Giago Has Plans to Buy It for $3.9 Million," *ICT [Indian Country Today]*, September 13, 2018, https://indian countrytoday.com/archive/wounded-knee-sold-tim-giago-has-plans-to-buy-it-for-39-million; and Ward, "Selling Off Wounded Knee."

75. Walter Delrio, Diana Lenton, Marcelo Musante, Mariano Nagy, Alexis Papazian, and Pilar Pérez, "Discussing Indigenous Genocide in Argentina: Past, Present, and Consequences of Argentinian State Policies toward Native Peoples," *Genocide Studies and Prevention* 5 (2010): 138–59.

76. Mahmood Mamdami, *Define and Rule: Native as Political Identity* (Johannesburg: Wits University Press, 2013).

77. Treuer, *The Heartbeat of Wounded Knee*, 142. Treuer, while critical, also points out that some Indians liked the boarding schools (135, 137).

78. Brenda J. Child (Ojibwe), "U.S. Boarding Schools for Indians had a Hidden Agenda: Stealing Land," *Washington Post*, August 27, 2021, https://www.washingtonpost.com/outlook /2021/08/27/indian-boarding-schools-united-states/. See also Child, *Boarding School Seasons: American Indian Families 1900–1940* (Lincoln: University of Nebraska, 1998).

79. Albert Memmi, *The Colonizer and the Colonized* (Boston: Beacon Press, 1991), which is a reprint of the 1965 English edition translated by Howard Greenfeld. Memmi argues that the colonizer educates the colonized in ways that serve the long-term interest of the colonizers in preserving their own privileged position.

80. Andrew Denson, "Memories of Western Violence, Lost and Found," *Reviews in American History* 42 (2014): 277.

81. Among the many scholarly discussions of this construction is Philp J. Deloria, *Indians in Unexpected Places* (Lawrence: University Press of Kansas, 2004).

82. David Uahikeaikaleiʻohu Maile, "Threats of Violence: Refusing the Thirty Meter Telescope and Dakota Access Pipeline," in *Standing with Standing Rock: Voices from the #NoDAPL Movement*, ed. Nick Estes and Jaskiran Dhillon (Minneapolis, Minn., 2019), 329, 328–43.

83. Glen Coultard (Yellowknives Dene), *Red Skins, White Masks: Rejecting the Colonial Politics of Recognition* (Minneapolis: University of Minnesota Press, 2014), 121. What Catherine Lu says about the history of Japanese imperialism applies to colonialism everywhere: "Resistance against acknowledging responsibility for injustices committed in the context of colonial rule, that were distinct from the injustice of aggressive war and crimes against humanity committed in contexts of war, has persisted" (Catherine Lu, "Colonialism as Structural Injustice: Historical Responsibility and Contemporary Redress," *Journal of Political Philosophy* 19 [2011]: 265).

84. Blackhawk, *Violence over the Land*.

85. Sarah Maddison, "Indigenous Identity, 'Authenticity,' and the Structural Violence of Settler Colonialism," *Global Studies in Culture and Power* 20 (2013): 288–89.

86. Achille Mbembe, *On the Postcolony* (Berkeley: University of California Press, 2001).

87. Erica Doss, *Memorial Mania: Public Feeling in America* (Chicago: University of Chicago Press, 2010).

88. Gerald Vizenor (Chippewa), *Native Liberty: Natural Reason and Cultural Survivance* (Lincoln: University of Nebraska Press, 2009), 85.

89. Standing Bear (Ponca: Macunajin), "Standing Bear's Speech," *Timeless Truths*, reprinted from the *Indian Journal*, 1879, https://library.timelesstruths.org/texts/Stories_Worth_Rereading/Standing_Bears_Speech/.

90. 6. 25 F. Cas. 695 (C.C.D. Neb. 1879) (No. 14,891). For an excerpt, see Francis Paul Prucha, ed., *Documents of United States Indian Policy*, 3rd ed. (Lincoln: University of Nebraska Press, 2000), 151.

91. Mary Kathryn Nagle (Cherokee; Ponca), "*Standing Bear v. Crook*: The Case for Equality under Waaxe's Law," *Creighton Law Review* 45, no. 3 (2011): 455–502. See also her discussion of *Tee-Hit-Ton Indians v. United States* (348 U.S. 272 [1955]) on 493–97.

92. Chief Joseph (In-mut-too-yah-lat-lat; Nez Percé), in a speech in Washington, DC, that same year, made the same appeal—"We only ask an even chance to live as other men"—and displayed the same refusal of victimhood ("An Indian's Views of Indian Affairs," *North American Review* 128 [April 1879]: 433).

93. Joseph M. Marshall (Brulé Lakota, Sicangu Oyate), *Keep Going: The Art of Perseverance* (New York: Sterling Ethos, 2009). He emphasizes Lakota "power and ability to rebuild and strengthen our culture," a theme common among Indian writers who comment on the legacies of colonialism such as, prominently, Indians lands "scarred by . . . toxic pollution" (Marshall, *Crazy Horse Weeps: The Challenge of Being Lakota in White America* [Golden, CO: Fulcrum, 2019], xiv).

94. Stephen W. Silliman, "Practice and Memory: Native American Persistence in Colonial New England," *American Antiquity* 74 (2009): 211–30.

95. Treuer, *The Heartbeat of Wounded Knee*, 29.

96. Bea Medicine (Standing Rock Sioux), "Anthropologists and American Indian Studies Programs," in *Anthropology and the American Indian: A Symposium*, ed. Rupert Custo (San Francisco: The Indian Historian, 1973), 83.

97. Ella C. Deloria (Aŋpétu Wašté Wiŋ/Yankton Sioux), *Speaking of Indians* (New York: Friendship Press, 1944), 98.

98. Deloria, *Custer Died for Your Sins*, 16.

99. Christopher J. Colvin, "Trauma," in *New South African Keywords*, ed. Nick Shepherd and Steven Robbins (Johannesburg: Jacana, 2008), 231.

100. Eva Rask Knudsen, *The Circle and the Spiral: A Study of Australian Aboriginal and New Zealand Māori Literature* (Amsterdam: Rodopi, 2004), 11.

101. Treuer, *The Heartbeat of Wounded Knee*, 88.

102. For insightful commentary on some of these writers, see Anjelica Marie Lawson (Northern Arapaho), "Resistance and Resilience in the Work of Four Native American Authors" (PhD dissertation, University of Arizona, 2006). Resistance as well as resilience is present in this literature in many forms, including as resistance to the religion brought by Christian missionaries. Lawson discusses how Erdrich, for example, strongly objected to "the inappropriateness of using an imposed, foreign religion in an attempt to assimilate Native Americans" (115).

103. Harvey Markowitz, *Converting the Rosebud: Catholic Mission and the Lakotas 1886–1916* (Norman: University of Oklahoma Press, 2018), 204, 186, 215; and the entire chap. 12, "Pragmatism and Sicangu Catholicism," 182–202.

104. Graber, *The Gods of Indian Country*.

105. David Martinez (Akimel O'odham/Hia Ced O'odham), *Life of the Indigenous Mind: Vine Deloria and the Birth of the Red Power Movement* (Lincoln: University of Nebraska Press, 2019), 237.

106. Hale, "Hostiles and Friendlies," 120.

107. Treuer, *The Heartbeat of Wounded Knee*, 1.

108. Michelle Pesantubbee (Choctaw), "Wounded Knee: Site of Resistance and Recovery," in *Recovering Memory: Exposing Religion, Violence, and the Remembrance of Place*, ed. Oren Baruch Stier and J. Shawn Landres (Bloomington: University of Indiana Press, 2006), 75.

109. Frantz Fanon, *Black Skin, White Masks*, trans. Charles Lam Markmann (London: Pluto Press, 1986). In one introduction to the book (two are included in the volume, the other by Ziauddin Sardar), Homi Bahaba quotes Fanon: "If psychiatry is a medical technique that aims to enable a man no longer to be a stranger to his environment, I owe it to myself that the Arab, permanently an alien in his own country, lives in a state of absolute depersonalization" (xxiii).

110. Linda Tuhiwai Smith, *Decolonizing Methodologies: Research and Indigenous Peoples* (London: Zed Books, 1999), 1. Twenty years later Smith suggested possibilities for collaboration between Indigenous and non-Indigenous scholars in Linda Tuhiwai Smith, Michaela Benson, and Sara Salem, "Decolonising Methodologies, 20 Years On: An Interview with Professor Linda Tuhiwai Smith," *Sociological Review*, February 11, 2020, https://thesociologicalreview.org/collections/decolonising-methodologies/an-interview-with-professor-linda-tuhiwai-smith/.

111. Devon Abbott Mihesuah (Choctaw) and Angela Cavender Wilson (Waziyatawin—Upper Sioux Community), *Indigenizing the Academy: Transforming Scholarship and Empowering Communities* (Lincoln: University of Nebraska Press, 2004).

112. Bruce Robbins, *The Beneficiary* (Durham: Duke University Press, 2017), 6.

113. Michael Rothberg, *The Implicated Subject* (Stanford: Stanford University Press, 2019), 1.

114. Susannah Radstone, "Trauma Theory: Contexts, Politics, Ethics," *Paragraph* 30 (2007): 23.

Chapter Two

1. Maria Yellow Horse Braveheart (Lakota), "The Return to the Sacred Path: Healing the Historical Trauma and the Historical Unresolved Grief Response among the Lakota through a Psychoeducational Group Intervention," *Smith College Studies in Social Work* 68 (1998): 287.

2. Hilary N. Weaver (Lakota) and Maria Yellow Horse Braveheart, "Examining Two Facets of American Indian Identity: Exposure to Other Cultures and the Influence of Historical Trauma," *Journal of Human Behavior in the Social Environment* 2 (1999): 22.

3. Maria Yellow Horse Braveheart and Lemyra M. DeBruyn, "The American Indian Holocaust: Healing Historical Unresolved Grief," *American Indian and Alaska Native Mental Health Research* 8 (1998): 60, 61.

4. Kathleen Hankinson, "Willful Forgetting: 'White Indians,' Trauma, and Relationality in American Historical Literature" (PhD dissertation, Stony Brook University, 2016), 9.

5. Joseph P. Gone (Gros Ventre), "Redressing First Nations Historical Trauma: Theorizing Mechanisms for Indigenous Culture as Mental Health Treatment," *Transcultural Psychiatry* 50 (2013): 683–706. Gone cites a Gros Ventre spiritual leader on the return to traditional ritual practices: "They're working" (684). For Braveheart and some others who have focused on psychological problems of identity and belongingness in Indian communities, a return to religious life was the answer, inasmuch as it had the potential to restore a "constructive collective memory" (Braveheart, "The Return to the Sacred Path," 302).

6. J. Brooks Bouson, *Quiet as It's Kept: Shame, Trauma, and Race in the Novels of Toni Morrison* (New York: SUNY Press, 2000), 137.

7. Michelle Balaev, "Trends in Literary Trauma Theory," *Mosaic* 41 (2007): 158.

8. Lane Benjamin and Melike M. Fourie, "The Intergenerational Effects of Mass Trauma in Sculpting New Perpetrators," in *The Routledge International Handbook of Perpetrator Studies*, ed. S. C. Knittel and Z. J. Goldberg (Abingdon, UK: Routledge, 2019), 278.

9. Tlalho Sam Raditlhalo, "Disgrace, Historical Trauma, and the Extreme Edge of Civility," in *Trauma, Memory, and Narrative in the Contemporary South African Novel: Essays*, ed. Ewald Mengel, and Michela Borzaga (Amsterdam: Brill, 2012), 248.

10. Ibid., 247.

11. Paul Memmott, "On Regional and Cultural Approaches to Australian Indigenous Violence," *Australian and New Zealand Journal of Criminology* 43 (2010): 346.

12. Ibid., 345.

13. Judy Atkinson (Australia: Jiman/Bundjalung), "A Nation Is Not Conquered," *Aboriginal Law Bulletin* 3, no. 80 (1996): 7.

14. Merav Alush-Levron, "The Politics of Ethnic Melancholy in Israeli Film," *Social Identities* 21 (2015): 169, 171. Scholarly writing about the intergenerational transmission of trauma is extensive, and there is much debate. One starting point is Ira Brenner, "Intergenerational Transmission of Trauma," in his *Dissociation of Trauma* (Madison: International Universities Press, 2001), 91–104.

15. Jermaine Singleton, "Cryptic Conversations: Melancholy, Ritual, and the (African American) Literary Imagination" (PhD dissertation, University of Minnesota, 2005). Next I discuss Singleton's subsequent enlargement of his arguments in *Cultural Melancholy: Readings of Race, Impossible Mourning, and African American Ritual* (Urbana: University of Illinois Press, 2015).

16. Singleton, *Cultural Melancholy*, 55.

17. Margo Natalie Crawford, "The Twenty-First Century Black Studies Turn to Melancholy," *American Literary History* 29 (2017): 800.

18. Shelly A. Wiechelt, Jan Gryczynski, and Kelly Hawk Lessard (Shawnee), "Cultural and Historical Trauma among Native Americans," in *Trauma: Contemporary Directions in Trauma Theory, Research, and Practice*, ed. Jerrold C. Brandell and Shoshana Ringel (New York: Columbia University Press, 2019), 105–6. An early attempt to intersect personal and collective contexts in analyzing

the experiences of descendants of traumatized persons is in Dori Laub, "Testimonies in the Treatment of Genocidal Trauma," *Journal of Applied Psychoanalytic Studies* 4 (2002): 63–87.

19. Wiechelt, Gryczynski, and Lessard, "Cultural and Historical Trauma," 106.

20. Waziyatawin Angela Wilson (Upper Sioux Community), "Manipi Hena Owas'in Wikunkiksuyapi (We Remember All Those Who Walked)," in *In the Footsteps of Our Ancestors: The Dakota Commemorative Marches of the 21st Century*, ed. Waziyatawin Angela Wilson (St. Paul, MN: Living Justice Press, 2006), 9.

21. Adrienne Harris, "Haunted Talk: Healing Action: Commentary on Paper by Kimberlyn Leary," *Psychoanalytic Dialogues* 10 (2000): 656.

22. Marinus H. van IJzendoorn, Marian J. Bakermans-Kranenburg, and Abraham Sagi-Schwartz, "Are Children of Holocaust Survivors Less Well-Adapted? A Meta-Analytic Investigation of Secondary Traumatization," *Journal of Traumatic Stress* 16 (2003): 459–69. The sample was $n = 4{,}418$.

23. As this is a book about religion as well as race and violence, I draw on here and adapt Judith Weisenfeld's idea of the religio-racial as a way of referring to the linkage of religion with identity in African American communities (*New World A-Coming: Black Religion and Racial Identity during the Great Migration* [New York: NYU Press, 2018], 95–126). I use it in connection with some African American writers' characterizations of Black trauma as a spiritual predicament as much as a social one. I refer to that in chapter 6 in discussing melancholy.

24. Among African American scholars, for example, the discussion of trauma and grief recently has been refashioned, following leads by Judith Butler and others, into discussions of melancholy. I discuss some of this literature subsequently, but it includes studies by Jermaine Singleton, Joseph R. Winters, Margo Natalie Crawford, and Stephen Best.

25. Bryan Cheyette, in Stef Craps, Bryan Ceyette, Alan Gibbs, Sonya Andermahr, and Larissa Allwork, "Decolonizing Trauma Studies: Round-Table Discussion," *Humanities* 4 (2015): 918.

26. E. Ann Kaplan, *Trauma Culture: The Politics of Terror and Loss in Media and Literature* (New Brunswick: Rutgers University Press, 2005), 25.

27. Irene Visser, "Trauma in Non-Western Contexts," in *Trauma and Literature*, ed. J. Roger Kurtz (New York: Cambridge University Press, 2018), 125.

28. Benjamin and Fourie, "The Intergenerational Effects of Mass Trauma," 279.

29. American Psychological Association, "Trauma," accessed April 7, 2021, www.apa.org/topics/trauma.

30. Joanne Pettitt, "Holocaust Narratives: Second Generation 'Perpetrators' and the Problem of Liminality," *European Legacy* 23 (2018): 288–89.

31. Balaev, "Trends in Literary Trauma Theory," 150.

32. Hans Jonas, "Cultural Trauma? On the Most Recent Turn in Jeffrey Alexander's Cultural Sociology," *European Journal of Social Theory* 8 (2005): 368. Jonas refers to the "objective reality of subjective perspectives" (368).

33. Didier Fassin and Richard Rechtman, *The Empire of Trauma: An Inquiry into the Condition of Victimhood* (Princeton: Princeton University Press, 2009).

34. Michelle Balaev, "Literary Trauma Theory Reconsidered," in *Contemporary Approaches in Literary Trauma Theory*, ed. Michelle Balaev (New York: Palgrave, 2014), 7.

35. Joseph Breuer and Sigmund Freud, *Studien über Hysterie* (Leipzig: F. Deuticke, 1895). A useful discussion of the role of Freud's theorizing about trauma and anxiety, with reference to the third case in those studies (Katharina) is in Jan Plamper, *The History of Emotions: An Introduction* (Oxford: Oxford University Press, 2017), 195–201.

36. "Letter from Freud to Fliess, December 18, 1892," in *The Complete Letters of Sigmund Freud to Wilhelm Fliess, 1887–1904*, trans. and ed. Jeffrey Moussaieff Masson (Cambridge, MA: Harvard University Press, 1985), 37. For the developing discursive context of that statement, see Josef Breuer and Sigmund Freud, "Studies on Hysteria," in *The Standard Edition of the Complete Psychological Works of Sigmund Freud*, ed. James Strachey, 24 vols. (London: Hogarth, 1955–74), 2:7.

37. Sigmund Freud, "On the History of the Psycho-Analytic Movement" (1914), in *The Standard Edition of the Complete Psychological Works*, 14:16.

38. Freud, "On Repression" (1915), in *The Standard Edition of the Complete Psychological Works*, 14:147.

39. Freud, "Project for a Scientific Psychology" (1895), in *The Standard Edition of the Complete Psychological Works*, 1:409.

40. Freud, "Analysis Terminable and Interminable" (1937), in *The Standard Edition of the Complete Psychological Works*, 23:226.

41. This view is similar to a theorization, a century later, of remembering/forgetting, and especially Frederic C. Bartlett's theory, discussed here in chapter 4.

42. Katrien Libbrecht and Julien Quackelbeen propose that Freud's adoption of Charcot's ideas enabled him to frame a theory that in turn had particular relevance for PTSD sufferers ("On the Early History of Male Hysteria and Psychic Trauma: Charcot's Influence on Freudian Thought," *Journal of the History of the Behavioral Sciences* 31 [1995]: 370–84).

43. As far as what is relevant to this book.

44. Breuer and Freud, "Studies on Hysteria," in *The Standard Edition of the Complete Psychological Works*, 2:5.

45. Ibid., 10.

46. Ibid.

47. Matthew Hugh Erdelyi, "The Unified Theory of Repression," *Behavioral and Brain Sciences* 29 (2006): 504.

48. Peter H. Rudebeck, Paul T. Putnam, Teresa E. Daniels, Tianming Yang, Andrew R. Mitz, Sarah E. V. Rhodes, and Elisabeth A. Murray, "A Role for Primate Subgenual Cingulate Cortex in Sustaining Autonomic Arousal," *Proceedings of the National Academy of Sciences* 114 (2014): 5391–96.

49. Robin L. Carhart-Harris, Helen S. Mayberg, Andrea L. Malizia, and David Nutt, "Mourning and Melancholia Revisited: Correspondences between Freudian Metapsychology and Empirical Findings in Neuropsychiatry," *Annals of General Psychiatry* 7 (2008): 13, 15; online document pagination from https://annals-general-psychiatry.biomedcentral.com/track/pdf/10.1186/1744-859X-7-9.pdf..

50. Ibid., 15.

51. Pierre Gagnepain, Richard N. Henson, and Michael C. Anderson, "Suppressing Unwanted Memories Reduces Their Unconscious Influence via Targeted Cortical Inhibition," *Proceedings of the National Academy of Sciences* 11 (2014): 1310, 1311.

52. Ryan Smith and Richard D. Lane, "Unconscious Emotion: A Cognitive Neuroscientific Perspective," *Neuroscience and Biobehavioral Reviews* 69 (2016): 217.

53. Daniel L. Schacter, "Implicit Memory: History and Current Status," *Journal of Experimental Psychology: Learning, Memory, and Cognition* 13 (1987): 501–18. Many of the issues and much of the research are addressed in Ran R. Hussin, James S. Uleman, and John A. Bargh, eds., *The New Unconscious* (New York, Oxford University Press, 2005). See especially chap. 3, Elizabeth A. Phelps, "The Interaction of Emotion and Cognition: The Relation between the

Human Amygdala and Cognitive Awareness," 61–76; and chap. 7, Jack Glaser and John Kihl-strom, "Compensatory Automaticity: Unconscious Volition Is Not an Oxymoron," 171–95.

54. Commentary on the emergence of implicit knowledge as a topic in the study of culture is in Robert Wuthnow and Marsha Witten, "New Directions in the Study of Culture," *Annual Review of Sociology* 14 (1988): 49–67.

55. Michael Polanyi, *The Tacit Dimension* (Chicago: University of Chicago Press, 1966), 4.

56. Smith and Lane, "Unconscious Emotion," 217.

57. John F. Kihlstrom, Shelagh Mulvaney, Betsy A. Tobias, and Irene B. Tobis, "The Emotional Unconscious," in *Cognition and Emotion*, ed. Erich Eich, John F. Kihlstrom, Gordon H. Bower, Joseph P. Forgas, and Paula M. Niedenthal (New York: Oxford University Press, 2000), 42. Additionally, it is useful to observe that among psychologists there is "the standard view that memory is not strictly veridical and is subject to wide-ranging and ongoing distortions" (Erde-lyi, "The Unified Theory of Repression," 511).

58. Erdelyi, "The Unified Theory of Repression," 511. I have built on Erdelyi's statement to include all kinds of repressed material.

59. Michael Rothberg, *Multidirectional Memory: Remembering the Holocaust in the Age of Decolonization* (Stanford: Stanford University Press: 2009), 70; and Christine Van Boheemen-Saaf, *Joyce, Derrida, Lacan, and the Trauma of History: Reading, Narrative, and Postcolonialism* (Cambridge: Cambridge University Press, 1999).

60. Dominic LaCapra, *Representing the Holocaust: History, Theory, Trauma* (Ithaca: Cornell University Press, 1994); LaCapra, *History and Memory after Auschwitz* (Ithaca: Cornell University Press, 1998); LaCapra, *Writing History, Writing Trauma* (Baltimore: Johns Hopkins University Press, 2001); Shoshana Felman and Dori Laub, *Testimony: Crises of Witnessing in Literature Psychoanalysis and History* (New York: Routledge, 1992); Saul Friedländer, "Trauma, Transference and 'Working through' in Writing the History of the 'Shoah,'" *History & Memory* 4 (1992): 39–59; and Friedländer, "Trauma, Memory and Transference," in *Holocaust Remembrance: The Shapes of Memory*, ed. Geoffrey Hartman (Cambridge: Blackwell, 1995), 252–63. A useful overview of "the real" in Lacan and Derrida is in Michael Lewis, *Derrida and Lacan: Another Writing* (Edinburgh: Edinburgh University Press, 2014), 148–201.

61. LaCapra, *Writing History, Writing Trauma*, 38n6.

62. LaCapra articulated such a notion, asserting that "desirable empathy involves not full iden-tification but what might be termed empathic unsettlement in the face of traumatic limit events, their perpetrators, and their victims" (*Writing History, Writing Trauma*, 102). See also his *History in Transit: Experience, Identity, and Critical Theory* (Ithaca: Cornell University Press, 2004); and Car-olyn J. Dean, *The Fragility of Empathy after the Holocaust* (Ithaca: Cornell University Press, 2004).

63. Marc-Antoine Crocq and Louis Crocq, "From Shell Shock and War Neurosis to Posttrau-matic Stress Disorder: A History of Psychotraumatology," *Dialogues in Clinical Neuroscience* 2 (2000): 47–55; Edgar Jones and Simon Wessely, "A Paradigm Shift in the Conceptualization of Psychological Trauma in the 20th Century," *Journal of Anxiety Disorders* 21 (2007): 164–75. Also relevant to this project of writing trauma is Joshua Pederson, "Speak, Trauma: Toward a Revised Understanding of Literary Trauma Theory," *Narrative* 22 (2014): 333–53.

64. Kenneth Fuchsman, "Traumatized Soldiers," *Journal of Psychohistory* 36 (2008): 72–84; James S. Olson, and Randy Roberts, *My Lai: A Brief History with Documents* (Boston: Bedford/St. Martin's, 1998); and Kimberly A. Lee, George E. Vaillant, William C. Torrey, and Glen H. El-der Jr., "A 50-Year Prospective Study of the Psychological Sequelae of World War II Combat," *American Journal of Psychiatry* 152 (1995): 516–22.

65. Judith Herman, *Trauma and Recovery* (New York: Basic Books, 1992).

66. Robert Doran, *The Ethics of Theory: Philosophy, History, Literature* (London: Blooms-bury, 2017).

67. Ella Myers, "Introduction: Tracing the Ethical Turn," in *Worldly Ethics: Democratic Politics and Care for the World* (Durham: Duke University Press, 2013), 1–19.

68. Beschara Karam, "The Representation of Perpetrator Trauma in *Forgiveness*," *Communicatio* 45 (2019): 72.

69. Gayatri Spivak, "Can the Subaltern Speak?," in *Marxism and the Interpretation of Culture*, ed. Lawrence Grossberg and Cary Nelson (Urbana: University of Illinois Press, 1988), 271–313. Gayatri previously had translated Derrida's *On Grammatology* and was an important proponent of deconstructive critical theory.

70. The McMartin Preschool trial of 1987 is an example.

71. Elizabeth Loftus and Katherine Ketcham, *The Myth of Repressed Memory* (New York: St. Martin's Press, 1994).

72. Richard McNally's research has been at the forefront of studies that have questioned the reliability of theories of repressed memory, but his work also allows for leeway in understanding why some people have trouble remembering trauma. See McNally, *Remembering Trauma* (Cambridge, MA: Harvard University Press, 2005); and McNally, "Searching for Repressed Memory," in *True and False Recovered Memories*, ed. Robert F. Belli, Nebraska Symposium on Motivation 58 (New York: Springer, 2012), 112–47.

73. Rachel Yehuda and Joseph Ledoux, "A Response Variation Following Trauma: A Translational Neuroscience Approach to Understanding PTSD," *Neuron* 56 (2007): 19–32. Studies estimate that as many as 90 percent of people suffer trauma but only 7.8–8.7 percent develop PTSD. See S. Malan-Miller, S. Seedat, and S. M. J. Hemmings, "Understanding Posttraumatic Stress Disorder: Insights from the Methylome," *Genes, Brain, and Behavior* 13 (2014): 52–68; S. Galea, A. Nandi, and D. Vlahov, "The Epidemiology of Post-Traumatic Stress Disorders after Disasters," *Epidemiologic Reviews* 27 (2005): 78–91; and Amarendra M. Singh, "Contribution of Epigenesis towards the Etiology, Prevention, and Treatment of Post-Traumatic Stress Disorder," *International Medical Journal* 27 (2020): 646–50.

74. Alan Gibbs, *The Trauma Paradigm and Its Discontents* (Edinburgh: Edinburgh University Press, 2014), 5.

75. Bessel A. van der Kolk, "The Body Keeps the Score: Memory and the Evolving Psychobiology of Posttraumatic Stress," *Harvard Review of Psychiatry* 1 (1994): 253–65: and van der Kolk, *Psychological Trauma* (Washington, DC: American Psychiatric Press, 1987).

76. Barry Gordon, "The Myth of Repressed Memory: False Memories and Allegations of Sexual Abuse," *New England Journal of Medicine* 333 (1995): 134.

77. Cathy Caruth, *Unclaimed Experience: Trauma, Narrative, and History* (Baltimore: Johns Hopkins University Press, 1996), 181.

78. Ibid., 72. See also Caruth, *Trauma: Explorations in Memory* (Baltimore: Johns Hopkins University Press, 1995).

79. Caruth, *Unclaimed Experience*, 3–4.

80. Ibid., 11.

81. Jean Laplanche and Jean-Bertrand Pontalis, *The Language of Psycho-Analysis* (London: Hogarth Press, 1973), 465.

82. Ruth Leys, in Ruth Leys and Marlene Goldman, "Navigating the Genealogies of Trauma, Guilt, and Affect: An Interview with Ruth Leys," *University of Toronto Quarterly* 79 (2010): 666,

667, 668. Leys's comments follow on her *Trauma: A Genealogy* (Chicago: University of Chicago Press, 2000), a polemical guide to the trauma theory debate, and anticipate her criticism of affect theory—which similarly is germane to my discussions in this book (Leys, *The Ascent of Affect: Genealogy and Critique* [Chicago: University of Chicago Press, 2017]). In the interview quoted here, Leys speaks to clarify her thinking about trauma theory with regard to several points that were underdeveloped in *Trauma: A Genealogy*.

83. An early effort in this regard, among others, is the mention by Kaplan, *Trauma Culture*, 37–38.

84. I have in mind here the theoretical forays of Brian Massumi, Sara Ahmed, and a widening circle of other scholars who took affect as prelinguistic. Some of those scholars, however, also tried to assert that "circulation of affect" in populations was political. See Sara Ahmed, *The Cultural Politics of Emotion* (London: Routledge, 2004); and Brian Massumi, *Politics of Affect* (Cambridge: Polity, 2015). Criticism of affect theory is described in Leys, *The Ascent of Affect*.

85. Richard J. McNally, "Debunking Myths about Trauma and Memory," *Canadian Journal of Psychiatry* 50 (2005): 817.

86. Richard J. McNally, *Remembering Trauma* (Cambridge, MA: Harvard University Press, 2003), 2.

87. Richard J. McNally, Brett T. Litz, Adrienne Prassas, Lisa M. Shin, and Frank W. Weathers, "Emotional Priming of Autobiographical Memory in Post-Traumatic Stress Disorder," *Cognition and Emotion* 8 (1994): 351–67.

88. Roger Luckhurst, *The Trauma Question* (London: Routledge, 2008), 55–56.

89. Rick Crownshaw, "Review Essay of Roger Luckhurst, *The Trauma Question*," *Textual Practice* 23 (2009): 507.

90. Gibbs, *The Trauma Paradigm and Its Discontents*.

91. Jacques Lacan, *The Seminar Book I: Freud's Papers on Technique, 1953–54*, ed. Jacques-Alain Miller; trans. John Forrester (Cambridge: Cambridge University Press, 1988), 66.

92. Dino Felluga, *Critical Theory: The Key Concepts* (London: Routledge, 2015), 264.

93. Antonio Traverso and Mick Broderick, "Interrogating Trauma: Towards a Critical Trauma Studies," *Continuum: Journal of Media and Cultural Studies* 24 (2010): 9.

94. LaCapra, *Writing History, Writing Trauma*, 64, 77.

95. Roger Luckhurst, *The Trauma Question* (London: Routledge, 2008), 212.

96. LaCapra warns against muddling punctual ("historical" in his phrasing) trauma with structural trauma (*Writing History, Writing Trauma*, xxiv, 72–83).

97. Laura S. Brown, "Not Outside the Range: One Feminist Perspective on Psychic Trauma," *American Imago* 48 (1991): 122.

98. Herman, *Trauma and Recovery*, 3.

99. Stef Craps and Gert Buelens, "Introduction: Postcolonial Trauma Novels," *Studies in the Novel* 40 (2008): 3–4, 3.

100. Susannah Radstone, "Trauma Theory: Contexts, Politics, Ethics," *Paragraph* 30 (2007): 22.

101. Stef Craps, "Wor(l)ds of Grief: Traumatic Memory and Literary Witnessing in Cross-Cultural Perspective," *Textual Practice* 24 (2010): 56.

102. Kai Tal, *Worlds of Hurt: Reading the Literatures of Trauma* (Cambridge: Cambridge University Press, 1995), 53–54, 59.

103. Balaev, "Literary Trauma Theory Reconsidered," 7.

104. Michael Rothberg, *The Implicated Subject: Beyond Victims and Perpetrators* (Stanford: Stanford University Press, 2019); and Rothberg, *Multidirectional Memory: Remembering the Holocaust in the Age of Decolonization* (Stanford: Stanford University Press: 2009).

105. Vine Deloria Jr., "Indian Affairs: Hebrews 13:8," in *Eating Fire, Tasting Blood: An Anthology of the American Indian Holocaust*, ed. MariJo Moore (New York: Thunder's Mouth Press, 2006), 62.

106. Iva Vukušić, "Understanding Perpetrators and Perpetration of Mass Violence," *Journal of Perpetrator Research* 3 (2020): 1.

107. Margaret Urban Walker, "Restorative Justice and the Challenge of Perpetrator Accountability," in *Routledge International Handbook of Perpetrator Studies*, ed. Susanne Knittel and Zachary J. Goldberg (London: Routledge, 2019), 255. See also Kara Critchell, Susanne C. Knittel, Emiliano Perra, and Uğur Ümit Üngör, "Editor's Introduction," *Journal of Perpetrator Research* 1 (2017): 1–27.

108. Sebastian Köthe, Laura Kater, and Juliane Dryoff, "Models of Perpetration and Transgression: Borderline Cases in Violence and Trauma Research," *Journal of Perpetrator Studies* 2 (2018): 164.

109. LaCapra, *Representing the Holocaust*, 210–11.

110. LaCapra, *History in Transit*, 113.

111. LaCapra, *Writing History, Writing Trauma*.

112. Dominick LaCapra, "Trauma, History, Memory, Identity: What Remains?," *History and Theory* 55 (2016): 375.

113. Even while LaCapra appeared open to the possibility of perpetrator trauma, he wrote that historians nevertheless should practice "empathy with the victim and revulsion toward the perpetrator," arguing that "the distinction between victims, perpetrators, and bystanders is crucial" (LaCapra, *Writing History, Writing Trauma*, 133, 79). LaCapra voiced his concern that the material particularities and context of the precipitating historical event might be lost in a theory of trauma that was too expansive, confusing absence—the transhistorical, abstract, metaphysical, nonevent—with loss, so that "the significance or force of particular historical losses (for example, those of apartheid or the Shoah) may be obfuscated or rashly generalized. As a consequence, one encounters the dubious ideas that everyone (including perpetrators and collaborators) is a victim, that all history is trauma" (64). Alan Gibbs criticizes that thinking as ideological and steeped in Western bias (Gibbs, *Contemporary American Trauma Narratives* [Edinburgh: Edinburgh University Press, 2014], 205).

114. See his discussion in LaCapra, "Trauma, History, Memory, Identity," 378–79.

115. Gabrielle Schwab, *Haunting Legacies: Violent Histories and Transgenerational Trauma* (New York: Columbia University Press, 2010).

116. Radstone, "Trauma Theory," 26.

117. Saira Mohamed, "Of Monsters and Men: Perpetrator Trauma and Mass Atrocity," *Columbia Law Review* 115 (2015): 1157.

118. Sigmund Freud, *Moses and Monotheism* (London: Hogarth Press, 1939). Freud's first writings about trauma were about perpetrator trauma. Pertinent commentary is in Jan Assmann, *Religion and Cultural Memory: Ten Studies*, trans. Rodney Livingstone (Stanford: Stanford University Press, 2006), chap. 2, "Monotheism, Memory, and Trauma: Reflections on Freud's Book of Moses," 46–63.

119. Jan Assmann, *Religion and Cultural Memory*, 50.

120. Desmond Tutu, *Opening Address*, HRVC Hearing, East London, Monday, April 15, 1996, in Desmond Tutu, *No Future without Forgiveness* (New York: Doubleday, 1999), 114.

121. Erin McGlothlin, "Theorizing the Perpetrator in Bernard Schlink's *The Reader* and Martin Amis's *Time's Arrow*," in *After Representation?: The Holocaust, Literature, and Culture*, ed. R. Clifton Spargo and Robert Ehrenreich (New Brunswick: Rutgers University Press, 2009), 213.

122. Ibid.

123. Alexander Hinton, *Man or Monster?: The Trial of a Khmer Rouge Torturer* (Durham: Duke University Press, 2016).

124. Hinton, drawing on Hannah Arendt's discussion of "the banality of evil," observes that "there is a need to critically reflect about how we are framing, including framings suggesting interpretations of self and other. Given the Judeo-Christian and often naturalized uses of the word "evil," perhaps we should consider not just the "banality of evil" but also the way the acts we call "evil" are intimately bound up with the "banality of everyday thought," our everyday ways of framing and categorizing the world—and all that, in so doing, we erase" (ibid., 31).

125. Critchell et al., "Editor's Introduction," 8.

126. Timothy Williams, "The Complexity of Evil: A Multi-Faceted Approach to Genocide Perpetration," *Zeitschrift für Friedens- und Konfliktforschung* 3 (2014): 74.

127. Köthe, Kater, and Dryoff, "Models of Perpetration and Transgression," speak of perpetrators as "perfectly ordinary people" (159). For examples of this approach, see the contributions to *Perpetrators and Perpetration of Mass Violence*, edited by Timothy Williams and Susanne Buckley-Zistel (London: Routledge, 2018). Scott Strauss, a contributor, observes: "The authors in this volume lean towards viewing perpetrators as 'ordinary' people" ("Is a Comparative Theory of Perpetrators Possible?," 204).

128. Iva Vukušić, "Understanding Perpetrators," 3.

129. Richard Crownshaw, "Perpetrator Fictions and Transcultural Memory," *parallax* 17 (2011): 80.

130. Roy Baumeister, *Evil: Inside Human Cruelty and Violence* (New York: W. H. Freeman, 1996), 386.

131. Ibid.

132. Craps et al., "Decolonizing Trauma Studies," 916.

133. Gibbs, *Contemporary American Trauma Narratives*, 247.

134. Primo Levy, *The Drowned and the Saved* (New York: Simon and Schuster, 2017), 26. See also Rothberg, *The Implicated Subject*; and Jonathan Drucker, "Ethical Grey Zones: On Coercion and Complicity in the Concentration Camp and Beyond," in *A Companion to the Holocaust*, ed. Simone Gigliotti and Hilary Ear (Hoboken: John Wiley, 2020), 487–502.

135. Lane Benjamin and Melike M. Fourie, "The Intergenerational Effects of Mass Trauma in Sculpting New Perpetrators," in *The Routledge International Handbook of Perpetrator Studies*, ed. S. C. Knittel and Z. J. Goldberg (Abingdon, UK: Routledge, 2019), 276–86.

136. Marinella Rodi-Risberg, "Problems in Representing Trauma," in *Trauma and Literature*, ed. J. Roger Kurtz (New York: Cambridge University Press, 2018), 119.

137. Schwab, "Haunting Legacies," 181.

138. Bill Nichols, "Waltzing with Bashir: Perpetrator Trauma and Cinema," *Studies in Documentary Film* 8 (2014): 83.

139. Raya Morag, *Waltzing with Bashir: Perpetrator Trauma and Cinema* (London: Palgrave, 2012), 27–32.

140. Robert S. Laufer, "Symptom Patterns Associated with Posttraumatic Stress Disorder among Vietnam Veterans Exposed to War Trauma," *American Journal of Psychiatry* 142 (1985): 1304–11; Erwin Randolph Parson, "The Reparation of the Self: Clinical and Theoretical Dimensions

in the Treatment of Vietnam Combat Veterans," *Journal of Contemporary Psychotherapy* 14 (1984): 4–56; Charles R. Figley, ed., *Stress Disorders among Vietnam Veterans* (Milton Park, UK: Brunner-Routledge, 1978); and Jesse O. Cavenar and James L. Nash, "The Effects of Combat on the Normal Personality: War Neurosis in Vietnam Returnees," *Comprehensive Psychiatry* 17 (1976): 647–53.

141. Ceri Evans sketches the history of forensic patient studies of perpetrators of violence in "The Trauma of Being Violent," in *Forensic Psychology*, ed. Graham J. Towl and David A. Crighton (Oxford: British Psychological Society and Blackwell Publishing, 2010), 329–345.

142. Maria Papanastassiou and John Boyle, "Post-Traumatic Stress Disorder in Mentally Ill Perpetrators of Homicide," *Journal of Forensic Psychiatry and Psychology* 15 (2004): 66–75; and C. W. J. Raeside, "Post-Traumatic Stress Disorder in Perpetrators of Violent Crime," *Australian and New Zealand Journal of Psychiatry* 34 (2000): A54.

143. Man Cheung Chung, Xiachu Di, and King Hung Wan, "Past Trauma, Alexithymisa, and Posttraumatic Stress among Perpetrators of Violent Crime," *Traumatology* 22 (2016): 104–12.

144. Rachel MacNair, *Perpetration-Induced Traumatic Stress: The Psychological Consequences of Killing* (Westport: Praeger, 2002), 7, passim.

145. Ervin Staub, "Reconciliation after Genocide, Mass Killing, or Intractable Conflict: Understanding the Roots of Violence, Psychological Recovery, and Steps toward a General Theory," *Political Psychology* 27 (2006): 874.

146. Susanne Vees-Gulani, *Trauma and Guilt: Literature of Wartime Bombing in Germany* (Berlin: Walter de Gruyter, 2003); Jean C. Beckham, Michelle E. Feldman, and Angela C. Kirby, "Atrocities Exposure in Vietnam Combat Veterans with Chronic Posttraumatic Stress Disorder: Relationship to Combat Exposure, Symptom Severity, Guilt, and Interpersonal Violence," *Journal of Traumatic Stress* 11 (1998): 777–85; and Gibbs, *Contemporary American Trauma Narratives*, chap. 4, "Gulf War Memoirs and Perpetrator Trauma," 161–200, and his discussion of theories of guilt offered by various writers (64, 169,171, 196). A closely argued critical overview of the trauma of the perpetrator set in a discussion of media and the repressed guilt of Israeli soldiers is in Morag, *Waltzing with Bashir*.

147. Chung, Di, and Wong, "Past Trauma," 104.

148. Ben Shepard, in *A War of Nerves: Soldiers and Psychiatrists in the Twentieth Century* (Cambridge, MA: Harvard University Press, 2001), wrote: "After Vietnam, many American soldiers on returning home began to develop intense feelings of guilt about what they had done because it conflicted with the underlying Christian values of their society and because their society did not endorse what they had done" (371–72).

149. On flashbacks, see A. S. Blank Jr., "Unconscious Flashback to the War in Vietnam Veterans: Clinical Mystery, Community Problem, and Legal Defense," in *The Trauma of War: Stress and Recovery in Vietnam War Veterans*, ed. Stephen M. Sonnenberg, Arthur S. Blank, and John A. Talbot (Washington, DC: American Psychiatric Press, 1985), 293–308. On flashbacks as "unconscious constructions," but with research showing no clear connection between different kinds of flashbacks, see Fred H. Frankel, "The Concept of Flashbacks in Historical Perspective," *International Journal of Clinical and Experimental Hypnosis* 42 (1994): 321–36. On flashbacks and continuing violent behavior, see Landy F. Sparr, Michael E. Reaves, and Roland M. Atkinson, "Military Combat, Posttraumatic Stress Disorder, and Criminal Behavior in Vietnam Veterans," *Bulletin of the American Academy of Psychiatry Law* 15 (1987): 141–62.

150. Rothberg, *Multidirectional Memory*, 90. For Rothberg, the category of implicated subject that he proposes as a useful way of thinking about trauma and mass violence "is not meant to replace the category of the perpetrator but to supplement it" (Susanne C. Knittel and Sofía

Forchieri, "Navigating Implication: An Interview with Michael Rothberg," *Journal of Perpetrator Research* 3 [2020]: 8).

151. Roger Luckhurst, *The Trauma Question* (New York: Routledge, 2008), 14.

152. A list of some recent work, with relevant discussion, is in Crownshaw, "Perpetrator Fictions," 75–89.

153. Toni Morrison, *A Mercy* (New York: Knopf, 2008); and Edward Jones, *The Known World* (New York: Amistad, 2003). In Alexie Sherman's *Flight* (New York: Grove, 2007), the main character, Zits, a half-Indian, half-Irish adolescent perpetrator, moves in and out of white men's and Native American's bodies as he lives in a dream state after an act of mass murder in which he was shot. Morrison's discussion of her "altruistic" approach to perpetration of mass murder is in her "Goodness: Altruism and the Literary Imagination," in *Toni Morrison: Goodness and the Literary Imagination*, ed. David Carrasco, Stephanie Paulsell, and Mara Willard (Charlottesville: University of Virginia Press, 2019), 13–19.

154. Sindiwe Magona, "Author's Preface," *Mother to Mother* (Boston: Beacon Press, 1998), v.

155. Kenneth Alan Adams, "Psychohistory and Slavery: Preliminary Issues," *Journal of Psychohistory* 43 (2015): 110.

156. Crownshaw, "Perpetrator Fictions," 80.

Chapter Three

1. The origins of the dance, the message of Wovoka, and the spread of the dance to other Native American communities have been the subjects of much scholarly writing. The starting point is James Mooney, *The Ghost-Dance Religion and the Sioux Outbreak of 1890* (Washington, DC: Government Publishing Office, 1896). Also useful as introductions are Rani-Henrik Andersson, *The Lakota Ghost Dance of 1890* (Lincoln: University of Nebraska Press, 2009); Cora Du Bois, *The 1870 Ghost Dance* (Lincoln: University of Nebraska Press, 2007); and Gregory E. Smoak, *Ghost Dances and Identity: Prophetic Religion and American Indian Ethnogenesis in the Nineteenth Century* (Berkeley: University of California Press, 2006).

2. Abby A. Judson, *Why She Became a Spiritualist* (Boston: Colby and Rich, 1892), 52.

3. Benjamin G. Armstrong and Thomas P. Wentworth, *Early Life among the Indians* (Ashland, WI: A. W. Bowron, 1892), 106.

4. Frederick Morgan Davenport, *Primitive Traits in Religious Revivals* (New York: Macmillan, 1906), 34.

5. Simeon Henry West, *Life and Times of S. H. West* (Bloomington, IN: Pantagraph Printing and Stationery Co., 1908).

6. *New York World*, November 18, 1890, 1.

7. Quoted in Benjamin J. Kracht, "The Kiowa Ghost Dance, 1894–1916: An Unheralded Revitalization Movement," *Ethnohistory* 39 (1992): 464. He cites B. F. Gassaway, "Letter to Kiowa Superintendent Ernest Stecker, 6 June," National Archives Record Service, Washington, DC.

8. Marion P. Maus, "The New Indian Messiah," *Harper's Weekly* 34 (1890): 944.

9. Carlyle Boynton Haynes, *Spiritualism versus Christianity* (Nashville: Southern Publishing Association, 1918), 70.

10. Jeffrey Ostler, *The Plains Sioux and U.S. Colonialism from Lewis and Clark to Wounded Knee* (Cambridge: Cambridge University Press, 2004), 350.

11. Tiffany Hale (Afro-Cherokee), "Hostiles and Friendlies: Memory, U.S. Institutions, and the 1890 Ghost Dance" (PhD dissertation, Yale University, 2017), 25.

12. Important recent analyses include Louis S. Warren, *God's Red Son: The Ghost Dance Religion and the Making of Modern America* (New York: Viking, 2017), which discusses Indian adaptation to wage work; and Heather Cox Richardson, *Wounded Knee: Party Politics and the Road to an American Massacre* (Basic Books, 2010), which parses the national politics leading up to the massacre. For a broader view of the personalities involved, see Nathaniel Philbrick, *The Last Stand: Custer, Sitting Bull, and the Battle of the Little Big Horn* (New York: Viking, 2010). Jeffrey Ostler argued that the army essentially acted according to its own interests as a state bureaucracy ("Conquest and the State: Why the United States Employed Massive Military Force to Suppress the Lakota Ghost Dance," *Pacific Historical Review* 65 [1996]: 217–48).

13. William P. Blankenburg, "The Role of the Press in an Indian Massacre," *Journalism Quarterly* 45 (1968): 61–70.

14. Hugh J. Reilly, *The Frontier Newspapers and the Coverage of the Plains Indian Wars* (Santa Barbara: Praeger, 2010), 134.

15. *New York Times*, January 19, 1867, 1.

16. Treuer uses this term to describe the psychological frame of the soldiers under Chivington at Sand Creek (David Treuer [Ojibwe], *The Heartbeat of Wounded Knee: Native America from 1890 to the Present* [New York: Corsair, 2019], 93).

17. Linda Charlton, "Army Denies Wounded Knee Massacre," *New York Times*, December 30, 1975, https://www.nytimes.com/1975/12/30/archives/army-denies-a-wounded-knee-massacre.html.

18. Hale, *Hostiles and Friendlies*, 98.

19. "Congressional Testimony of John S. Smith, March 14, 1865," in "Four Documents on the Sand Creek Massacre," *Digital History*, accessed June 23, 2021, https://www.digitalhistory.uh.edu/disp_textbook.cfm?smtID=3&psid=1150.

20. *Black Elk Speaks: Being the Life Story of a Holy Man of the Oglala Sioux*, as told to John G. Neihardt (New York: William Morrow, 1932), 270.

21. Lydia Maria Child, "The Indians," *National Standard*, May 1, 1870.

22. S. F. Tappan, "Our Indian Relations," *National Standard*, June 1, 1870.

23. *Omaha World-Herald*, December 30, 1890, 1.

24. Elaine Goodale Eastman, *Sister to the Sioux: The Memoirs of Elaine Goodale Eastman 1885–1891*, ed. Kay Graber (Lincoln: University of Nebraska Press, 1978), 162.

25. The book was published at a moment when interest in Native American history was surging, both in popular forms (Hollywood movies) and academic research (dissertations). See Donald L. Parman and Catherine Price "'A Work in Progress': The Emergence of Indian History as a Professional Field," *Western Historical Quarterly* 20 (1989): 185–96.

26. Daisy Alioto, "10 Books for a Good Cry," *Christian Science Monitor*, January 9, 2012, https://www.csmonitor.com/Books/2012/0109/10-books-for-a-good-cry/Bury-My-Heart-at-Wounded-Knee-An-Indian-History-of-the-American-West-by-Dee-Brown.

27. Thomas Jefferson, *Notes on the State of Virginia* (Philadelphia: Prichard and Hall, 1788), 173.

28. David L. Sills, ed., *International Encyclopaedia of the Social Sciences* (New York: Macmillan, 1968).

29. Walter Laqueur, *No End to War: Terrorism in the Twenty-First Century* (New York: Continuum, 2003), 7; and Laqueur, *The New Terrorism: Fanaticism and the Arms of Mass Destruction* (New York: Oxford University Press, 2000).

30. Early exceptions include Albert Parry, *Terrorism: From Robespierre to Arafat* (New York: Vanguard, 1976); Martha Crenshaw Hutchinson, *Revolutionary Terrorism: The FLN in Algeria*

1954-1962 (Stanford: Stanford University Press, 1978); Martha Crenshaw and John Pimlott, *En-cyclopedia of World Terrorism* (Armonk, NY: Sharpe, 1997); and John Bowyer Bell, *The Irish Troubles, A Generation of Violence 1967-1992* (Dublin: Gill and MacMillan, 1993). Examples of the subsequent gradual turn to historical interpretation include Walter Laqueur, *A History of Terrorism* (New Brunswick: Transaction Books, 2001); Michael Burleigh, *A Cultural History of Terrorism* (London: HarperPress, 2010); and Jussi M. Hanhimäki and Bernhard Blumenau, eds., *An International History of Terrorism: Western and Non-Western Experiences* (New York: Routledge, 2013).

31. "For most commentators terrorism has no history, or at least they would have us believe that the 'terrorist problem' had no significance until the 1960s, when the full impact of modern technology was felt, endowing most individuals as individuals or as members of small groups, with capacities they never had before" (David C. Rapoport, "Introduction," in David C. Rapoport and Yonah Alexander, eds., *The Morality of Terrorism: Religious and Secular Justifications* [New York: Columbia University Press, 1989], xii).

32. Isabelle Duyvesteyn, "How New Is the New Terrorism?," *Studies in Conflict and Terrorism*, 27 (2004): 443. Calling for more robust historical study of terrorism, Duyvesteyn noted some exceptions to the neglect of that history but pointed out the meagerness of historical engagement overall.

33. Audrey Kurth Cronin, "Behind the Curve: Globalization and International Terrorism," *International Security* 27 (2002–3): 33. "Religious terrorism is not new; rather it is a continuation of an ongoing modern power struggle between those with power and those without it" (38).

34. Rochdi Mohan Nazala, "New Terrorism: What Can the History of Terrorism Contribute?," *Jurnal Hubungan Internasional* 8 (2019): 112–20.

35. David C. Rapoport, "Terrorism in Three Religious Traditions," *American Political Science Review* 78 (1984): 659.

36. Bruce Hoffman, *Inside Terrorism* (London: Victor Gollancz, 1998), 87, 112.

37. Additionally, because religion was constructed in Western scholarship with an emphasis on the centrality of "internal states," the category of religion itself provided cover for freewheeling forays into analyses of fear, hatred, and anger in religious groups associated with violence.

38. Ersun N. Kurtulus, "The 'New Terrorism' and Its Critics," *Studies in Conflict and Terrorism* 34 (2011): 478.

39. Those volumes, edited by Martin E. Marty and R. Scott Appleby in collaboration with other scholars and published by the University of Chicago Press, are *Fundamentalisms Observed* (1991), *Fundamentalisms and Society: Reclaiming the Sciences, the Family, and Education* (1993), *Fundamentalisms and the State: Remaking Polities, Economies, and Militance* (1994), *Accounting for Fundamentalisms: The Dynamic Character of Movements* (1994), and *Fundamentalisms Comprehended* (1995).

40. William Shepard, "'Fundamentalism' Christian and Islamic," *Religion* 17 (1987): 362.

41. Gabriel A. Almond, Emmanuel Sivan, and R. Scott Appleby, "Fundamentalism: Genus and Species," in Martin and Appleby, *Fundamentalisms Comprehended*, 412, 408.

42. Jakobus Martinus Vorster, "Analytical Perspectives on Religious Fundamentalism," *Journal for the Study of Religions and Ideologies* 6 (2007): 185.

43. Michael O. Emerson and David Hartman, "The Rise of Religious Fundamentalism," *Annual Review of Sociology* 32 (2006): 134.

44. Emery J. Hyslop-Margisaon and Ayaz Naseem, *Scientism and Education: Empirical Research as a Neo-Liberal Ideology* (New York: Springer, 2007), ix.

45. Raoul Adam, "An Epistemic Theory of Religious Fundamentalism," *International Journal of Religion and Spirituality in Society* 1 (2011): 81. Adam notes that relational ways of knowing can include relativism to a certain extent and can be cyclical, with binaries collapsing at times.

46. Sara Savage, "Four Lessons from the Study of Fundamentalism and Psychology of Religion," *Journal of Strategic Security* 4 (2011): 131, 135, 137, 139, 140, 145.

47. Mark Juergensmeyer, "The Worldwide Rise of Religious Nationalism," *Journal of International Affairs* 50 (1996): 15; and Juergensmeyer, "The Logic of Religious Violence: The Case of the Punjab," *Contributions to Indian Sociology* 22 (1988): 65–88. These themes are detailed in Juergensmeyer, *Terror in the Mind of God: The Global Rise of Religious Violence* (Berkeley: University of California Press, 2003).

48. Alex P. Schmid, "Frameworks for Conceptualising Terrorism," *Terrorism and Political Violence* 16 (2004): 211, 212.

49. Juergensmeyer, "The Worldwide Rise of Religious Nationalism," 5. The most recent edition of Juergensmeyer's *Terror in the Mind of God: The Global Rise of Religious Violence* (Berkeley: University of California Press, 2017), like previous editions, stated that "religion has supplied not only the ideology but also the social identity and organizational structure for the perpetrators" (4).

50. Magnus Ranstorp, "Terrorism in the Name of Religion," *Journal of International Affairs* 50 (1996): 51, 47. Crucially, this begs the question of why they felt their identity was threatened.

51. Jacobus Martinus Vorster, "Analytical Perspectives on Religious Fundamentalism," *Journal for the Study of Religions and Ideologies* 17 (2007): 17.

52. Andreas Hasenclever and Volker Rittberger, "Does Religion Make a Difference?: Theoretical Approaches to the Impact of Faith on Political Conflict," *Journal of International Studies* 29 (2000): 647, 658, 661.

53. Lorne L. Dawson, "Debating the Role of Religion in the Motivation of Religious Terrorism," *Nordic Journal of Religion and Society* 31 (2018): 98–117. Dawson juxtaposes his approach to those of Marc Sageman (*Misunderstanding Terrorism* [Philadelphia: University of Pennsylvania Press, 2017]) and Clark McCauley and Sophia Moskalenko ("Mechanisms of Political Radicalization: Pathways towards Terrorism," *Terrorism and Political Violence* 20 [2008], 415–33). An example of research on terrorism that deemphasizes ideology that sharply distinguishes one group from another is Mahmood Mamdani, *When Victims Become Killers: Colonialism, Nativism, and the Genocide in Rwanda* (Princeton: Princeton University Press, 2001).

54. David Matsumoto, Hyi Sung Wang, and Mark G. Frank, "The Role of Emotion in Predicting Violence," *FBI Law Enforcement Bulletin* 81 (2012): 1–11. This article takes a flawed approach in that it assumes that certain emotions, such as hate, anger, and disgust, exist as essences that surface whole in experience from exposure to stimuli and can be read in facial expressions of individuals and in other ways. Other studies, many of which are based on research by Matsumoto and Frank (funded by the Department of Defense and other government departments), are similarly flawed, and typically also frame the problem as the emotional response to discourse. See Jacquelien Stekelenburg, "Radicalization and Violent Emotions," *PS: Political Science and Politics* 50 (2017): 936–39; Mark G. Frank, David Matsumoto, and H. C. Hwang, "Intergroup Emotions and Political Violence: The ANCODI Hypothesis," in *Social Psychology and Politics*, ed. Joseph P. Forgas, Klaus Fiedler, and William D. Crano (London: Routledge, 2015), 173–90; and David Matsumoto, H. C. Hwang, and Mark G. Frank, "Emotions Expressed by Leaders in Videos Predict Political Aggression," *Behavioral Sciences of Terrorism and Political Aggression*, 6 (2014): 212–18.

55. For an overview see David Lemmings and Ann Brooks, "The Emotional Turn in the Humanities and Social Sciences," in *Emotions and Social Change: Historical and Sociological Perspectives*, ed. David Lemmings and Ann Brooks (New York: Routledge, 2014), 3–18.

56. I discuss later how neuroscience should play a role in such interdisciplinary research. Among others who affirm interdisciplinarity, the historian of emotions Rob Boddice urges that such research engage scientific studies about brain and body (Rob Boddice, "History Looks Forward: Interdisciplinarity and Critical Emotion Research," *Emotion Review* 12 [2020], 131–34; and Rob Boddice and Mark Smith, *Emotion, Sense, Experience* [Cambridge: Cambridge University Press, 2020]).

57. For a discussion of various kinds of histories of emotions, see Jan Plamper, *The History of Emotions: An Introduction* (Oxford: Oxford University Press, 2017). My own forays in this area, which indicate something of the social constructionist aspects of my approach as well as my attention to the complexities and paradoxes of emotional self/collective emotional self, include Corrigan, *Business of the Heart: Religion and Emotion in the Nineteenth Century* (Berkeley: University of California Press, 2001); Corrigan, *Emptiness: Feeling Christian in America* (Chicago: University of Chicago Press, 2015); and Corrigan, *Religious Intolerance, America and the World: A History of Forgetting and Remembering* (Chicago: University of Chicago Press, 2020).

58. Stephanie Cacioppo and John T. Cacioppo, *Introduction to Social Neuroscience* (Princeton: Princeton University Press, 2020), 14.

59. Ibid.

60. Vesa Talvitie and Juhani Ihanus propose an "interfield conception" involving "the interaction between the spheres of the brain, the mental unconscious, and the phenomenal states" ("On Neuropsychoanalytic Metaphysics," *International Journal of Psychoanalysis* 92 [2011]: 1586, 1590).

61. Society for Social Science, "Mission Statement," accessed July 5, 2021, https://www.s4sn.org/mission.

62. Bruce S. McEwen and Huda Akil, "Introduction to Social Neuroscience: Gene, Environment, Brain, Body," *Annals of the New York Academy of Sciences* 1231 (2011): vii.

63. Stephanie Cacioppo and John T. Cacioppo, "Social Neuroscience," *Perspectives on Psychological Science* 8 (2013): 668.

64. Jean Decety, Robert Pape, and Clifford I. Workman, "A Multilevel Social Neuroscience Perspective on Radicalization and Terrorism," *Social Neuroscience* 13 (2018): 511, 512, 524.

65. William James, "What Is an Emotion?," *Mind* 9 (1884): 193, 190, 194.

66. Martha Nussbaum, *Upheavals of Thought: The Intelligence of Emotion* (New York: Cambridge University Press, 2003), 3.

67. Vahid Nejati, Reyhaneh Majdi, Mohammad Ali Salehinejad, and Michael A. Nitsche, "The Role of Dorsolateral and Ventromedial Prefrontal Cortex in the Processing of Emotional Dimensions," *Scientific Reports* 11, no. 1971 (2021), n.p., https://www.nature.com/articles/s41598-021-81454-7.pdf.

68. Areas of the prefrontal cortex are involved in regulating the valences of emotional experience and also in limiting or extinguishing arousal arising from emotional stimuli (ibid.).

69. Joseph LeDoux, "The Emotional Brain, Fear, and the Amygdala," *Cellular and Molecular Neurobiology* 23 (2003): 733.

70. Jacek Debiec and Joseph LeDoux, "The Amygdala and the Neural Pathways of Fear," in *Post-Traumatic Stress Disorder: Basic Science and Clinical Practice*, ed. Priyattam J. Shiromani, Terence M. Keane, and Joseph E. LeDoux (New York: Humana Press, 2009), 23–38.

71. This research might be summarized as investigation of how "cognitive functions such as memory could interact with processing even in the sensory cortex" (Lars Muckli and Lucy S. Petro, "The Significance of Memory in Sensory Cortex," *Trends in Neuroscience* 40 [2017]: 255). One leading example is research from the lab of Wen Li, which offers substantial evidence for the role of the sensory cortex in the processing of fear and memory of it, and in so doing challenges what Li calls the "canonical" view, that the amygdala-prefrontal circuit fully accounts for fear processing. There is evidence that "long-term retention of conditioning in the basic sensory cortices supports the conserved role of the human sensory cortex in the long-term storage of aversive conditioning" (Yuqi You, Joshua Brown, and Wen Li, "Human Sensory Cortex Contributes to the Long-Term Storage of Aversive Conditioning," *Journal of Neuroscience* 41 [2021]: 3222). See also Yuqi You, Lucas R. Novak, Kevin J. Clancy, and Wen Li, "Pattern Differentiation and Tuning Shift in Human Sensory Cortex Underlie Long-Term Threat Memory," *Current Biology* 32, no. 9 (2022), 2063–75, https://doi.org/10.1016/j.cub.2022.02.076.

72. Joseph LeDoux, "Fear: The Awareness That You Are In Harm's Way," Supplementary Note 1, in "Viewpoints: Approaches to Defining and Investigating Fear," *Nature Neuroscience* 22 (2019): 1205–16. The supplementary notes are published separately online with no pagination, https://authors.library.caltech.edu/97316/2/41593_2019_456_MOESM1_ESM.pdf.

73. LeDoux writes: "Activation of subcortical circuits controlling behavioral and physiological responses that occur at the same time can intensify the experience by providing inputs to the cognitive circuits, but they do not determine the content of the experience. . . . The experience itself, in my model, is the result of pattern completion of one's personal fear schema, which gives rise to some variant of what you have come to know as one of the many varieties subsumed under the concept of 'fear' that you have built up by accumulating experiences over the course of your life" (ibid., 1206).

74. Kristen A. Lindquist and Lisa Feldman Barrett, "Constructing Emotion: The Experience of Fear as a Conceptual Act," *Psychological Science* 19 (2008): 899.

75. Ibid., 902.

76. Lisa Feldman Barrett, "Feeling Is Perceiving: Core Affect and Conceptualization in the Experience of Emotion," in *Emotion and Consciousness*, ed. Lisa Feldman Barrett, P. M. Niedenthal, and P. Winkelman (New York: Guilford Press, 2005): 255–84; James A. Russell and Lisa Feldman Barrett, "Core Affect," in *The Oxford Companion to Emotion and the Affective Sciences*, ed. David Sander and Klaus R. Scherer (Oxford: Oxford University Press, 2009); and James A. Russell, "Core Affect and the Psychological Construction of Emotion," *Psychological Review* 110 (2003): 145–72.

77. Lisa Feldman Barrett and Kristen A. Lindquist, "Constructing Emotion: The Experience of Fear as a Conceptual Act," *Psychological Science* 19 (2008): 898–903. Emphasis mine. The theory of "core affect" and how it is involved in the production of the emotion of fear is generally compatible with my own understanding of the feeling of forgetting and the anxiety that comes with repressed collective trauma. Instead of "core affect" it will be more precise later to speak about anxiety, which can take various forms. Anxiety is a specific "core feeling," like "tension" for Barrett and for James A. Russell ("Core Affect, Prototypical Emotional Episodes, and Other Things Called Emotion: Dissecting the Elephant," *Journal of Personality and Social Psychology* 76 [1999]: 805–19).

78. Lisa Feldman Barrett, "Emotions Are Real," *Emotion* 12 (2012): 413.

79. Lisa Feldman Barrett *How Emotions Are Made: The Secret Life of the Brain* (Boston: Houghton Mifflin Harcourt, 2017): 137.

80. Leys discusses this issue with respect to the "affective turn" in Ruth Leys and Marlene Goldman, "Navigating the Genealogies of Trauma, Guilt, and Affect: An Interview with Ruth Leys," *University of Toronto Quarterly* 79 (2010): 666, 667, 668, and, with particular relevance, on 666–71.

81. Michael Boiger and Bajta Mesquita, "The Construction of Emotion in Interactions, Relationships, and Culture," *Emotion Review* 4 (2012): 221.

82. Ibid., 226. There is a rich literature on the variety of ways in which an emotion is constructed, or not constructed, in different social contexts.

83. Monique Scheer, "Are Emotions a Kind of Practice (and Is That What Makes Them Have a History)? A Bourdieuian Approach to Understanding Emotion," *History and Theory* 51 (2012): 200.

84. Ibid.

85. Pierre Bourdieu, *The Logic of Practice* (Stanford: Stanford University Press, 1990), 56.

86. Rainer Muhlhoff, "Affective Resonance," in Jan Schlaby and Christian von Scheve, *Affective Societies* (New York: Routledge, 2019), 189–200; and Daniel Stern, *The Interpersonal World of the Infant: A View from Psychoanalysis and Developmental Psychology* (New York: Basic Books, 1985; repr., 2019).

87. Tim Groves, "Rapport *sans* Rapport: The Affective Bond in Suggestion and Transference," *Subjectivity* 12 (2019): 247.

88. Felicity Callard and Constantina Papoulias, "Affect and Embodiment," in *Memory: Histories, Theories, Debates*, ed. Susannah Radstone and Bill Schwarz (New York: Fordham University Press, 2010), 258.

89. Margaret Wetherell, "Circulating Affect: Waves of Feeling, Contagion, and Affective Transmission," in *Affect and Emotion: A New Social Science Understanding* (London: Sage, 2012), 140–60.

90. Aletta Diefenback, Antje Kahl, Dina Wahba, et al., *The Politics of Affective Societies: An Interdisciplinary Essay* (Bielefeld: transcript Verlag—Bielefeld University Press, 2020), https://library.oapen.org/handle/20.500.12657/24344. The authors write, "If indeed there is a change in the ways politics and the political are presently taking shape—and we tend to agree that there is—this change is best understood qualitatively in terms of changing affective relations, rather than as a simple quantitative rise" (12).

91. Gavin Brent Sullivan, "Collective Emotions," *Social and Personality Psychology Compass* 9, no. 8 (2015): 383–93, 384.

92. Joseph de Rivera, "Emotional Climate: Social Structure and Emotional Dynamics," in *International Review of Studies on Emotion*, vol. 2, ed. K. T. Strongman (New York: John Wiley & Sons, 1992), 197–218; and Joseph De Rivera, Rahael Kurrien, and Nina Olsen, "The Emotional Climate of Nations and Their Culture of Peace," *Social Issues* 63 (2007): 255–71.

93. Véronique Christophe and Bernard Rimé, "Exposure to the Social Sharing of Emotion," *European Journal of Social Psychology* 27 (1997): 37.

94. Barbara H. Rosenwein, *Emotional Communities in the Middle Ages* (Ithaca: Cornell University Press, 2006).

95. A starting point for understanding collective emotion across such disciplines is *Collective Emotions: Perspectives from Psychology, Philosophy, and Sociology*, ed. Christian von Scheve and Mikko Salmela (Oxford: Oxford University Press, 2014). Discussion of relevant aspects of the psychology and sociology of social identity and emotion is in Jochen I. Menges and Martin Kilduff, "Group Emotions: Cutting the Gordian Knots Concerning Terms, Levels of Analysis,

and Processes," *Academy of Management Annals* 9 (2015): 845–928; Amit Goldenberg, Eran Halperin, Martijn van Zomeren, and J. J. Gross, "The Process Model of Group-Based Emotion: Integrating Intergroup Emotion and Emotion Regulation Perspectives," *Personality and Social Psychology Review* 20 (2016): 118–41; Brian Parkinson, Agneta Fischer, and Antony S. R. Manstead, *Emotion in Social Relations: Cultural, Group, and Interpersonal Processes* (New York: Psychology Press, 2005); Eliot R. Smith and Diane M. Mackie, "Group-level Emotions," *Current Opinion in Psychology* 11 (2016): 15–19; Ian Burkitt, *Emotions and Social Relations* (London: Sage, 2014); and Arlie Russell Hochschild, *The Managed Heart: Commercialization of Human Feeling* (Berkeley: University of California Press, 1983). Overviews of the history of emotions that attend to various issues in the academic discussion of collective emotion include Barbara Rosenwein, "Problems and Methods in the History of Emotion," *Passions in Context* 1 (2010): 1–32; Rosenwein and Riccardo Cristiani, *What Is the History of Emotions?* (Cambridge: Polity, 2018); William M. Reddy, "Historical Research on the Self and Emotions," *Emotion Review* 1 (2009): 302–15; Reddy, *The Navigation of Feeling: A Framework for the History of Emotions* (New York: Cambridge University Press, 2001); Peter N. Stearns, *Shame: A Brief History* (Urbana: University of Illinois Press, 2017); Stearns, "Histories of Emotions: Issues of Change and Impact," in *Handbook of Emotions*, 3rd ed., ed. Michael Lewis, Jeannette M. Haviland-Jones, and Lisa Feldman Barrett (New York: Guilford Press, 2008), 17–31; Susan J. Matt and Peter N. Stearns, eds., *Doing Emotions History* (Urbana: University of Illinois Press, 2014); Jan Plamper, *The History of Emotions: An Introduction* (Oxford: Oxford University Press, 2017); and Laura Kounine, "Emotions, Mind, and Body on Trial: A Cross-Cultural Perspective," *Journal of Social History* 51 (2017): 219–30.

96. Christian von Scheve and Sven Ismer, "Towards a Collective Theory of Emotions," *Emotion Review* 5 (2013): 406.

97. Daniel Bar-Tal, "Why Does Fear Override Hope in Societies Engulfed by Intractable Conflict, as It Does in Israeli Society?," *Political Psychology* 22 (2001): 606.

98. Myriam Jimeno, Daniel Varela, and Angela Castillo, "Violence, Emotional Communities, and Political Action in Colombia," in *Resisting Violence: Emotional Communities in Latin America*, ed. Morna Macleod and Natalia De Marinis (New York: Palgrave Macmillan, 2018), 23.

99. Von Scheve and Ismer, "Towards a Collective Theory of Emotions," 408, 409–10, 411.

100. Bar-Tal, "Why Does Fear Override Hope in Societies Engulfed by Intractable Conflict," 607.

101. Maurice Halbwachs, *On Collective Memory*, ed. and trans. Lewis A. Coser (Chicago: University of Chicago Press, 1992), 38. For a relevant interpretation of Halbwachs's thinking about collective memory, see Jan Assmann, *Das kulturelle Gedächtnis Schrift, Erinnerung und Politische Identität in Frühen Hochkulturen* (Munich: Verlag C. H. Beck, 1992).

102. Todd H. Hall and Andrew A. G. Ross, "Rethinking Affective Experience and Popular Emotion: World War I and the Construction of Group Emotion in International Relations," *Political Psychology* 40 (2019): 1359.

103. J. Turner, M. Hogg, P. Oakes, S. Reicher, and M. Wetherell, *Rediscovering the Social Group: A Self-categorization Theory* (Oxford: Blackwell, 1987); and Brett E. Sasley, "Theorizing States' Emotions," *International Studies Review* 13 (2011): 454.

104. Henri Tajfel, *Human Groups and Social Categories: Studies in Social Psychology* (Cambridge: Cambridge University Press, 1981): 255.

105. Jonathan Mercer, "Feeling Like a State: Social Emotion and Identity," *International Theory* 6 (2014): 515–35.

106. Ibid., 517.

107. Ibid., 520.

108. Hochschild, *The Managed Heart*.

109. Von Scheve and Ismer, "Towards a Collective Theory of Emotions," 408–9.

110. Simon Koschut, "The Structure of Feeling: Emotional Culture and National Self-Sacrifice in World Politics," *Millennium: Journal of International Studies* 45 (2017): 175.

111. Burkitt rejects as not useful for his analyses distinctions between affect, feeling, and emotions, arguing that all three are braided together. The distinction also is rejected by Mercer ("Feeling Like a State," 516), and critically questioned by Ruth Leys at the categorical level (*The Ascent of Affect: Genealogy and Critique* [Chicago: University of Chicago Press, 2017]).

112. Ian Burkitt, *Emotions and Social Relations* (London: Sage, 2014), 94, 6. "Feelings and emotions only arise in patterns of relationship, which include the way we look at and perceive the world, and these also result in patterns of activity that can become dispositions—ways of acting in particular situations that are not wholly within our conscious control and are, thus, partly involuntary" (6); Piotr Winkielman, "Bob Zajonc and Unconscious Emotion," *Emotion Review* 2 (2010): 353–62.

113. Ben Wang, *Illuminations from the Past: Trauma, Memory, and History in Modern China* (Stanford: Stanford University Press, 2004), 114. A more forceful view is that trauma is actually "incurable" (Manfred Weinberg, "Trauma—Geschichte, Gespenst, Literatur—und Gedächtnis," in *Trauma: Zwischen Psychoanalyse und kulturellem Deutungsmuster*, ed. Elizabeth Bronfen, Birgit Erdle, and Sigrid Weidel [Cologne: Böhlau, 1999], 173–206).

114. Sharon Macdonald, *Memorylands: Heritage and Identity in Europe Today* (London: Routledge, 2013), 60.

115. Alex Pillen, "Language, Translation, Trauma," *Annual Review of Anthropology* 45 (2016): 98.

116. Jeffrey C. Alexander, "Toward a Theory of Cultural Trauma," in *Cultural Trauma and Collective Identity*, ed. Jeffrey C. Alexander (Berkeley: University of California Press, 2004), 5. Emphasis mine. Alexander is discussing what he calls "lay trauma theory" of a psychoanalytic bent, which some academics have embraced.

117. Jeffrey Prager, "Danger and Deformation: A Social Theory of Trauma Part II: Disrupting the Intergenerational Transmission of Trauma, Recovering Humanity, and Repairing Generations," *American Imago* 72 (2015): 145.

118. Gilad Hirschberger, "Collective Trauma and the Social Construction of Meaning," *Frontiers in Psychology* 10, no. 9 (2018): 2.

119. Emma Hutchison, *Affective Communities in World Politics: Collective Emotions after Trauma* (New York: Cambridge University Press, 2016).

120. Ibid., 3.

121. Bernhard Giesen, "The Trauma of Perpetrators," in *Triumph and Trauma*, ed. Bernhard Giesen and S. N. Eisenstadt (New York: Routledge, 2004), 145.

122. Many writers, including several cited here, such as Vamik Volkan and Hutchison, have addressed this in various ways. A discussion drawing together several salient aspects of theory is in Piotr Stompka, "Cultural Trauma: The Other Face of Social Change," *European Journal of Social Theory* 3 (2000): 457.

123. Vamik D. Volkan, "Transgenerational Transmissions and Chosen Traumas: An Aspect of Large-Group identity," *Group Analysis* 34 (2001): 79–98.

124. Adam B. Lerner, "Theorizing Collective Trauma in International Political Economy," *International Studies Review* 21 (2019): 549–71.

125. Ibid.

126. Alexander, "Toward a Theory of Cultural Trauma," 10.

127. Yael Danieli, "Introduction: Historical and Conceptual Foundations," in *International Handbook of Multigenerational Legacies of Trauma*, ed. Yale Danieli (New York: Plenum Press, 1998), 2.

128. Hirschberger, "Collective Trauma and the Social Construction of Meaning," 1.

129. Ibid., 11. See also the reference to the peculiar makeup of an American group that carried the memory of the Mountain Meadows Massacre of 1857 in Shannon A. Novak and Lars Rodseth, "Remembering Mountain Meadows: Collective Violence and the Manipulation of Social Boundaries," *Journal of Anthropological Research* 62 (2006): 10–12.

130. Adam B. Lerner, "Theorizing Collective Trauma in International Political Economy," *International Studies Review* 21 (2019): 554.

131. Volkan, "Transgenerational Transmissions," 8.

132. Paul Connerton, *How Societies Remember* (Cambridge: Cambridge University Press, 1989), 4.

133. Geoffrey White, "Violent Memories/Memory Violence," *Reviews in Anthropology* 46 (2017): 20.

134. On Spain itself, see William A. Christian Jr., "Provoked Religious Weeping in Early Modern Spain," in *Religious Organization and Religious Experience*, ed. J. Davis (London: Academic Press, 1982), 97–114.

135. Hutchison (*Affective Communities in World Politics*) discusses how collective trauma, specifically, relies on such media.

136. Von Scheve and Ismer, "Towards a Collective Theory of Emotions," 411.

137. Matsumoto, Wang, and Frank, "The Role of Emotion in Predicting Violence," 5.

138. White, "Violent Memories/Memory Violence," 21.

139. Licata Laurent and Aurélie Mercy, "Social Psychology of Collective Memory," in *The Institutional Encyclopedia of the Social and Behavioral Sciences*, 2nd ed., vol. 4, ed. James D. Wright (Oxford: Elsevier, 2015), 196.

140. Michael J. A. Wohl, Nassim Tabri, and Eran Halperin, "Emotional Sources of Intergroup Atrocities," in *Confronting Humanity at Its Worst: Social Psychological Perspectives on Genocide*, ed. Leonard S. Newman (New York: Oxford University Press, 2020), 95.

141. Gabriele Schwab, "Haunting Legacies: Trauma in Children of Perpetrators," *Postcolonial Studies* 7 (2004): 184.

142. Edwin Hutchins, *Cognition in the Wild* (Cambridge, MA: MIT Press, 1995).

143. Three early influential efforts in these three fields are Arlie Hochschild, *The Managed Heart: Commercialization of Human Feeling* (Berkeley: University of California Press, 1983); James R. Averill, "The Social Construction of Emotion: With Special Reference to the Emotion of Love," in *The Social Construction of the Person*, ed. Kenneth J. Gergen and Keith E. Davis (New York: Springer Verlag, 1985), 89–109; and Michelle Zimbalist Rosaldo, *Knowledge and Passion: Ilongot Notions of Self and Social Life* (New York: Cambridge University Press, 1980). An overview of some of the early relevant literature, especially for the study of religion, is in John Corrigan, "Appendix 1: History, Religion, and Emotion: A Historiographical Survey," in Corrigan, *Business of the Heart: Religion and Emotion in the Nineteenth Century* (Berkeley: University of California Press, 2002), 269–80.

144. Neil J. Smelser, "Psychological Trauma and Cultural Trauma," in Alexander, *Cultural Trauma and Collective Identity*, 37.

145. Hans Joas, "Book Review: Cultural Trauma? On the Most Recent Turn in Jeffrey Alexander's Cultural Sociology," *European Journal of Social Theory* 8 (2005): 368.

146. There is a growing body of research about this, but a recent study that is relevant to this discussion is Hutchison, *Affective Communities in World Politics*. Hutchison summarizes her thinking about this in the Preface, xi–xiii. She also writes: "One of the distinguishing features of my inquiry is that it explicitly addresses the disjuncture between the two very different conceptualizations of trauma. I focus on understanding how seemingly individual traumatic encounters can acquire larger societal and political importance. I do so by underlining the key role that processes of representation play in making traumatic events collectively meaningful, including to those who do not experience trauma directly, but only bear witness, from a distance. By giving voice to or visually depicting what are unique and somewhat incommunicable experiences of shock and pain, representational practices craft understandings of trauma that have social meaning and significance. In particular circumstances, such practices and the shared meanings that are produced resonate with shared, culturally ascribed notions of mutual bereavement, loss and solidarity. A community bound by shared understandings and a common purpose of working through trauma may ensue. The primary contribution—and argument—of the book emerges from the observation that emotions are a crucial, though largely underappreciated element of the process through which traumatic events construct political communities" (3).

147. Catherine Malabou, "Is Psychic Phylogenesis Only a Fantasy? New Biological Developments in Trauma Inheritance," in *Freud and Monotheism: Moses and the Violent Origins of Religion*, ed. Gilad Sharvit and Karen S. Feldman, University of California, Berkeley Forum in the Humanities (New York: Fordham University Press, 2018), 193.

148. Ibid., 189.

149. Alexander Miller, Catherine Malabou, Emily Apter, Peter Szendy, Emanuela Bianchi, and Alexander R. Galloway, "On Epigenesis," *October* 175 (2021): 109.

150. Ibid., 111.

151. A recent overview of some aspects of epigenetic transmission relevant here is in Johannes Bohacek and Isabelle M. Mansuy, "Molecular Insights into Transgenerational Non-genetic Inheritance of Acquired Behaviours," *Nature Reviews Genetics* 16 (2015): 641–52.

152. Other processes include acetylation, deacetylation, histone modification, and the attachment of noncoding RNA to coding RNA.

153. Grégoire Rondelet and Johan Wouters, "Human DNA (cytosine-5)-methyltransferases: A Functional and Structural Perspective for Epigenetic Cancer Therapy," *Biochimie* 139 (2017): 137–47; and Keqin K. Li, Fangcheng Li, Qiushi S. Li, Kun Yang, and Bilian Jin, "DNA Methylation as a Target of Epigenetic Therapeutics in Cancer," *Anticancer Agents in Medicinal Chemistry* 13 (2013): 242–47.

154. Amarendra M. Singh, "Contribution of Epigenesis towards the Etiology, Prevention, and Treatment of Post-Traumatic Stress Disorder," *International Medical Journal* 27 (2020): 646.

155. Jordan W. Smoller, "The Genetics of Stress-related Disorders: PTSD, Depression, and Anxiety Disorders," *Neuropsychopharmacology* 41 (2016): 313.

156. Ibid., 306.

157. Thomas Elbert and Maggie Schauer, "Epigenetic, Neural, and Cognitive Memories of Traumatic Stress and Violence," in *Psychology Serving Humanity: Proceedings of the 30th International Congress of Psychology, Volume 2: Western Psychology*, ed. Saths Cooper and Kopano Ratele (London: Psychology Press, 2014), 215, 216.

158. Ibid., 216.

159. Rachel Yehuda and Amy Lerner, "Intergenerational Transmission of Trauma Effects: Putative Role of Epigenetic Mechanisms," *World Psychiatry* 17 (2018): 243.

160. There are a number of important studies involving mice, bees, and other animals. Illustrative studies of worms—which focuses not on methylation but on RNA levels—include Leah Houri-Zeevi, Yael Korem Kohanim, Olgo Antonova, and Oded Rechavi, "Three Rules Explain Transgenerational Small RNA Inheritance in C. elegans," *Cell* 182 (2020): 1186–97; and Oded Rechavi, Leah Houri-Zeevi, Sarit Anava, Wee Siong Sho Goh, Sze Yen Kerk, Gregory J. Hannon, and Oliver Hobert, "Starvation-Induced Transgenerational Inheritance of Small RNAs in C. elegans," *Cell* 158 (2014): 277–87.

161. Smoller, "The Genetics of Stress-Related Disorders," 301.

162. Rachel Yehuda and Amy Lerner, "Intergenerational Transmission of Trauma Effects," 251.

163. Qian Zihao Wang, Wenfeng Zhang, Qingbo Wen, et al., "The Memory of Neuronal Mitochondrial Stress Is Inherited Transgenerationally via Elevated Mitochondrial DNA levels," *Nature Cell Biology* 23 (2021): 870–80.

164. Brian R. Herb, Florian Wolshin, Kasper D. Hansen, Martin J. Aryee, Ben Langmead, Rafael Irizarry, Gro V. Amden, and Andrew P. Feinberg, "Reversible Switching between Epigenetic States in Honeybee Behavioral Subcastes," *Nature Neuroscience* 15 (2012): 1371–73.

165. Bastiaan T. Heijmansa, Elmar W. Tobia, Aryeh D. Steinb, Hein Putterc, Gerard J. Blauwd, Ezra S. Sussere, P. Eline Slagbooma, and L. H. Lumeye, "Persistent Epigenetic Differences Associated with Prenatal Exposure to Famine in Humans," *Proceedings of the National Academy of Sciences* 105 (2008): 17048.

166. F. Serpeloni, K. Radtke, S. G. de Assis, F. Henning, D. Nätt, and T. Elbert, "Grandmaternal Stress during Pregnancy and DNA Methylation of the Third Generation: An Epigenome-Wide Association Study," *Translational Psychiatry* 7 (2017): 1202.

167. Rachel Yehuda, Nikolaos P. Daskalakis, Linda M. Bierer, Heather N. Bader, Torsten Klengel, Florian Holsboer, and Elisabeth B. Binder, "Holocaust Exposure Induced Intergenerational Effects on FKBP5 Methylation," *Biological Psychiatry* 80 (2016): 372.

168. L. Ly, D. Chan, and J. M. Trasler, "Developmental Windows of Susceptibility for Epigenetic Inheritance Through the Male Germline," *Seminars in Cell and Developmental Biology* 43 (2015): 96–105; and O. J. Rando, "Intergenerational Transfer of Epigenetic Information in Sperm," *Cold Spring Harbor Perspectives in Medicine* 6 (2016): 6. See also, for a broad view, H. J. Clarke and K. F. Vieux, "Epigenetic Inheritance through the Female Germ-line: The Known, the Unknown, and the Possible," *Seminars in Cell and Developmental Biology* 43 (2015): 106–16.

169. An overview of this area of study is in Ali Jawaid, Martin Roszkowski, and Isabelle M. Mansuy, "Transgenerational Epigenetics of Traumatic Stress," *Progress in Molecular Biology and Translational Science* 158 (2018): 273–98. A review article of this area is Sriya Bhattacharya, Audrey Fontaine, Phillip E. MacCallum, James Drover, and Jacqueline Blundell, "Stress across Generations: DNA Methylation as a Potential Mechanism Underlying Intergenerational Effects of Stress in Both Post-Traumatic Stress Disorder and Pre-Clinical Predator Stress Rodent Models," *Frontiers in Behavioral Neuroscience* 13 (2019): 1–12.

170. Charlotte E. Wittekind, Lena Jelinek, Michael Kellner, Steffen Moritz, and Christoph Muhtz, "Intergenerational Transmission of Biased Information Processing in Posttraumatic Stress Disorder (PTSD) Following Displacement after World War II," *Journal of Anxiety Disorders* 24 (2010): 953–57; and Ann C. Davidson and David J. Mellor, "The Adjustment of Children of Australian Vietnam Veterans: Is There Evidence for the Transgenerational Transmission of the Effects of War-Related Trauma?," *Australian and New Zealand Journal of Psychiatry* 35 (2001): 345–51.

171. Connie Svob, Norman R. Brown, Vladimir Taksic, Katarina Katulic, and Valnea Žauhar, "Intergenerational Transmission of Historical Memories and Social-Distance Attitudes in Post-War Second-Generation Croatians," *Memory and Cognition* 44 (2016): 846–55.

172. Nigel P. Field, Sophear Muong, and Vannavuth Sochanvimean, "Parental Styles in the Intergenerational Transmission of Trauma Stemming from the Khmer Rouge Regime in Cambodia," *American Journal of Orthopsychiatry* 83 (2013): 483–94.

173. Ian G. Barron and Ghassan Abdallah, "Intergenerational Trauma in the Occupied Palestinian Territories," *Journal of Child and Adolescent Trauma* 8 (2015): 103–10.

174. Maria Roth, Frank Neuner, and Thomas Elbert, "Transgenerational Consequences of PTSD: Risk Factors for the Mental Health of Children Whose Mothers Have Been Exposed to the Rwandan Genocide," *International Journal of Mental Health Systems* 8 (2014): 1–12; and Nader Perroud, Eugene Rutembesa, Ariane Paoloni-Giacobino, Jean Mutabaruka, Léon Mutesa, Ludwig Stenz, Alain Malafosse, and Felicien Karege, "The Tutsi Genocide and Transgenerational Transmission of Maternal Stress: Epigenetics and Biology of the HPA Axis," *World Journal of Biological Psychiatry* 15 (2014): 334–45.

175. Beverley Raphael, Patricia Swan, and Nada Martinek, "Intergenerational Aspects of Trauma for Australian Aboriginal People," in *International Handbook of Multigenerational Legacies of Trauma*, ed. Yael Danieli (Boston: Springer, 1998), 327–39.

176. Leonie Pihama, Paul Reynolds, Cherryl Smith, John Reid, Linda Tuhiwai Smith, and Rihi Te Nana, "Positioning Historical Trauma Theory within Aotearoa New Zealand," *AlterNative: An International Journal of Indigenous Peoples* 10 (2014): 248–62.

177. Hatsantour Karenian, Miltos Livaditis, Sirpouhi Karenian, Kyriakos Zafiriadis, Valentini Bochtsou, and Kiriakos Xenitidis, "Collective Trauma Transmission and Traumatic Reactions among Descendants of Armenian Refugees," *International Journal of Social Psychiatry* 57 (2011): 327–37; and Natasha Azarian-Ceccato, "Reverberations of the Armenian Genocide: Narrative's Intergenerational Transmission and the Task of Not Forgetting," *Narrative Inquiry* 20 (2010): 106–23.

178. Ron Eyerman, *Cultural Trauma: Slavery and the Formation of African American Identity* (New York: Cambridge University Press, 2001).

179. Dora L. Costa, Noelle Yetter, and Heather DeSomer, "Intergenerational Transmission of Paternal Trauma among US Civil War ex-POWs," *Proceedings of the National Academy of Sciences* 115 (2018): 11215–20.

180. Connie Mulligan, Nicole D'Errico, Jared Stees, and David Hughes, "Methylation Changes at NR3C1 in Newborns Associate with Maternal Prenatal Stress Exposure and Newborn Birth Weight," *Epigenetics* 7 (2012): 853–57.

181. For example, the MemoTV (Memories of Traumatic Stress and Violence) project at the University of Konstanz Centre of Excellence for Psychotraumatology.

182. Connie J. Mulligan, "Systemic Racism Can Get under Our Skin and into Our Genes," *American Journal of Physical Anthropology* 175 (2021): 401.

183. Ibid.

184. Élodie Grossi, "New Avenues in Epigenetic Research about Race: Online Activism around Reparations for Slavery in the United States," *Social Science Information* 59 (2020): 108. Grossi discusses how lay interpretation of scientific research has extended scientific findings into "truths" that at times overreach, based on what has been evidenced by academic studies.

185. Ibid.

186. Ute Deichmann, "Epigenetics: The Origins and Evolution of a Fashionable Topic," *Developmental Biology* 416 (2016): 249–54.

187. Irene Lacai and Rossella Ventrura, "Epigenetic Inheritance: Concepts, Mechanisms, Perspectives," *Frontiers in Molecular Neuroscience* 11 (2018): 1–22.

188. Rachel Yehuda and Amy Lehrner, "Intergenerational Transmission of Trauma Effects," 243. Emphasis mine.

Chapter Four

1. Tiffany Hale (Afro-Cherokee), "Hostiles and Friendlies: Memory, U.S. Institutions, and the 1890 Ghost Dance" (PhD dissertation, Yale University, 2017), 18, 19.

2. Lawrence E. Hedges, "Listening Perspectives for Emotional-Relatedness Memories," *Psychoanalytic Inquiry* 25 (2005): 455.

3. Felicity Callard and Constantina Papoulias, "Affect and Embodiment," in *Memory: Histories, Theories, Debates*, ed. Susannah Radstone and Bill Schwarz (New York: Fordham University Press, 2010), 246.

4. Roberto Cubelli, "A New Taxonomy of Memory and Forgetting," in *Forgetting*, ed. Sergio Della Sala (London: Routledge, 2010), 41.

5. Peter Goldie, *The Mess Inside: Narrative, Emotion, and the Mind* (Oxford: Oxford University Press, 2021), 11.

6. Ralf Babinsky, Pasquale Calabrese, Herbert F. Derwen, Hans J. Markowitsch, Michael Würker, Dirk Brechtelsbauer, Lothar Heuser, and Walter Gehlen, "The Possible Contribution of the Amygdala to Memory," *Behavioral Neurology* 6 (1993): 167.

7. Hans J. Markowitsch and Pasquale Calabrese, "The Amygdala's Contribution to Memory—A Study on Two Patients with Urbach-Wiethe Disease," *NeuroReport* 5 (1994): 1349.

8. Kelsi J. Hall, Emily J. Fawcett, Kathleen L. Hourihan, and Jonathan M. Fawcett, "Emotional Memories Are (Usually) Harder to Forget: A Meta-Analysis of the Item-Method Directed Forgetting Literature," *Psychonomic Bulletin and Review* 28 (2021): 1322.

9. Pierre Gagnepain, Justin Huilbert, and Michael C. Anderson, "Parallel Regulation of Memory and Emotion Supports the Suppression of Intrusive Memories," *Journal of Neuroscience* 37 (2017): 6423.

10. Ibid., 6440.

11. Mary Douglas, *Evans-Pritchard* (Glasgow: Fontana, 1980), 22–26.

12. Frederic C. Bartlett, *Remembering: A Study in Experimental and Social Psychology* (Cambridge: Cambridge University Press, 1932), 311, 214, 303, 85. For his theory of feeling, see his previous "Feeling, Imaging, and Thinking," *British Journal of Psychology* 16 (1925): 16–28.

13. Ibid., 53ff.

14. Leading researcher in the area of implicit memory (nonconscious forms of memory) Daniel L. Schacter attributed his research direction to Bartlett ("Implicit Memory, Constructive Memory, and Imagining the Future: A Career Perspective," *Perspectives on Psychological Science* 14 [2019]: 257).

15. Daniel. L. Schacter, "The Seven Sins of Memory: Insight from Psychology and Cognitive Neuroscience," *American Psychologist* 54 (1987): 182–203; Matthew Hugh Erdelyi, *The Recovery of Unconscious Memories: Hyperamnesia and Reminiscence* (Chicago: University of Chicago Press, 1996); Erdelyi, "Subliminal Perception and Its Cognates: Theory, Indeterminacy, and

Time," *Consciousness and Cognition* 13 (2004): 73–91; and R. R. Hassin, J. S. Uleman, and J. A. Bargh, eds., *The New Unconscious* (Oxford: Oxford University Press, 2005).

16. Matthew Hugh Erdelyi, "Forgetting and Remembering in Psychology: Commentary on Paul Connerton's 'Seven Types of Forgetting,'" *Memory Studies* 1 (2008): 276.

17. I. H. Paul, "Studies in Remembering," *Psychological Issues* 1 (1959): 4.

18. David Rapaport, "The Experimental Contributions of General Psychology," in Rapaport, *Emotions and Memory,* 2nd unaltered ed. (Madison, CT: International Universities Press, 1942), 41.

19. Bartlett, *Remembering,* 299, 296.

20. John Shotter, "The Social Construction of Remembering and Forgetting," chap. 7 in *Collective Remembering,* ed. David Middleton and Derek Edwards (London: Sage Publications, 1990), 120.

21. Garrett A. Sullivan Jr., *Memory and Forgetting in English Renaissance Drama* (Cambridge: Cambridge University Press, 2005), 22, 45–48.

22. A representative recent discussion of the value of forgetting in personal life is in Jonathan M. Fawcett, "The Many Faces of Forgetting: Toward a Constructive View of Forgetting in Everyday Life," *Journal of Applied Research in Memory and Cognition* 9 (2020): 1–18. Fawcett lists serenity, stability, clarity, revision, abstraction, inspiration, and rediscovery all as personal virtues of "organized forgetting" (3).

23. Marc Augé, *Oblivion,* trans. Marjolijn de Jager (Minneapolis: University of Minnesota Press, 2004), 18.

24. *The Odyssey,* bk. 24, ll. 480–90.

25. Winston Churchill, in *The Sinews of Peace: Postwar Speeches by Winston S. Churchill,* ed. Randolph S. Churchill (London: Cassell, 1948), 10. I draw from Aleida Assmann's writing about this speech.

26. Tony Judt, "The Rehabilitation of Europe," in Judt, *Postwar: A History of Europe since 1945* (New York: Penguin, 2005), 61–62.

27. Tony Judt, "From the House of the Dead: On Modern European Memory," *New York Review of Books* 52 (October 2005): 16.

28. Shannon Walsh, "In Defence of Forgetting," in *Memory,* ed. Philippe Tortell, Mark Turin, and Margot Young (Vancouver: Peter Wall Institute for Advanced Studies, 2018), 173.

29. Debbora Battaglia, "At Play in the Fields (and Borders) of the Imaginary: Melanesia Transformations of Forgetting," *Cultural Anthropology* 8 (1993): 430–42.

30. David Rieff, *In Praise of Forgetting: Historical Memory and Its Ironies* (New Haven: Yale University Press, 2016).

31. Andocides, *On the Mysteries,* 87:1, in *Minor Attic Orators,* vol. 1 of 2 vols., with an English translation by K. J. Maidment (Cambridge, MA: Harvard University Press, 1968). See Christopher T. Joyce, "The Athenian Amnesty and Scrutiny of 403," *Classical Quarterly,* 58 (2008): 507–18.

32. *A Treaty of Peace between the Empire and Sweden, 24th of October, 1648,* art. 3, para 1. See the English translation at Oxford Public International Law, 2020, https://opil.ouplaw.com /view/10.1093/law:oht/law-oht-1-CTS-1.regGroup.1/law-oht-1-CTS-1; and the document, 2020, 201, https://opil.ouplaw.com/view/10.1093/law:oht/law-oht-1-CTS-119.regGroup.1/1_CTS_119 _eng.pdf.

33. *Treaty of Peace between France and Great Britain, 20 September 1697,* art. 3. See the document, 2020, 445, https://opil.ouplaw.com/view/10.1093/law:oht/law-oht-21-CTS-409.regGroup .1/21_CTS_409_eng.pdf.

34. A full discussion of this "rhetoric of amnesia" in the edicts is in Andrea Frisch, "Learning to Forget," in *Forgetting Differences: Tragedy, Historiography, and the French Wars of Religion* (Edinburgh: Edinburgh University Press, 2015), 1–25. The various edicts over four decades that ended the fighting, leading up to Nantes, are discussed in Cornel Zwierlein, "Forgotten Religions, Religions That Cause Forgetting," in *Forgetting Faith? Negotiating Confessional Conflict in Early Modern Europe*, ed. Isabel Karremann, Cornel Zwierlein, and Inga Mai Groote (Berlin: DeGruyter, 2012), 117n2.

35. Black Moon (Miniconjou Lakota), quoted in "Document 2.23. From: Volume 26 (1897–98): The Sioux and Their Apostles," in *Lakotas, Black Robes, and Holy Women: German Reports from the Indian Missions in South Dakota, 1886–1900*, ed. Karl Markus Kreis, trans. Corinna Dally-Starna (Lincoln: University of Nebraska Press, 2000), 258. I discuss his speech in chapter 2.

36. Glen Coultard, *Red Skins, White Masks: Rejecting the Colonial Politics of Recognition* (Minneapolis: University of Minnesota Press, 2014), 108, 121.

37. This is Mary Douglas's economical phrasing of Evans-Pritchard's project (*Edward Evans-Pritchard*, in *Mary Douglas Collected Works*, vol. 7 of 7 vols. [London: Routledge, 2003], 320–21).

38. Mary Douglas, *How Institutions Think* (Syracuse: Syracuse University Press, 1986), 72.

39. Ibid.; see esp. chap. 6, "Institutions Remember and Forget."

40. Douglas, *Edward Evans-Pritchard*, 77.

41. Douglas, *How Institutions Think*, 72.

42. Laura Bohannan, "A Genealogical Charter," *Africa* 22 (1952): 301–15; and Bohannan and Paul Bohannan, *The Tiv of Central Nigeria* (London: International African Institute, London, 1953). See also the discussion in Michael Thompson, *Rubbish Theory: The Creation and Destruction of Value* (Oxford: Oxford University Press, 1979), 77–83. A critical and constructive overview of salient research is in Edward Peck and Perri Six, *Memory, Forgetting, Time Horizons, and Capability in Organisations* (New York: Palgrave, 2006), 50–77.

43. Steven D. Brown and Paula Reavey, "Memory in the Wild: Life Space, Setting-Specificity, and Ecologies of Experience," in *Memory in the Wild*, ed. Brady Wagoner, Ignacio Brescó de Luna, and Sophie Zadeh (Charlotte: Information Age Publishing, 2020), 37.

44. On "state regimes of forgetting," see Mneesha Gellman, *Democratization and Memories of Violence: Ethnic Rights Movements in Mexico, Turkey, and El Salvador* (London: Routledge, 2017), 174, 176–77.

45. Wulf Kansteiner, "Of Media Scandals and Regimes of Forgetting: Strauss-Kahn, Public History, and Memory Studies," *Memory Studies* 8 (2015): 385–89.

46. Guy Beiner, "Disremembering 1798? An Archaeology of Social Forgetting and Remembrance in Ulster," *History and Memory* 25 (2013): 9.

47. "L'essence d'une nation est que tous les individus aient beaucoup de choses en commun, et aussi que tous aient oublié bien des choses" (Ernest Renan, "Qu'est-ce qu'une nation?," in *Oeuvres complètes*, vol. 1 of 10 vols. [Paris: Calmann Lévy, 1947–61], 892).

48. The historian and political theorist Benedict Anderson was particularly interested in remembering and forgetting. He wrote that there is a "vast pedagogical industry," present in America as well as in France and elsewhere, that "works ceaselessly to oblige young Americans to remember/forget the hostilities of 1861–5 as a great 'civil' war between brothers rather than between—as they briefly were—two sovereign nation-states." That is, the national narrative is a story of fratricide. For Anderson, Americans have settled on a story about the violence between North and South as fighting between kin, and that view is extended to understandings of the relationship of whites to enslaved Blacks and Native Americans in North America, with white

Americans imagining a kind of kin association as they practiced a broader racially inflected fratricide. "In the United States of America," wrote Anderson, "this paradox is particularly well exemplified" (Anderson, *Imagined Communities: Reflections on the Origin and Spread of Nationalism*, rev. ed. [London: Verso, 1991], 199–200, 202, 205).

49. Ibid., 35, 36.

50. The wording here is from Susanne Buckley-Zistel, "Between Pragmatism, Coercion, and Fear: Chosen Amnesia after the Rwandan Genocide," in *Memory and Political Change*, ed. Aleida Assmann and Linda Shortt (London: Palgrave, 2012), 74.

51. Stanley Cohen, *States of Denial: Knowing about Atrocities and Suffering* (Cambridge: Polity, 2001), 132. He writes: "Whole societies have an astonishing ability to deny the past—not really forgetting, but maintaining a public culture that seems to have forgotten" (138).

52. Ibid., 34.

53. Friedrich Nietzsche, *On the Genealogy of Morality*, trans. Maudemarie Clark and Alan J. Swensen (Indianapolis: Hackett Publishing, 1998), 35.

54. Petar Ramadanovic, "From Haunting to Trauma: Nietzsche's Active Forgetting and Blanchot's Writing of the Disaster," in *Trauma: Essays on the Limit of Knowledge and Experience*, ed. Petar Ramadanovic, special issue of *Postmodern Culture: An Electronic Journal of Interdisciplinary Criticism* 11 (2001): 13.

55. Andy Clark describes this as "a new kind of cognitive scientific collaboration involving neuroscience, physiology, and social, cultural, and technological studies in about equal measure" (*Mindware: An Introduction to the Philosophy of Cognitive Science* [Oxford: Oxford University Press, 2000], 154).

56. Kourken Michaelian and John Sutton, "Distributed Cognition and Memory Research: History and Current Directions," *Review of Philosophy and Psychology* 4 (2013): 1, 2, 14.

57. Meghan Tinsley, "Memory and Melancholia in the Garden of Tropical Agronomy," *Memory Studies* 14 (2021): 536. The literature that Tinsley cites in support of this claim is on memory and war.

58. Matthew Hugh Erdelyi, "The Unified Theory of Repression," *Behavioral and Brain Sciences* 29 (2006): 499.

59. Jo-Berger Schmeing, Aram Kehyayan, Henrik Kessler, Anne T. A. Do Lam, Juergen Fell, and Anna Christine Schmidt, "Can the Neural Basis of Repression Be Studied in the MRI Scanner? New Insights from Two Free Association Paradigms," *PLOS ONE* 8 (2013): 12.

60. Erdelyi, "The Unified Theory of Repression," 499.

61. Examples include van der Kolk and like-minded writers (such as in Caruthian literary studies) who believe that trauma is unconsciously repressed but remains "under the skin." See Bessel A. van der Kolk, "The Body Keeps the Score: Memory and the Evolving Psychobiology of Posttraumatic Stress," *Harvard Review of Psychiatry* 1 (1994): 253–65; and van der Kolk, *Psychological Trauma* (Washington, DC: American Psychiatric Press, 1987).

62. Darinka Trübutschek, Sébastien Marti, Andrés Ojeda, Jean-Rémi King, Yuanyuan Mi, Misha Tsodyks, and Stanislaus Dehaene, "A Theory of Working Memory without Consciousness or Sustained Activity," *eLife* 6 (2017): 2, 21.

63. Hakwan C. Lau and Richard E. Passingham, "Unconscious Activation of the Cognitive Control System in the Human Prefrontal Cortex," *Journal of Neuroscience* 27 (2007): 5809.

64. Ibid., 5805.

65. Joseph E. LeDoux and Daniel S. Pine, "Using Neuroscience to Help Understand Fear and Anxiety: A Two-System Framework," *American Journal of Psychiatry* 173 (2016): 1086.

66. Shih-kuen Cheng, I-Chun Liu, Jun Ren Lee, Daisy L. Hung, and Ovid J.-L. Tzeng, "Intentional Forgetting Might Be More Effortful Than Remembering: An ERP Study of Item-Method Directed Forgetting," *Biological Psychology* 89 (2012) 283– 292; Hall et al., "Emotional Memories are (Usually) Harder to Forget."

67. I borrow wording here from Edward S. Casey's summary of the discussion of this in Heidegger, in *Remembering: A Phenomenological Study*, 2nd ed. (Bloomington: Indiana University Press, 2000), 8. The text in Heidegger is: "The fact that curiosity always already keeps to what is nearest by, and has forgotten what went before, is not something resulting from curiosity, but the ontological condition for curiosity itself" (*Being and Time: A Translation of Sein Und Zeit*, trans. Joan Stambaugh [Albany: State University of New York Press, 1996], 319).

68. Aleida Assmann, "Cultural and Political Frames of Forgetting," in *Forgetting: An Interdisciplinary Conversation*, ed. C. Giovanni Galizia and David Dean Shulman (Jerusalem: Hebrew University Magnes Press, 2015), 16.

69. Avery A. Rizio and Mancy A. Denis, "The Neural Correlates of Cognitive Control: Successful Remembering and Intentional Forgetting," *Journal of Cognitive Neuroscience* 25 (2013): 297.

70. Literature reviews include Michael C. Anderson and Simon Hanslmayr, "Neural Mechanisms of Motivated Forgetting," *Trends in Cognitive Sciences* 18 (2014): 279–92; Matthias Brand and Hans J. Markowitsch, "Aspects of Forgetting in Psychogenic Amnesia," in *Forgetting*, ed. Sergio Della Sala (London: Psychology Press, 2010), 239–51; and Colin M. Macleod, "Directed Forgetting," in *Intentional Forgetting: Interdisciplinary Approaches*, ed. Colin M. Macleod and Jonathan M. Golding (Mahwah: Erlbaum, 1997), 1–57.

71. Anderson and Hanslmayr, "Neural Mechanisms of Motivated Forgetting," 279.

72. Michael C. Anderson and Ean Huddleston, "Towards a Cognitive and Neurobiological Model of Motivated Forgetting," in *True and False Recovered Memories: Toward a Reconciliation of the Debate*, ed. Robert F. Belli (New York: Springer, 2012), 83, 84, 100, 53, 57.

73. Michael C. Anderson and Justin C. Hulbert, "Active Forgetting: Adaptation of Memory by Prefrontal Control," *Annual Reviews of Psychology* 72 (2021): 20.

74. Ibid.

75. Ibid., 27.

76. Ibid., 4.

77. Jonathan M. Fawcett, Tracy L. Taylor, and Lynn Nadel, "Intentional Forgetting Diminishes Memory for Continuous Events," *Memory* 21 (2013): 675–94.

78. Nicolai Axmacher, Anne T. A. Do Lam, Henrik Kessler, and Juergen Fell, "Natural Memory beyond the Storage Model: Repression, Trauma, and the Construction of a Personal Past," *Frontiers in Neuroscience* 4 (2010): 1, 6, 9. In the long wake of the charged debates about "recovered memory" that drew its battle lines in the 1990s, there remains a minority who resist the idea of repression of memories in general and "recovered memory" in particular. See Henry Otgaar, Mark L. Howe, Olivier Dodier, Scott O. Lilienfeld, Elizabeth F. Loftus, Steven ay Lynn, Harald Merckelbach, and Lawrence Patihis, "Belief in Unconscious Repressed Memory Persists," *Perspectives on Psychological Science* 16 (2021): 454–60; and Olivier Dodier, Anne-Laure Gilet, and Fabienne Colombel, "What Do People Really Think of When They Claim to Believe in Repressed Memory? Methodological Middle Ground and Applied Issues," *Memory*, January 24, 2021, 744–752, https://doi.org/10.1080/09658211.2020.1868524. In a recent comprehensive study, Chris R. Brewin has concluded that such resistance to the theory of repression imagines "a problem for which little objective evidence can be found" ("Tilting at Windmills: Why Attacks on Repression Are Misguided," *Perspectives on Psychological Science* 16 [2020]: 443).

79. Brewin, "Tilting at Windmills," 444.

80. Celia B. Harris, John Sutton, and Amanda J. Barneier, "Autobiographical Forgetting, Social Forgetting, and Situated Forgetting: Forgetting in Context," in *Current Issues in Memory*, ed. Jan Rummel (London: Routledge, 2021), 159.

81. Howard Caygill, "Physiological Memory Systems," in *Memory: History, Theories, Debates*, ed. Susannah Radstone and Bill Schwarz (New York: Fordham, 2010), 227.

82. Ibid., 163.

83. Astrid Erll, "Cultural Memory Studies: An Introduction: Towards a Conceptual Foundation for Cultural Memory Studies," in *Cultural Memory Studies: An International and Interdisciplinary Handbook*, ed. Astrid Erll and Ansgar Nünning (Berlin: de Gruyter, 2008), 7.

84. Ibid., 2.

85. David Manier and William Hirst, "A Cognitive Taxonomy of Collective Memories," in Erll and Nünning, *Cultural Memory Studies*, 260.

86. Episodic memories are memories of events in which a person participates; semantic memories are memories that people can recite without having participated in the event (e.g., Washington crossed the Delaware); procedural memory, or "implicit memory," is held in community traditions and rituals that remind, in their performance, of the past. Manier and Hirst offer the following example: "The meaning of Mass that parishioners learn about in catechism, that is, parishioners' collective semantic memories about the meaning of Mass, are more likely to be retained over an extended period of time than are the collective episodic memories that parishioners might form of particular Masses they have attended. Still more likely to be retained, however, are the collective procedural memories parishioners have for Mass. . . . They are likely to remember quite accurately, until they die, how to participate in the Mass" (Ibid., 260).

87. Ibid.

88. Ludmila Isurin, drawing on quantitative and qualitative data and scientific and humanistic research, demonstrates the possibilities of systematically exploring that intertwining in a study of migrations of Russians in *Collective Remembering: Memory in the World and in the Mind* (New York: Cambridge University Press, 2017). She writes: "*Collective Remembering* provides a new theoretical framework for memory studies that incorporates both content analysis of texts and empirical data from human participants, thus demonstrating that methodologies from the humanities and the social sciences can complement each other to create a better understanding of how memory works in the world and in the mind" (front matter); and "I am attempting to merge two types of memory as they relate to a group (collective memory) and the individual (autobiographical memory)" (1).

89. Aleida Assmann, "Memory, Individual and Collective," in *Contextual Political Analysis*, ed. Robert E. Goodin and Charles Tilly (Oxford: Oxford University Press, 2006), 211.

90. Manier and Hirst, "A Cognitive Taxonomy of Collective Memories," 253.

91. Aleida Assmann, "Memory, Individual and Collective," 223.

92. A concise statement by Pierre Nora is in "Between Memory and History: Les Lieux de Mémoire," *Representations* 26 (1989). "Perhaps the most tangible sign of the split between history and memory has been the emergence of a history of history, the awakening, quite recent in France, of a historiographical consciousness. . . . The study of lieux de mémoires, then, lies at the intersection of two developments that in France today give it meaning: one a purely historiographical movement, the reflexive turning of history upon itself, the other a movement that is, properly speaking, historical: the end of a tradition of memory" (9, 11).

93. Frank Wilker, "Individual Trauma and the Study of Literature," in Wilker, *Cultural Memories of Origin: Trauma, Memory and Imagery in African American Narratives of the Middle Passage* (Heidelberg: Universitätsverlag Winter, 2017), 52. He writes: "On an analytical level it does not make sense for the individual and the collective to be differentiated in a strictly oppositional manner. In order to understand what it means to survive, individual and cultural trauma need to be read together" (52).

94. Aleida Assmann, "Memory, Individual and Collective," 222.

95. Jan Assmann writes: "Remembrance is a matter of emotional ties, cultural shaping, and a conscious reference to the past that overcomes the rupture between life and death. These are the elements that characterize cultural memory and take it far beyond the reaches of tradition" (*Cultural Memory and Early Civilization: Writing, Remembrance, and Political Imagination* [Cambridge: Cambridge University Press, 2011], 20). Commenting on Halbwachs's view of families and collective memory, for example, Astrid Erll observes: "To Halbwachs, family memory is a type of collective memory which is characterized by the strength of its group allegiances and its powerful emotional dimension" ("Locating Family in Cultural Memory Studies," *Journal of Comparative Family Studies* 42 [2011]: 306).

96. Halbwachs, *La topographie légendaire des évangiles en Terre sainte* (Paris: Presses Universitaires, 1941), is his fullest treatment of feeling and collective memory in discussing biblical sites of memory.

97. Daniele Hervieu-Léger, *Religion as a Chain of Memory* (New Brunswick: Rutgers University Press, 2000). See also Dominique MacNeill, "Extending the Work of Halbwachs: Danièle Hervieu-Léger's Analysis of Contemporary Religion," *Durkheimian Studies/Études Durkheimiennes*, n.s., 4 (1998): 73–86.

98. "For Halbwachs, therefore, collective memory and history stand as antinomies. Whereas collective memory seeks to confirm the similarities between past and present, history prefers to establish a critical distance between them. Memory evokes deep emotion, whereas history prides itself on its dispassion" (Patrick H. Hutton, "Collective Memories and Collective Mentalities: The Halbwachs-Ariès Connection," *Historical Reflections / Réflexions Historiques* 15 (1988): 317). Jan Assmann notes of Halbwachs's attempt to link feeling and memory: "Strictly speaking, it is the emotions rather than the memories that are individual because emotions are closely connected with our bodies, whereas memories have their origins in the thoughts of the different groups to which we belong" (*Cultural Memory and Early Civilization: Writing, Remembrance, and Political Imagination* [Cambridge: Cambridge University Press, 2011]: 23).

99. See Hutton, "Collective Memories and Collective Mentalities."

100. Two of the leading proponents of the idea of cultural memory are Aleida Assmann and Jan Assmann. I draw directly on their work in conceptualizing cultural memory and its relation to trauma. In addition to their writings cited elsewhere in this book, see Aleida Assmann, *Cultural Memory and Western Civilization: Functions, Media, Archives*; Aleida Assmann, "Cultural Memory" in *Social Trauma: An Interdisciplinary Textbook*, ed. Andreas Hamburger, Camellia Hancheva, and Vamik D. Volkan (New York: Springer, 2021), 25–36; and Jan Assmann, "Communicative and Cultural Memory," in *Cultural Memories*, ed. Peter Meusberger, Michael Heffernan, and Edgar Wunder (New York: Springer, 2011), 15–27. I note, however, that the Assmanns (contra Halbwachs) do not foreground emotion as the binding element in community life, but instead emphasize the importance of symbols, communication, and language, in a process dependent on canonization and archives (see "Conversation with Jan Assmann: Memory Goes Hand-in-Hand

with Forgetting," interview led by Caroline Gaudriault, 2013, http://www.zigzag-blog.com/spip
.php?page=article&id_article=3).

101. Erll, "Cultural Memory Studies," 2.

102. Qi Wang, "On The Cultural Constitution of Collective Memory," *Memory* 16 (2008): 305.

103. Marita Sturken, *Tangled Memories: The Vietnam War, the AIDS Epidemic, and the Politics of Remembering* (Berkeley: University of California Press, 1997), 3.

104. Ibid., 2.

105. Friedrich Nietzsche, *Untimely Meditations*, trans. R. J. Hollingdale (1874; repr., Cambridge: Cambridge University Press, 1997), 62, 63. The phrase reads in full: "the unhistorical and the historical are necessary in equal measure for the health of an individual, of a people and of a culture," but the context clearly is forgetting versus remembering.

106. Johannes Fabian, "Forgetful Remembering: A Colonial Life in the Congo," *Africa: Journal of the International African Institute* 73 (2003): 490.

107. "Disremembering 1798? An Archaeology of Social Forgetting and Remembrance in Ulster," *History and Memory* 25 (2013): 9.

108. Paul Ricoeur, *Memory, History, Forgetting* (Chicago: University of Chicago Press, 2004), 426. An insightful discussion of Ricoeur's thinking about cultural memory in comparison to that of Jan and Aleida Assmann is in Suzi Adams, "A Note on Ricoeur's Early Notion of Cultural Memory," *Études Ricoeuriennes/Ricoeur Studies* 10 (2019): 112–24.

109. "Conversation with Jan Assmann."

110. Aleida Assmann, "Memory, Individual and Collective," 220.

111. Ricoeur, *Memory, History, Forgetting*, 414; and Ricoeur, "Aux origines de la mémoire, l'oubli de réserve," *Esprit* 266–267 (2000): 32–47.

112. Charles B. Stone, Amanda J. Barnier, John Sutton, and William Hurst, "Building Consensus about the Past: Schema Consistency and Convergence in Socially Shared Retrieval-Induced Forgetting," *Memory* 18 (2010): 182.

113. Battaglia, "At Play in the Fields," 430; David Berliner, "The Abuses of Memory: Reflections on the Memory Boom in Anthropology," *Anthropological Quarterly* 78 (2005): 205.

114. Janet Carsten, "The Politics of Forgetting: Migration, Kinship, and Memory on the Periphery of the Southeast Asian State," *Journal of the Royal Anthropological Institute*, n.s., 1 (1995): 318.

115. Ibid., 331.

116. Battaglia, "At Play in the Fields," 440.

117. Erika Doss, *Memorial Mania: Public Feeling in America* (Chicago: University of Chicago Press, 2010), 143, 15.

118. Ananda Abeysekara, "Active Forgetting of History: The Impossibility of Justice," in *The Politics of Postsecular Religion: Mourning Secular Futures*, ed. Ananda Abeysekara (New York: Columbia University Press, 2008), 200.

119. A utilization of "memoryscape" in this way is in Hamsah Muzaini and Brenda S. A. Yeoh, "War Landscapes as 'Battlefields' of Collective Memories; Reading the *Reflections at Bukit Chandu*, Singapore," *Cultural Geographies* 12 (2005): 345.

120. Avishai Margalit, *The Ethics of Memory* (Cambridge, MA: Harvard University Press, 2002), 78. Benedict Anderson identifies a similarly ironic—or paradoxical—scene in discussing French memory of St. Barthelemy massacres (*Imagined Communities: Reflections on the Origin and Spread of Nationalism* [London: Verso, 2008], 203–5).

121. Margalit, *The Ethics of Memory*, 56.

122. Jan Assmann, *Religion and Cultural Memory: Ten Studies*, esp. 46–62.

123. Over 1,000 images are included on the panels. A website that includes images of panels is Mnemosyne: Meandering through Aby Warburg's *Atlas*, accessed July 19, 2021, https://warburg.library.cornell.edu/.

124. Susanne Küchler, "The Place of Memory," in *The Art of Forgetting*, ed. Adrian Forty and Susanne Küchler (Oxford: Berg, 1999), 54.

125. Ibid., 58.

126. Ibid., 59.

127. Ibid., 63.

128. Michel de Certeau, *The Practice of Everyday Life*, trans. S. Rendall (Berkeley: University of California Press, 1984), 87. Certeau writes: "Far from being the reliquary or trash can of the past, it sustains itself by *believing* in the existence of possibilities and by vigilantly awaiting them, constantly on the watch for their appearance" (87).

129. Howard Williams, "Remembering and Forgetting the Medieval Dead: Exploring Death, Memory, and Material Culture in Monastic Archaeology," in *Archaeologies of Remembrance: Death and Memory in Past Societies*, ed. Howard Williams (New York: Springer, 2003), 233.

130. Ibid., 232, 246.

131. Ibid., 246.

132. Barbara J. Mills, "Recent Research on Chaco: Changing Views on Economy, Ritual, and Society," *Journal of Archaeological Research* 10 (2002): 98.

133. Ibid., 85.

134. Buckley-Zistel, "Between Pragmatism, Coercion, and Fear," 74. Buckley-Zistel focuses on the manner in which such buried/unburied memories frustrate social transformation that potentially would undermine the practice of ethnic killings.

135. Dominick LaCapra, "Trauma, History, Memory, Identity; What Remains?," *History and Theory* 55 (2016): 391.

136. In addition to the material cited earlier in this chapter, see Brown and Reavey, "Memory in the Wild"; and Sophie Zadeh, "Remembering and Forgetting in the Wild: A Social Representations Perspective," in *Memory in the Wild*, ed. Brady Wagoner, Ignacio Brescó de Luna, and Sophie Zadeh (Charlotte: Information Age Publishing, 2020), 143–61, 7.

137. David Middleton and Derek Edwards, "Introduction," in *Collective Remembering*, ed. David Middleton and Derek Edwards (London: Sage Publications, 1990), 1. In the same volume see the chapters by Michael Schudson, "Ronald Reagan Misremembered" (chap. 6), and John Shotter, "The Social Construction of Remembering and Forgetting" (chap. 7).

138. Zadeh, "Remembering and Forgetting in the Wild," 151.

139. Brown and Reavey, "Memory in the Wild," 32.

140. Debbora Battaglia, "The Body in the Gift: Memory and Forgetting in Sabari Mortuary Exchange," *American Ethnologist* 19, no. 1 (1992): 12.

141. Battaglia, "At Play in the Fields," 430.

142. Douglas, "How Institutions Think," 71.

143. Ibid., 72.

144. Middleton and Edwards, "Introduction," 10.

145. Ibid., 112–13.

146. Mircea Eliade, *The Sacred and the Profane: The Nature of Religion*, trans. Willard R. Trask (New York: Harcourt, 1959), 101.

147. Hervieu-Léger, *Religion as a Chain of Memory*, 124.

148. Jonathan Smith, "Prologue: In Comparison a Magic Dwells," in *A Magic Still Dwells: Comparative Religion in the Postmodern Age*, ed. Kimberley C. Patton and Benjamin C. Ray (Berkeley: University of California Press, 2000), 24–25.

149. Jan Assmann's work, cited in several places in this book, addresses this. Some especially direct discussion of the theme is in his *Cultural Memory and Early Civilization: Writing, Remembrance, and Political Imagination*.

150. Machiavelli quoted in Cornel Zwierlein, "Forgotten Religions, Religions That Cause Forgetting," in *Forgetting Faith? Negotiating Confessional Conflict in Early Modern Europe*, ed. Isabel Karremann, Cornel Zwierlein, and Inga Mai Groot (Berlin: de Gruyter, 2012), 118.

151. Ibid., 119, 126.

152. Edward Gibbon, "The Destruction of Paganism and the Rise of the Cult of Saints," chap. 27 in *History of the Decline and Fall of The Roman Empire*, vol. 3, 1782 (written), 1845 (revised), https://sourcebooks.fordham.edu/source/gibbon-decline28.asp.

153. Robert W. Goodfellow, "Sing Wis, ya Wis: What Is Past Is Past: Forgetting What It Was to Remember the Indonesian Killings of 1965" (PhD dissertation, University of Wollongong, 2003), 97–99; and James Wilce, "Genres of Memory and the Memory of Genes: 'Forgetting' Lament in Bangladesh," *Comparative Studies in Society and History* 44 (2002): 175.

154. Wilce, "Genres of Memories," 175.

155. Sverrir Jakobsson, "Conversion and Cultural Memory in Medieval Iceland," *Church History* 88 (2019): 2.

156. Wilce, "Genres of Memory," 159.

157. See the discussion of "Devout Forgetting" in Galizia and Schulman, *Forgetting*, 141–88.

158. Gadi Sagiv, "Some Notes on Forgetting in Jewish Mysticism," in Galizia and Shulman, eds., 152–53.

159. Michael Ebstein, "The Mercy in Forgetting: A Short Reading in Ibn al-ʿArabī's *al-Futūḥāt al-Makkiyya* ('The Meccan Revelations')," in Galizia and Shulman, *Forgetting*, 149.

160. Timothy Longman and Théoneste Rutagengwa, "Religion, Memory, and Violence in Rwanda," in *Religion, Violence, Memory, and Place*, ed. Oren Baruch Stier and J. Shawn Landres (Bloomington: Indiana University Press, 2006), 132–49.

161. Björn Krondorfer, "Is Forgetting Reprehensible? Holocaust Remembrance and the Task of Oblivion," *Journal of Religious Ethics* 36 (2008): 234.

162. Anderson, *Imagined Communities*, 43.

163. Andrea G. Arai, "Notes to the Heart: New Lessons in National Sentiment and Sacrifice from Recessionary Japan," in *Global Futures in East Asia*, ed. Ann Anagnost, Andrea Arai, and Hai Ren (Stanford: Stanford University Press, 2013), 175.

164. Aleida Assmann, *Is Time Out of Joint?: The Rise and Fall of the Modern Time Regime*, trans. Sarah Clift (Ithaca: Cornell University Press, 2020), 81. Assmann proposes that the promise of the future is diminished in modernity, and that time accordingly is out of joint, which complicates both remembering and forgetting.

165. Augé, *Oblivion*, 57.

166. John Corrigan, *Emptiness: Feeling Christian in America* (Chicago: University of Chicago Press, 2015).

167. Ellen G. White, *God's Amazing Grace* (Hagerstown: Review and Herald Publishing Association, 1973), 230.

168. Corrigan, *Emptiness*, 91–98.

169. "The true fast . . . is the making of an emptiness about the soul that the higher fulness

may fill it" (nineteenth-century Episcopal clergyman Phillips Brooks, quoted in the *New York Observer*, April 20, 1911, 508).

170. Corrigan, *Emptiness*, 40–81.

171. John Calvin, *Institutes of the Christian Religion*, ed. John T. McNeill, trans. Ford Lewis Battles (Philadelphia: Westminster, 1977), 912. See the germane discussion of this in Bradford Vivian, *Public Forgetting: The Rhetoric and Politics of Beginning Again* (University Park: Pennsylvania State University Press, 2021), 1–60.

172. David Attwell, "Trauma Refracted: J. M. Coetzee's *Summertime*," in *Trauma, Memory, and Narrative in the Contemporary South African Novel*, ed. Ewald Mengel and Michela Borzaga (Amsterdam: Rodopi, 2012), 287.

173. Gabriele Schwab, "Haunting Legacies: Trauma in Children of Perpetrators," *Postcolonial Studies* 7 (2004): 181.

174. Aleida Assmann, "Ghosts of the Past," *East European Memory Studies* 8 (2011): 1–5.

175. *The Friend: A Religious and Literary Journal*, July 15, 1876, 383.

176. Washington Irving, "Traits of the Indian Character," *Analectic Magazine*, February 1, 1814, 148. I borrow the quotation (and add my own differing citation), from Renée Bergland, *The National Uncanny: Indian Ghosts and American Subjects* (Hanover: Dartmouth/University Press of New England, 2000), 2.

177. Daniel Dorchester, *Christianity in the United States* (New York: Hunt and Eason, 1890), 170.

178. "Reviews," *Journal of the Military Service Institution of the United States*, vol. 6 (New York: G. P. Putnam's Sons, 1885), 288.

179. Mary C. Greenleaf, *Life and Letters of Mary C. Greenleaf* (Boston: Massachusetts Sabbath School Society, 1858), 84.

180. Charles Colcock Jones, *Indian Remains in Southern Georgia* (Savannah: J. M. Cooper and Co., 1859), 18. Amy Kaplan writes of the U.S "process of securing the continental borders that now define it, through a series of 'forgotten' Indian wars." ("Nation, Religion, and Empire," in *The Columbia History of the American Novel*, ed. Emory Elliott [New York: Columbia University Press, 1991], 242).

181. Zuzanna Dziuban, "Memory as Haunting," *HAGAR Studies in Culture, Polities, and Identity* 12 (2014): 117.

182. Bergland, *The National Uncanny*, 9.

183. The secondary literature is extensive. The best starting point is ibid. Other studies that are germane to the discussion here are Lucy Maddox, *Removals: Nineteenth-Century Literature and the Politics of Indians Affairs* (New York: Oxford University Press, 1991); Jean O'Brien, *Firsting and Lasting: Writing Indians Out of Existence in New England* (Minneapolis: University of Minnesota Press, 2010); Andrew Newman, *On Records: Delaware Indians, Colonists, and the Media of History and Memory* (Lincoln: University of Nebraska Press, 2012); and Richard Slotkin, *Regeneration through Violence: The Mythology of the American Frontier, 1600–1860* (Norman: University of Oklahoma Press, 1973). For discussion of the overlap with white religion, see Molly McGarry, *Ghosts of Futures Past: Spiritualism and the Cultural Politics of Nineteenth-Century America* (Berkeley: University of California Press, 2008). A study of post-nineteenth-century American literature is in Kathleen Brogan, *Cultural Haunting: Ghosts and Ethnicity in Recent American Literature* (Charlottesville: University of Virginia Press, 1998).

184. "He Cursed the Town," *Morning Olympian*, May 17, 1901, 54; and "The Dismal Swamp Is Full of Legend," *Pawtucket Times*, January 30, 1920, 26.

185. Bergland, *The National Uncanny*, 19.

186. Philip J. Deloria, *Playing Indian* (New Haven: Yale University Press, 1998).

187. Carroll Smith-Rosenberg discusses this with respect to nineteenth-century New York City's Tammany Society in *This Violent Empire: The Birth of an American National Identity* (Chapel Hill: University of North Carolina Press, 2010), 194.

188. Shari M. Huhndorf, *Going Native: Indians in the American Cultural Imagination* (Ithaca: Cornell University Press, 2001).

189. "The wilderness masters the colonist. It finds him a European in dress, industries, tools, modes of travel, and thought. It takes him from the railroad car and puts him in the birch canoe. It strips off the garments of civilization and arrays him in the hunting shirt and moccasin. It puts him in the log cabin of the Cherokee and Iroquois and runs an Indian palisade around him" (Frederick Jackson Turner, *The Significance of the Frontier in American History* [1893], in *Rereading Frederick Jackson Turner: "The Significance of the Frontier in American History" and Other Essays*, ed. John Mach Faragher [New Haven: Yale University Press, 1996], 33).

190. Alan Trachtenberg, *Shades of Hiawatha: Staging Indians, Making Americans, 1880-1920* (New York: Hill and Wang, 2004), 115.

191. A helpful broader discussion of the staging of Indians is in Rosemarie K. Bank, "Staging the 'Native': Making History in American Theatre Culture, 1828-1838," *Theatre Journal* 45 (1993): 461-86.

192. Ibid.

193. For a discussion of the ghost as part of "the spectral turn" in literary scholarship that was prompted in part by Jacques Derrida's *Specters of Marx: The State of the Debt, the Work of Mourning & the New International*, trans. Peggy Kamuf (New York: Routledge, 1993), see María del Pilar Blanco and Esther Pereen, "The Spectral Turn," in *The Spectralities Reader: Ghosts and Haunting in Contemporary Cultural Theory*, ed. María del Pilar Blanco and Esther Pereen (London: Bloomsbury, 2013), 29-88.

194. Kathryn Troy, *The Specter of the Indian: Race, Gender, and Ghosts in American Séances, 1848-1890* (Albany: State University of New York Press, 2017), xxiii. The movement did not peak until the latter part of the century, but its rapid mid-century growth and geographical breadth are documented in David Nartonis, "The Rise of 19th-Century American Spiritualism, 1854-1873," *Journal for the Scientific Study of Religion*, 49 (2010): 361-73.

195. John Wetherbee, *"Shadows": Being a Familiar Presentation of Thoughts and Experiences in Spiritual Matters* (Boston: Colby and Rich, 1885), 197, 198.

196. "Mrs. Helen Palmer, Portland ME," *Facts*, vol. 1 (Boston: Facts Publishing Company, 1882), 258-62. Palmer reported that the girl ghost was present at the Cheyenne Massacre of 1866.

197. Emily Suzanne Clark has documented, for example, how a Black Spiritualist community received messages from an array of white American and European civic leaders, from Thomas Jefferson to Napoleon (*A Luminous Brotherhood: Afro-Creole Spiritualism in Nineteenth-Century New Orleans* [Chapel Hill: University of North Carolina Press, 2016]).

198. McGarry, *Ghosts of Futures Past*, 173, 72-73.

199. Feeling the presence of a spirit was a physical experience, sometimes no more than a chill or a buzzing in the head, or a quick breath, but it could be more than that, and usually was when during a séance: "He felt the presence of many persons. Innumerable hands stroked his head and face, patted his shoulders, and demonstrated their presence very powerfully, then suddenly were gone" ("L. L. Whitlock," *Facts*, vol. 1 [Boston: Facts Publishing Company, 1882], 440).

200. Wetherbee, "'Shadows,'" 109.

201. In addition to works already cited, see Ann Braude, *Radical Spirits: Spiritualism and Women's Rights in Nineteenth-Century America* (Boston: Beacon, 1989).

202. Bridget Bennett, *Transatlantic Spiritualism and Nineteenth-Century American Literature* (New York: Palgrave, 2007), 11. Bennett is discussing Bergland in this passage.

203. John J. Kucich, *Ghostly Communion: Cross-Cultural Spiritualism in Nineteenth-Century American Literature* (Hanover: Dartmouth College Press, 2015), xxxii.

204. Jeffrey Jerome Cohen, "Monster Culture: Seven Theses," in *Classic Readings in Monster Theory: Demonstrare*, vol. 1, ed. Asa Simon Mittman and Marcus Hensel (Leeds, UK: ARC, 2018), 44–54. He writes, "Fear of the monster is really a kind of desire" (52). See also the essays in Cohen, ed., *Monster Theory: Reading Culture* (Minneapolis: University of Minnesota Press, 1996).

205. Ciano Aydin, "How to Forget the Unforgettable? On Collective Trauma, Cultural Identity, and Mnemotechnologies," *Identity: An International Journal of Theory and Research* 17 (2017): 131.

Chapter Five

1. On the American penchant for converting and its occurrence across denominations, see Lincoln A. Mullen, *The Chance of Salvation: A History of Conversion in America* (Cambridge, MA: Harvard University Press, 2017).

2. Michelle Cox, "5 Bible Verses to Help You Let Go of Past Mistakes," *Guideposts*, accessed October 3, 2022, https://www.guideposts.org/bible-verses/bible-verses-about-strength/5-bible-verses-to-help-you-let-go-of-past-mistakes.

3. "How Do I Ask God for Forgiveness?," World Faith Harvest Fellowship Church, 2022, https://thrive.worldfaithharvest.org/.

4. "Forget the Past and God Will Bring Better Things," *Bibliatodo Tip of the Day*, December 4, 2021, https://www.bibliatodo.com/En/christian-pictures/forget-the-past-and-god-will-bring-better-things-en-con-2152/.

5. Matt James, "How to Forgive Yourself and Move on from the Past," *Psychology Today*, October 22, 2014, https://www.psychologytoday.com/us/blog/focus-forgiveness/201410/how-forgive-yourself-and-move-the-past.

6. Miroslav Volf, *The End Of Memory: Remembering Rightly in a Violent World* (Grand Rapids: Eerdmans, 2004).

7. T. Denise Anderson, "February 24, Epiphany 7C (Genesis 45:3–11, 15; Luke 6:27–38)," *Christian Century*, January 15, 2019, https://www.christiancentury.org/article/living-word/february-24-epiphany-7c-genesis-453-11-15-luke-627-38.

8. Bob Jackson, "Top 13 Bible Verses—Forget the Past," *Everyday Servant*, February 13, 2019, https://everydayservant.com/top-13-bible-verses-forget-the-past/.

9. Vanessa Sanders, "Forgetting the Past," Pinterest, accessed October 3, 2022, https://www.pinterest.com/vanessasanders9/forgetting-the-past/.

10. Synergy Designs, Travel mug with handle (Forget the past, Christian, Motivation), Spreadshirt, accessed October 3, 2022, https://www.spreadshirt.com/shop/design/forget+the+past+christian+motivation+travel+mug-D5c30290120517636a6d85cd4?sellable=Bqk3XJYbMlIDYRORX0wr-773-39.

11. J. B. Cachilla, "Forgetting the Past Requires This One Thing," *Christian Today*, December 11, 2016, https://www.christiantoday.com/article/forgetting-the-past-requires-this-one-thing/102860.htm.

12. Ibid.

13. Ibid.

14. Ann Steiner, "Four Steps to Putting the Past behind You," *Active Christianity*, accessed October 5, 2021, https://activechristianity.org/forget-the-past-12-bible-verses-about-moving-on..

15. Ibid.

16. Forget The Past Forgive Yourself Begin Again: Portable Christian Journal: 6"x9" Journal Notebook with Christian Quote: Inspirational Gifts for Religious Men & Women (Christian Journal), accessed October 3, 2022, https://www.goodreads.com/book/show/52134886-forget-the -past-forgive-yourself-begin-again.

17. Ronald C. Christie, "Philippians 3:13–14—Looking to the Future, Forgetting the Past," *Christian Library*, accessed October 4, https://www.christianstudylibrary.org/article/philippians -313-14-looking-future-forgetting-past. The article appears to have been published originally in the *Monthly Record* in 1992.

18. William Samuel Long, "Forgetting the One—Reaching after the Other," *Herald of Gospel Liberty*, April 11, 1918, 15.

19. "The Art of Forgetting," *Christian Index*, April 30, 1885, 6.

20. "Forgetting Oneself," *Reformed Church Messenger*, March 8, 1906, 4.

21. "The Open Door for Missions," *Watchman*, January 21, 1904, 12.

22. George L. Chaney, "Self-Culture, Self-Sacrifice, and Self-Forgetting," *Unitarian Review and Religious Magazine*, May 1877, 531, 542, 543.

23. "The Grace of Forgetting," *Zion's Herald*, February 12, 1890, 52.

24. "Forgetting Wrongs," *Christian Observer*, October 30, 1901, 2.

25. "The Home: The Freedom of Forgetting," *Christian Union*, April 18, 1889, 492.

26. "Tuesday Meeting at Dr. Palmer's, New York," *Christian Advocate*, September 21, 1876, 302. Belden's words are referenced in the article. Belden founded a church in Washingtonville, a short distance north of New York City.

27. "The Art of Forgetting," *Christian Observer*, December 28, 1910, 2.

28. "Forgetting," *Christian Advocate*, May 9, 1889, 299.

29. "On 'Forgetting Those Things Which Are Behind,'" *Adviser, or, Vermont Evangelical Magazine*, July 1810, 212.

30. Rev. Samuel T. Spears, "Sermon II: The Retributive Power of Memory," *National Preacher and Village Pulpit*, January 1861, 12–13.

31. "The Fountain of Oblivion," *Western Messenger Devoted to Religion, Life, and Literature*, December 1836, 309–10, 311. Emphasis mine.

32. "Freaks of Memory," *Christian Union*, May 17, 1888, 633.

33. "Forgetting the Things That Are Behind," *Christian Union*, December 26, 1889, 834.

34. Wayland Hoyt, "Things Good to Forget," *Christian Union*, March 29, 1883, 257.

35. "City Religious Press," *New York Evangelist*, January 15, 1863, 7. The article appears to be a partial reprint of material from the *Methodist*.

36. Jon Butler, *Awash in a Sea of Faith: Christianizing the American People* (Cambridge, MA: Harvard University Press, 1990), 129–63.

37. Deirdre M. Moloney, *American Catholic Lay Groups and Transatlantic Social Reform in the Progressive Era* (Chapel Hill: University of North Carolina Press, 2002), 207.

38. Vincent J. Cheng, *Amnesia and the Nation: History, Forgetting, and James Joyce* (London: Palgrave Macmillan, 2018), 93–95.

39. Robert J. Swan, "Prelude and Aftermath of the Doctors' Riot of 1788: A Religious Interpretation of White and Black Reaction to Grave Robbing," *New York History* 81 (2000): 419.

40. Cited in Joyce Hansen and Gary McGowan, *Breaking Ground, Breaking Silence: The Story of New York's African Burial Ground* (New York: Henry Holt, 1998), 33.

41. Marc Howard Ross, *Slavery in the North: Forgetting History and Recovering Memory* (Philadelphia: University of Pennsylvania Press, 2018), 170.

42. Ibid.

43. Kami Fletcher, "Founding Baltimore's Mount Auburn Cemetery and Its Importance to Understanding African American Burial Rites," in *Till Death Do Us Part: American Ethnic Cemeteries as Borders Uncrossed*, ed. Alan Amanik and Kami Fletcher (Jackson: University of Mississippi Press, 2020), 132.

44. Helen C. Blouet, "Spatial and Material Transformations in Commemoration on St. John, U.S. Virgin Islands," in *Materialities of Ritual in the Black Atlantic*, ed. Akinwumi Ogundiran and Paula Sanders (Bloomington: Indiana University Press, 2014), 289.

45. Robert K. Fitts, "The Landscapes of Northern Bondage," *Historical Archaeology* 30 (1996): 62.

46. Jubilee Marshall, "Race, Death, and Public Health in Early Philadelphia, 1750–1793," *Pennsylvania History: A Journal of Mid-Atlantic Studies* 87 (2020): 364–89.

47. Ira Berlin, *Many Thousands Gone: The First Two Centuries of Slavery in America* (Cambridge, MA: Harvard University Press, 1998), 62.

48. Vered Vinitzky-Seroussi and Chana Teeger, "Unpacking the Unspoken: Silence in Collective Memory and Forgetting," *Social Forces* 88 (2010): 1104.

49. Thomas P. Reilly and Office of the Attorney General, Commonwealth of Massachusetts, "The Sexual Abuse of Children in the Roman Catholic Archdiocese of Boston: A Report by the Attorney General," 2003, 73.

50. Marie Keenan, *Child Sexual Abuse and the Catholic Church: Gender, Power, and Organizational Culture* (New York: Oxford University Press, 2012), 142; and Mary Gail Frawley-O'Dea, *Perversion of Power: Sexual Abuse in the Catholic Church* (Nashville: Vanderbilt University Press, 2007), 121.

51. Donald B. Cozzens, *Sacred Silence: Denial and the Crisis in the Church* (Collegeville, MN: Liturgical Press, 2002).

52. Keenan, *Child Sexual Abuse and the Catholic Church*; Frawley-O'Dea, *Perversion of Power*; and Jason Berry and Gerald Renner, *Vows of Silence: The Abuse of Power in the Papacy of John Paul II* (New York: Free Press, 2004).

53. Hans Küng, "Hans Kung Open Letter to Catholic Bishops," *Independent Catholic News*, May 3, 2010, https://www.indcatholicnews.com/news/15996.

54. John Cornwell, *Hitler's Pope: The Secret History of Pius XII* (1999; repr., New York: Penguin, 2008). On similar behavior from his predecessor, Pius XI, see David I. Kertzer, *The Pope and Mussolini: The Secret History of Pius XI and the Rise of Fascism in Europe* (New York: Random House, 2015).

55. *Declaration on the Relation of the Church to Non-Christian Religions. Nostra Aetate. Proclaimed by His Holiness Pope Paul VI on October 28, 1965*, Article 3, https://www.vatican.va/archive/hist_councils/ii_vatican_council/documents/vat-ii_decl_19651028_nostra-aetate_en.html..

56. Avonia Jones-Blanca, *Daily Missouri Republican*, February 3, 1853; "Examinations," in *The Encyclopedia Britannica*, 9th ed., ed. T. S. Barnes (New York: Charles Scribner's Sons, 1878–1889);

"Knew He Had Forgotten Something," *Leader* (Washington, DC), May 18, 1889, 1; "A Fin Do Steele Mother," *Minneapolis Journal*, February 27, 1895, 4; "Mother, Leaving Car, Forgets 3-Year Old Baby," *Fort Worth Star-Telegram*, October 4, 1910, 1; "Breaking Down and Breaking Up," *Philadelphia Inquirer*, January 21, 1900, 7; *Daily Inter Ocean* (Chicago), June 16, 1881, 4.

57. Depending on the academic discipline in which the discussion is situated, the terms *metacognitive feeling, epistemic feeling*, and *noetic feeling* can appear to show aspects of detail that differentiate them in some ways. However, there is more similarity than difference, and the kinds of analytical parsing that a strictly philosophical or psychological treatise would endeavor are not germane to the current discussion.

58. Philosophers and psychologists sometimes also list the "feeling of not knowing" as a distinct, but related, epistemic feeling. I have found it more productive, in the context of this feature, to discuss the feeling of forgetting and to point to its similarity to the feeling of not knowing. In any case, the mental process is the same—both are epistemic emotions, "feelings about knowing."

59. Santiago Arango-Muñoz, "The Nature of Epistemic Feelings," *Philosophical Psychology* 27 (2014): 193–211; Arango-Muñoz, "Metacognitive Feelings, Self-Ascriptions, and Mental Actions," *Philosophical Inquiries* 2 (2014): 145–62; Arango-Muñoz, "Scaffolded Memory and Metacognitive Feelings," *Review of Philosophy and Psychology* 4 (2013): 135–52; Sven Bernecker, "Remembering without Knowing," in *Memory: A Philosophical Study* (New York: Oxford University Press, 2009), 65–103; Paul Connerton, "Seven Types of Forgetting," *Memory Studies* 1 (2008): 59–71; Jérôme Dokic and Jean-Rémy Martin, "Felt Reality and the Opacity of Perception," *Topoi* 36 (2017): 299–309; Michael E. Harkim, "Feeling and Thinking in Memory and Forgetting," *Ethnohistory* 50 (2003): 261–84; C. B. Martin, and Max Deutscher, "Remembering," *Philosophical Review* 75 (1966): 161–96; Anne Meylan, "Epistemic Emotions: A Natural Kind?," *Philosophical Inquiries* 2 (2014): 173–90; Eda Mizrak and Ilke Öztekin, "The Relationship between Emotion and Forgetting," *Emotion* 16 (2016): 33–42; B. Kenneth Payne and Elizabeth Corrigan, "Emotional Constraints on Intentional Forgetting," *Journal of Experimental Social Psychology* 43 (2007): 780–86; Ali I. Tekcan, and Melis Aktürk, "Are You Sure You Forgot? Feeling of Knowing in Directed Forgetting," *Journal of Experimental Psychology* 27 (2001): 1487–90; and Kourken Michaelian, Dorothea Debus, and Denis Perrin, eds., *New Directions in the Philosophy of Memory* (London: Routledge, 2018), "Part III: The Affective Dimension of Memory," 137–78.

60. I use the terms *feeling* and *emotion* mostly interchangeably here because I will be referring to a kind of feeling that straddles the categories of culture and body and I wish at various times to emphasize one or another of those features.

61. A partial list of epistemic feelings is in Kourken Michaelian and Santiago Arango-Muñoz, "Epistemic Feelings, Epistemic Emotions: Review and Introduction to the Focus Section," *Philosophical Inquiries* 2 (2014): 99–122. See also Ronald de Sousa, *Emotional Truth* (Oxford: Oxford University Press, 2011); and de Sousa, "Epistemic Feelings," in *Epistemology and Emotions*, ed. Georg Brun, Ulvi Doğuoğlu, and Dominique Kuenzle (Aldershot, UK: Ashgate, 2008), 185–204; Jérôme Dokic, "Seeds of Knowledge: Noetic Feelings and Metacognition," in *Foundations of Metacognition*, ed. Michael J. Beran, Johannes Brandl, Josef Perner, and Joelle Proust (Oxford: Oxford University Press, 2012), 302–20; Vered Halamish, Shannon McGillivray, and Alan D. Castel, "Monitoring One's Own Forgetting in Younger and Older Adults," *Psychology and Aging* 26 (2011): 631–35; William F. Brewer and Cristina Sampiano, "The Metamemory Approach to Confidence: A Test Using Semantic Memory," *Journal of Memory and Language* 67 (2012): 59–77; Asher Koriat, "The Feeling of Knowing: Some Metatheoretical Implications for Consciousness

and Control," *Consciousness and Cognition* 9 (2000): 149–71; Karen Jones, "Trust as an Affective Attitude," *Ethics* 107 (1996): 4–25; Bruce Mangan, "What Feeling Is the 'Feeling-of-Knowing?'" *Consciousness and Cognition* 9 (2000): 538–44; Adam Morton, "Epistemic Emotions," in *Oxford Handbook of Philosophy of Emotion*, ed. Peter Goldie (Oxford: Oxford University Press, 2010), 385–99; Lynne M. Reder, *Implicit Memory and Metacognition* (Mahwah: Erlbaum, 1996); Steven Ravett Brown, "Tip-of-the-Tongue States: An Introductory Phenomenological Analysis," *Consciousness and Cognition* 9 (2000): 516–37; and Israel Scheffler, *In Praise of the Cognitive Emotions and Other Essays in the Philosophy of Education* (New York: Routledge, 1991).

62. Santiago Arango-Muñoz, "Cognitive Phenomenology and Metacognitive Feelings," *Mind and Language* 34 (2019): 258.

63. Alexander Bain, *The Emotions and the Will* (London: John W. Parker and Sons, 1859), 199–200, 205.

64. Jesse J. Prinz, *Gut Reactions: A Perceptual Theory of Emotion* (Oxford: Oxford University Press, 2004), 14–17, 52–78, 163–64, 241–42.

65. Discussion of types of cues and heuristics that lead to metacognitive feelings is in Christopher A. Paynter, Lynne M. Reder, and Paul D. Kieffaber, "Knowing We Know Before We Know: ERP Correlates of Initial Feeling of Knowing," *Neuropsychologia* 47 (2009): 796–803; Valerie A. Thompson, Jamie A. Prowse Turner, and Gordon Pennycook, "Intuition, Reason, and Metacognition," *Cognitive Psychology* 63 (2011): 107–40; and Bruce W. A. Whittlesea and Lisa D. Williams, "The Source of Feelings of Familiarity: The Discrepancy-Attribution Hypothesis," *Journal of Experimental Psychology* 26 (2001): 547–65.

66. Arango-Muñoz, "Cognitive Phenomenology and Metacognitive Feelings," 248. "Metacognitive feelings serve as a conscious summary representation of a variety of unconscious processes" (Koriat, "The Feeling of Knowing," 163).

67. Arango-Muñoz, "The Nature of Epistemic Feelings," 194.

68. Ibid., 198–99.

69. Ibid.

70. William James, *Principles of Psychology*, vol. 1 (1890; repr., New York: Holt, 1910), 251. See also Clotide Calabi, "Tip-of-the Tongue Experiences: A Modest Proposal on Cognitive Phenomenology," *Phenomenology and Mind* 10 (2016): 86–93.

71. James, *Principles of Psychology*, 259. See also William James, "A World of Pure Experience," *Journal of Philosophy, Psychology, and Scientific Methods* 1 (1904): 533–43.

72. Koriat, "The Feeling of Knowing," 152–53.

73. Ibid., 163.

74. Pablo Fernández Velasco and Roberto Casati, "Subjective Disorientation as a Metacognitive Feeling," *Spatial Cognition and Computation* 4 (2020): 294.

75. Joëlle Proust, "Metacognition and Metarepresentation: Is a Self-Directed Theory of Mind a Precondition for Metacognition?," *Synthese* 159 (2007): 271–95; and Proust, *The Philosophy of Metacognition: Mental Agency and Self-Awareness* (Oxford: Oxford University Press, 2013), 39–78.

76. Jérôme Dokic, "Feelings of (Un)Certainty and Margins of Error," *Philosophical Inquiries* 2 (2014): 128.

77. Asher Koriat, "The Self-Consistency Model of Affective Confidence," *Psychological Review* 119 (2012): 82.

78. Asher Koriat, "The Feeling of Knowing: Some Metatheoretical Implications for Consciousness and Control," *Consciousness and Cognition* 9 (2000), 164.

79. Hakwan C. Lau and Richard E. Passingham, "Unconscious Activation of the Cognitive Control System in the Human Prefrontal Cortex," *Journal of Neuroscience* 27 (2007): 5805.

80. Arango-Muñoz, "The Nature of Epistemic Feelings," 198–99. He proposes also that some epistemic feelings can manifest as nonconceptual experiences. Because "feeling certain of something does not consist in having second-order thoughts about oneself . . . , or self-ascribing the concept of certainty," it stands that "a subject does not need to possess the concepts of CERTAINTY or UNCERTAINTY in order to undergo E-feelings such as feeling certain or uncertain about something" (197–98).

81. Ibid., 200.

82. Dokic, "Feelings of (Un)Certainty," 311.

83. Ibid.

84. Koriat, 159.

85. Dokic, "Feelings of (Un)Certainty," 207. The reference is to William James, *The Principles of Psychology* (New York: Holt, 1890), 686.

86. Jonathan M. Fawcett, Tracy L. Taylor, and Lynn Nadel, "Intentional Forgetting Diminishes Memory for Continuous Events," *Memory* 21 (2013): 693.

87. Hans J. Markowitsch, Alexander Thiel, Josef Kessler, Hans-Martin von Stockhausen, and Wolf-Dieter Heiss, "Ecphorizing Semi-Conscious Information via the Right Temporopolar Cortex—A PET Study," *Neurocase* 3 (1997): 448.

88. Valerie F. Reyna, "A New Intuitionism: Meaning, Memory, and Development in Fuzzy-Trace Theory," *Judgment and Decision Making* 7 (2012): 332–59.

89. Sara Dellantonio and Luigi Pastore, "How Can You Be Sure? Epistemic Feelings as a Monitoring System for Cognitive Contents," in *Model-Based Reasoning in Science and Technology*, ed. Ángel Nepomuceno-Fernández, Lorenzo Magnani, Francisco Salguero-Lamillar, Cristina Barés-Gómez, and Mattheiu Fontaine (New York: Springer, 2019), 420.

90. Valerie A. Thompson, "What Intuitions Are . . . and Are Not," *Psychology of Learning and Motivation* 60 (2014): 62.

91. Ibid., 54, 62, 57, 63, 60.

92. William James, *The Varieties of Religious Experience* (1902; repr., New York: Philosophical Library, 2015), 90.

93. Robert L. West and Brendan Conway-Smith, "Put Feeling into Cognitive Models: A Computational Theory of feeling," *Proceedings of the 17th International Conference of Cognitive Modelling*, 2019, 295, https://iccm-conference.neocities.org/2019/proceedings/ICCM2019Proceedings.pdf.

94. David B. Yaden, Khoa D. Le Nguyen, Margaret L. Kern, et al., "The Noetic Quality: A Multimethod Exploratory Study," *Psychology of Consciousness: Theory, Research, and Practice* 4 (2017): 54.

95. Janet Metcalfe, "Feelings and Judgments of Knowing: Is There a Special Noetic State?," *Consciousness and Cognition* 9 (2000): 184.

96. Marie Vanderkecrckhove and Jaak Panksepp, "A Neurocognitive Theory of Higher Mental Emergence: From Anoetic Affective Experiences to Noetic Knowledge and Autonoetic Awareness," *Neuroscience and Biobehavioral Reviews* 35 (2011): 2021, 2017.

97. Lisa Feldman Barrett, *How Emotions Are Made: The Secret Life of the Brain* (Boston: Houghton Mifflin Harcourt, 2017), 137.

98. Koriat, "The Self-Consistency Model of Affective Confidence," 163.

99. Peter N. Stearns, with Carol Z. Stearns, "Emotionology: Clarifying the History of Emotions and Emotional Standards," *American Historical Review* 90 (1985): 813–36.

100. Payne and Corrigan, "Emotional Constraints on Intentional Forgetting," 784.

101. Sigmund Freud, "The 'Uncanny,'" in *The Standard Edition of the Complete Psychological Works of Sigmund Freud, Volume XVII (1917–1919): An Infantile Neurosis and Other Works*, ed. James Strachey (London: Hogarth Press, 1953–74), 219.

102. Ibid., 220.

103. Ibid., 249.

104. Ibid., 241.

105. Timothy Beal, *Religion and Its Monsters* (New York: Routledge, 2002), 3.

106. Jan H. Blits, "Hobbesian Fear," *Political Theory* 17 (1989): 424; Noel Boulting, "An Architecture of Fear: The Relevance of Hobbes's Tripartite Contribution," *Distinktion: Journal of Social Theory* 12 (2011): 142; Chad Lavin, "Fear, Radical Democracy, and Ontological Methadone," *Polity* 38 (2006): 256; and Thomas Hobbes, *Leviathan*, ed. Richard Flathman and David Johnston (New York: W. W. Norton, 1997), chap. 12.

107. Fredrik Zvanaeus, "Freud's Philosophy of the Uncanny," *Scandinavian Psychoanalytic Review* 22 (1999): 243.

108. Cathy Caruth emphasized that the unknowable quality of trauma is present from the beginning of a person's experience of it, and it is that "unknown" that haunts a person: "Trauma is not locatable in the simple violent or original event in an individual's past, but rather in the way its unassimilated nature—the way it was precisely not known in the first instance—returns to haunt the survivor later on" (Cathy Caruth, *Unclaimed Experience: Trauma, Narrative, and History* [Baltimore: Johns Hopkins University Press, 1996], 4).

109. Anneleen Masschelein, *The Unconcept: The Freudian Uncanny in Late Twentieth Century Theory* (Albany: State University of New York Press, 2011), 4, 6, 16, 49, 70–71.

110. Yolanda Gampel, "Reflections on the Prevalence of the Uncanny in Social Violence," in *Cultures under Siege: Collective Violence and Trauma*, ed. Antonius C. G. M. Robben and Marcelo M. Suarez-Orozco (Cambridge: Cambridge University Press, 2000), 49, 50.

111. Ibid., 51.

112. Julia Kristeva, *Powers of Horror: An Essay on Abjection*, trans. Leon S. Roudiez (New York: Columbia University Press, 1982), 6.

113. Caruth, *Unclaimed Experience*, 3.

114. Santiago Arango-Muñoz and Kourken Michaelian, "Epistemic Feelings, Epistemic Emotions: Review and Introduction to the Focus Section," *Philosophical Inquiries* 2 (2014): 103, 104.

115. Freud initially, in writing about the unconscious in 1915, supposed that anxiety was the consequence of repression; that is, that repression of libidinal impulses produced anxiety. In 1926, in altering his positions on a number of theoretical points, he proposed that repression was the result, rather than the cause, of anxiety. The two differing articulations of the theory of the relation of anxiety to the unconscious have been debated by scholars since. For our purposes, it is not a crucial distinction because Freud continued to argue that repression was recognizable in anxiety. This book is more concerned with the fact of American forgetting and the anxiety associated with that rather than with establishing a priority of order. In fact, debate about that issue "merely circumvents the problem we are discussing," namely, the paradoxical relationship "of awareness and repression," the state of "having to know something in order not to know it" (J. R. Maze and R. M. Henry, "Problems in the Concept of Repression and Proposals for Their Resolution," in Rachael M. Henry, *Psychologies of Mind: The Collected Papers of John Maze* [London:

Bloomsbury, 2012], 223, 229). See also Freud, "The Unconscious," in *Standard Edition*, 14:159–215; and Freud, "Inhibitions, Symptoms, and Anxiety," in *Standard Edition*, 20:77–175.

116. Freud, "Anxiety and Instinctual Life," in *Standard Edition*, 22:95. This was one of the lectures Freud gave in the 1915–1917 series delivered at the Vienna Psychiatric Clinic.

117. Heidi Schlipphacke, "The Future of Melancholia: Freud, Fassbinder, and Anxiety after the War. President's Address," *Pacific Coast Philology* 52 (2017): 12.

118. P. S. Wong, "Anxiety, Signal Anxiety, and Unconscious Anticipation: Neuroscientific Evidence for an Unconscious Signal Function in Humans," *Journal of the American Psychoanalytic Association* 47 (1999): 817.

119. Michelle G. Kraske, "Phobic Fear and Panic Attacks: The Same Emotional States Triggered by Different Cues?," *Clinical Psychology Review* 5 (1991): 599.

120. Gordon D. Baumbacher, "Signal Anxiety and Panic Attacks," *Psychotherapy* 26 (1989): 75.

121. Nicole S. Smith, Brian J. Albanese, Norman B. Schmidt, and Daniel W. Capron, "Intolerance of Uncertainty and Responsibility for Harm Predict Nocturnal Panic Attacks," *Psychiatry Research* 273 (2019): 82–88.

122. Cristina M. Wood, José M. Salguero, Antonio Can-Vindel, and Sandro Galea, "Perievent Panic Attacks and Panic Disorder after Mass Trauma: A 12-Month Longitudinal Study," *Journal of Traumatic Stress* 26 (2013): 338–44. The importance of emotion in panic attacks (anxiety especially) alongside cognition is discussed in Matthew T. Tull, "Extending an Anxiety Sensitivity Model of Uncued Panic Attack Frequency and Symptom Severity: The Role of Emotion Dysregulation," *Cognitive Therapy and Research* 30 (2006): 177–84; and Tull, "Emotion Regulation Difficulties Associated with the Experience of Uncued Panic Attacks: Evidence of Experiential Avoidance, Emotional Nonacceptance, and Decreased Emotional Clarity," *Behavior Therapy* 38 (2007): 378–91.

123. Jacques Lacan, "Seminar I: Wednesday, November 14, 1962," in *The Seminar of Jacques Lacan. Book X. Anxiety. 1962–1963*, trans. Cormac Gallagher, in *Jacques Lacan in Ireland: Collected Translations and Papers by Cormac Gallagher*, 2, https://esource.dbs.ie/bitstream/han dle/10788/160/Book-10-Anxiety.pdf; and Gilbert Diatkine, "A Review of Lacan's Seminar on Anxiety," *International Journal of Psychoanalysis* 897 (2006): 1051.

124. Such a view is comparable to the philosophical position, mentioned previously, that noetic feelings—so important in religion—are experienced as pointers to what is "real."

125. Lisa Feldman Barrett, "Are Emotions Natural Kinds?," *Perspectives on Psychological Science* 1 (2006): 48.

126. Ibid.

127. Tor D. Wager and Lisa Feldman Barrett, "From Affect to Control: Functional Specialization of the Insula in Motivation and Regulation," *BioRxiv*, January 24, 2017, https://doi .org/10.1101/102368. See also, for a philosophical discussion, Andrea Scarantino, "Core Affect and Natural Affective Kinds," *Philosophy of Science* 76 (2009): 940–57. Scarantino writes: "I believe the case for unconscious emotions is strong" (943).

128. James A. Russell, "Core Affect and the Psychological Construction of Emotion," *Psychological Review* 110 (2003): 145.

129. Scarantino, "Core Affect and Natural Affective Kinds," 948.

130. Russell, "Core Affect," 155, 162.

131. Ibid., 149.

132. Lisa Feldman Barrett, "Ten Common Misconceptions about Psychological Construction Theories of Emotion," in *The Psychological Construction of Emotion*, ed. Lisa Feldman Barret and James A. Russell (New York: Guilford, 2015), 51.

133. Kristen A. Lindquist, Karen S. Quigley, Erika H. Siegel, and Lisa Feldman Barrett, "The Hundred-Year Emotion War: Are Emotions Natural Kinds or Psychological Constructions? Comment on Lench, Flores, and Bench," *Psychological Bulletin* 139 (2013): 259.

134. James A. Russell, "Psychological Construction of Episodes Called Emotions," *History of Psychology* 24 (2021): 119.

135. Ruth Leys has made the issue of intentionality the centerpiece of her criticism of psychological research about affect. As part of that, she criticizes James A. Russell for writing intentionality out of emotion. Russell has responded that Leys misunderstands his constructionist approach. See Leys, "The Trouble with Affect," *History of Psychology* 24 (2021): 126–29; Leys, "Critical Response II. Affect and Intention: A Reply to William E. Connolly," *Critical Inquiry* 37 (2022): 799–805; Leys, *The Ascent of Affect: Genealogy and Critique* (Chicago: University of Chicago Press, 2017), 366–68; and Russell, "Psychological Construction of Episodes Called Emotions," 119.

136. Lindquist et al., "The Hundred-Year Emotion War," 259.

137. For a more detailed diagram see Michelle Yik, James A. Russell, and James H. Steiger, "A 12-Point Circumplex Structure of Core Affect," *Emotion* 11 (2011): 722.

138. James A. Russell, "Emotion in Human Consciousness Is Built on Core Affect," *Journal of Consciousness Studies* 12 (2005): 34.

139. Jacob B. Hirsch, Raymond A. Mar, and Jordan B. Peterson, "Psychological Entropy: A Framework for Understanding Uncertainty-Related Anxiety," *Psychological Review* 119 (2012): 304.

140. Rajagopal Raghunathan and Michel Tuan Pham, "All Negative Moods Are Not Equal: Motivational Influences of Anxiety and Sadness on Decision Making," *Organizational Behavior and Human Decision Processes* 79 (1999): 56.

141. Yauanyuan Gu, Simeng Gu, and Hong Li, "From Uncertainty to Anxiety: How Uncertainty Fuels Anxiety in a Process Mediated by Intolerance of Uncertainty," *Neural Plasticity*, November 22, 2020, 1, https://doi.org/10.1155/2020/8866383.

142. Ibid., 2.

143. Donna Britt, "A Stolen BLM Banner, Its White Defender, and Giving Thanks," *Washington Post*, November 25, 2021, in "Social Issues. Perspective" section, https://www.washingtonpost.com/dc-md-va/2021/11/25/blm-banner-saved-by-white-man/.

144. William M. Reddy, "The Unavoidable Intentionality of Affect: The History of Emotions and the Neurosciences of the Present Day," *Emotion Review* 12 (2020): 173.

145. "Psychologists read and cite mainly other psychologists. Future generations of emotional researchers must integrate work across disciplines. It is a scandal that we work in isolated disciplinary silos" (Russell, "Psychological Construction of Episodes Called Emotions," 118).

146. Michael A. Hogg, Janice R. Adelman, and Robert D. Blagg, "Religion in the Face of Uncertainty: An Uncertainty Identity Theory Account of Religiousness," *Personality and Social Psychology Review* 14 (2010): 72–83.

147. Ian McGregor, Mark P. Zanna, John G. Holmes, and Steven J. Spencer, "Compensatory Conviction in the Face of Uncertainty: Going to Extremes and Being Oneself," *Journal of Personality and Social Psychology* 80 (2001): 479.

148. Michael A. Hogg, "Uncertainty-Identity Theory," *Advances in Experimental Social Psychology* 39 (2007): 77.

149. Kees van den Bos, Jitse van Ameijde, and Hein van Gorp, "On the Psychology of Religion: The Role of Personal Uncertainty in Religious Worldview Defense," *Basic and Applied Social Psychology* 28 (2006): 333–41.

150. McGregor et al., "Compensatory Conviction," 485.

151. Timothy Williams, "The Complexity of Evil: A Multi-Faceted Approach to Genocide Perpetration," *Zeitschrift für Friedens- und Konfliktforschung* 3 (2014): 84. Williams stresses uncertainty, over hate and ideology, as the correct starting point in understanding motivation.

152. Michael J. A. Wohl, Nassim Tabri, and Eran Halperin, "Emotional Sources of Intergroup Atrocities," in *Confronting Humanity at Its Worst: Social Psychological Perspectives on Genocide*, ed. Leonard S. Newman (Oxford: Oxford University Press, 2020), 92.

153. Laura Stoler, *Along the Archival Grain: Epistemic Anxieties and Colonial Common Sense* (Princeton: Princeton University Press, 2008), 1-2. Stoler writes that "disquiet and anxieties registered the uncommon sense of events and things; epistemic uncertainties repeatedly unsettled the imperial conceit that all was in order" (1-2).

154. Michael A. Hogg, "Self-Uncertainty, Social Identity, and the Solace of Extremism," in *The Claremont Symposium on Applied Social Psychology: Extremism and the Psychology of Uncertainty*, ed. Michael A. Hogg and D. L. Blaylock (Oxford: Wiley-Blackwell, 2012), 19. See also Michael A. Hogg and Danielle L. Blaylock, "Preface: From Uncertainty to Extremism," in *Extremism and the Psychology of Uncertainty*, ed. Michael A. Hogg and Danielle L. Blaylock (Oxford: Wiley-Blackwell, 2012), xxvff.

155. Aaron L. Wichman, "Uncertainty and Religious Reactivity: Uncertainty Compensation, Repair, and Innoculation," *European Journal of Social Psychology* 40 (2010): 35-42; Mathew D. Francis and Kim Knott, "How Do Religious and Other Ideological Minorities Respond to Uncertainties?," in *Minority Religions and Uncertainty*, ed. Matthew D. Francis and Kim Knott (London: Routledge, 2020), 1-21; Hogg, "Self-Uncertainty, Social Identity, and the Solace of Extremism"; and Hogg, Adelman, and Blagg, "Religion in the Face of Uncertainty."

156. Robert Gellately, "The Third Reich, the Holocaust, and Visions of Serial Genocide," in *The Specter of Genocide: Mass Murder in Historical Perspective*, ed. Robert Gellately (New York: Cambridge University Press, 2003), 241-64.

157. Gregory H. Stanton, "The Ten Stages of Genocide," *Genocide Watch*, 2013, n.p., http://legacy.wss.sd73.bc.ca/pluginfile.php/17146/mod_resource/content/1/The-Ten-Stages-of-Genocide-handout.pdf.

158. Laurence Miller, "Serial Killers: II. Development, Dynamics, and Forensics," *Aggression and Violent Behavior* 19 (2014): 12-22.

159. When social scientists and historians discuss the roles of hatred and fear, they refer to hatred and fear of other social groups. On hatred, see James L. Gibson, Christopher Classen, and Joan Barceló, "Is Hatred the Main Emotional Source of Political Intolerance?," May 5, 2017, https://ssrn.com/abstract=2981528.

160. Jerold Lee Shapiro, "We Hate What We Fear: Interpersonal Hate from a Clinical Perspective," in *The Psychology of Love and Hate in Intimate Relationships*, ed. Katherine Aumer (New York: Springer, 2016), 156.

161. See the discussion of relatively low levels of hate in the Rwandan genocide in Andrew A. G. Ross, *Mixed Emotions: Beyond Hate and Fear in International Conflict* (Chicago: University of Chicago Press, 2014), chap. 4, "Emotions and Ethnic Conflict," 93-122. For a discussion of fear as mediated by hatred in political intolerance, see Eran Halperin, Daphna Canetti-Nisim, and Sivan Hirsch-Hoefler, "The Central Role of Group-Based Hatred as an Emotional Antecedent of Political Intolerance: Evidence from Israel," *Political Psychology* 30 (2009): 93-123. On hatred as a distinct emotion, see Halperin, "Hatred in Intractable Conflict in Israel," *Journal of Conflict Resolution* 52 (2008): 713-36.

162. For Barrett and other emotional constructionists, the "construction processes are not unique to emotions (or to visual illusions): the processes are at play in memories" ("Ten Common Misconceptions," 51).

163. Shapiro, "We Hate What We Fear," 158. I have, with regard to this statement, extrapolated from a discussion of interpersonal relationships to group interrelationships.

164. When social scientists and historians discuss the roles of hatred and fear, they refer to hatred and fear of other social groups. On hatred, see Gibson, Classen, and Barceló, "Is Hatred the Main Emotional Source of Political Intolerance?."

165. Daniel Bar-Tal, "Why Does Fear Override Hope in Societies Engulfed by Intractable Conflict, as It Does in Israeli Society?," *Political Psychology* 22 (2001): 608.

166. Hutchison summarizes her thinking about this in the Preface to *Affective Communities in World Politics: Collective Emotions after Trauma* (New York: Cambridge University Press, 2016), xi–xiii.

167. Ross, *Mixed Emotions*, 18.

168. Catherine Lutz, *Unnatural Emotions: Everyday Sentiments on a Micronesian Atoll and Their Challenge to Western Theory* (Chicago: University of Chicago Press, 1988), 115.

169. Ross, *Mixed Emotions*, title.

170. Todd H. Hall and Andrew A. G. Ross, "Rethinking Affective Experience and Popular Emotion: World War I and the Construction of Group Emotion in International Relations," *Political Psychology* 40 (2019): 1359.

171. Ross criticizes the expression as a stereotype in *Mixed Emotions*, 154.

172. The usefulness of the term in certain instances can be seen in Jobb Arnold, "A Psychological Investigation of Individual and Social Transformations in Post-Genocide Rwanda," in *Confronting Genocide*, ed. René Provost and Payam Akhavan (New York: Springer, 2011), 305–17; Pritam Singh, "The Political Economy of the Cycles of Violence and Non-Violence in the Sikh Struggle for Identity and Political Power: Implications for Indian Federalism," *Third World Quarterly* 28 (2007): 555–70; and Ervin Staub, "The Origins and Prevention of Genocide, Mass Killing, and Other Collective Violence," *Peace and Conflict: Journal of Peace Psychology* 5 (1999): 303–36. "Genocide proceeds in a downward cycle of killings until, like a whirlpool, it reaches the vortex of mass murder. Killings by one group may provoke revenge killings by the other" (Gregory H. Stanton, "The Seven Stages of Genocide," Working Paper GS01, Yale Center for International and Area Studies Working Paper Series, 1998, 4).

173. Jeffrey Prager, "Danger and Deformation: A Social Theory of Trauma Part II: Disrupting the Intergenerational Transmission of Trauma, Recovering Humanity, and Repairing Generations," *American Imago* 72 (2015): 151, 153.

174. Jan T. Gross, *Fear: Anti-Semitism in Poland after Auschwitz: An Essay in Historical Interpretation* (New York: Random House, 2007).

175. See, for example, the discussion of soldiers' behavior in Nick Turse, "Kill Anything That Moves: U.S., War Crimes, and Atrocities in Vietnam, 1965–1973" (PhD dissertation, Columbia University, 2005); and Michael Sallah and Mitch Weiss, *Tiger Force: A True Story of Men and War* (New York: Little, Brown, 2006). Lifton (*Home from the War: Vietnam Veterans: Neither Victims nor Executioners* [London: Wildwood House, 1974]), in an interpretation that some scholars subsequently have adopted, theorized that killing intensifies a specific fear, the fear of death, in the killer and that the killer is driven to further killing in an attempt to manage that fear. A perceived similarity to the victim is thought to advance that process.

176. Stanley Milgram, *Obedience to Authority: An Experimental View* (London: Tavistock, 1974).

177. Andy Martens, Spee Kosloff, Jeff Greenberg, Mark J. Landau, and Tomi Schmader, "Killing Begets Killing: Evidence from a Bug-Killing Paradigm That Initial Killing Fuels Subsequent Killing," *Personality and Social Psychology Bulletin* 33 (2007): 1262.

178. Ibid., 1252.

179. Scholars address the topic in different ways. See Barbara Harff, "A German-Born Genocide Scholar," in *Pioneers of Genocide Studies*, ed. S. Totten and S. L. Jacobs (New Brunswick: Transaction Publishers, 2002), 97–112; Lifton, *Home from the War*; Neil Kressel, *Mass Hate: The Global Rise of Genocide and Terror* (New York: Plenum, 1996); Ervin Staub, "The Psychology of Bystanders, Perpetrators, and Heroic Helpers," in *Understanding Genocide: The Social Psychology of the Holocaust*, ed. L. S. Newman and R. Erber (New York: Oxford University Press, 2002), 11–42; Jeffrey Goldstein, Roger Davis, and Dennis Herman, "Escalation of Aggression: Experimental Studies," *Journal of Personality and Social Psychology* 31 (1975): 167–70; and Israel W. Charny, "Leo Kuper: A Giant Pioneer," in Totten and Jacobs, *Pioneers of Genocide Studies*, 267–94.

180. Martens et al., "Killing Begets Killing," 1251.

181. Shapiro, "We Hate What We Fear," 160.

182. Ibid., 158. Hate "arises from an unconscious defense against facing the anxiety" caused by a neurosis, and in so doing it keeps the object of hatred close because that is the way to avoid coming to terms with the pain of anxiety (60).

183. Willard Gaylin, *Hatred: The Psychological Descent into Violence* (New York: Public Affairs, 2003), 26. Perpetrator attachment to victims might be characterized emotionally as a kind of Stockholm Syndrome, but with the attachment taking place from a position of power.

184. Jenny Adkins, *Trauma and the Memory of Politics* (Cambridge: Cambridge University Press, 2003), xv.

185. Neta C. Crawford, "Human Nature and World Politics: Rethinking 'Man,'" *International Relations* 23 (2009): 278.

186. Christopher L. Schilling, *Emotional State Theory: Friendship and Fear in Israeli Foreign Policy* (Lanham: Lexington Books, 2015), xviii.

Chapter Six

1. The state enforces amnesia about such things. In late 2021, North Dakota, like many other states, passed a law forbidding schools to teach "that racism is systematically imbedded in American society and the American legal system" (North Dakota, House Bill 1508, signed by Gov. Doug Burgum on November 15, 2021).

2. Poll data and focus groups in the year following the insurrection universally evidenced an eagerness to forget (Patrick Healy and Adrian J. Rivera, "Why Republican Voters Think Americans Have to Get Over Jan. 6," *New York Times*, January 7, 2022, https://www.nytimes.com/2022/01/07/opinion/republicans-focus-group.html).

3. Quotes are from Liz Goodwin, "What Capitol Attack? Amnesia Sets in among Republicans in Washington," *Boston Globe*, January 20, 2021.

4. Ann Steiner, "Four Steps to Putting the Past behind You," *Active Christianity*, accessed October 5, 2021, https://activechristianity.org/forget-the-past-12-bible-verses-about-moving-on.

5. J. B. Cachilla, "Forgetting the Past Requires This One Thing," *Christian Today*, December 11, 2016, https://www.christiantoday.com/article/forgetting-the-past-requires-this-one-thing/102860.htm.

6. Ralph Ellison, "Blues People," in *The Collected Essays of Ralph Ellison*, ed. John F. Callahan (New York: Modern Library, 2003), 280.

7. Toni Morrison, "Living Memory: A Meeting with Toni Morrison," in *Small Acts: Thoughts on the Politics of Black Culture*, ed. Paul Gilroy (London: Serpent's Tail, 1993), 179.

8. James Baldwin, "Many Thousands Gone," in *Notes of a Native Son* (Boston: Beacon, 1955), 29.

9. Richard Wright, *12 Million Black Voices* (1941; repr., New York: Thunder's Mouth Press, 1992), 146.

10. W. James Booth, "The Work of Memory: Time, Identity, and Justice," *Social Research: An International Quarterly* 75 (2008): 250.

11. Walter Ben Michaels, "'You Who Was Never There': Slavery and the New Historicism, Deconstruction, and the Holocaust," *Narrative* 4 (1996): 5.

12. Kate Riga, "McCarthy Comes Out against Bipartisan January 6 Commission Proposal," *Talking Points Memo*, May 18, 2021, https://talkingpointsmemo.com/news/mccarthy-january-6 -capitol-proposal.

13. David L. Eng and Shinhee Han, "A Dialogue on Racial Melancholia," in *Asian American Studies Now: A Critical Reader*, ed. Jean Yu-Wen Shen Yu and Thomas Chen (New Brunswick: Rutgers University Press, 2010), 55–79.

14. Vine Deloria Jr., "Indian Affairs: Hebrews 13:8," in *Eating Fire, Tasting Blood: An Anthology of the American Indian Holocaust*, ed. MariJo Moore (New York: Thunder's Mouth Press, 2006), 62.

15. Anne Anlin Cheng, *The Melancholy of Race* (New York: Oxford University Press, 2000), xi.

16. Ewald Mengel and Michela Borzaga, "Introduction," in *Trauma, Memory, and Narrative in the Contemporary South African Novel: Essays*, ed. Edwald Mengel and Michela Borzaga (Amsterdam: Rodopi, 2012), xi.

17. Frantz Fanon, *Black Skin, White Masks*, trans. Charles Lam Markmann (London: Pluto Press, 1986); Achille Mbembe, *On the Postcolony* (Berkeley: University of California Press, 2001); and Sara Nuttall, *Entanglement: Literary and Cultural Reflections on Post-Apartheid* (Johannesburg: Wits University Press, 2009).

18. David Atwell, "Trauma Refracted: J. M. Coetzee's *Summertime*," in Mengel and Borzaga, *Trauma, Memory, and Narrative in the Contemporary South African Novel*, 286.

19. Sigmund Freud, "Mourning and Melancholia" (1917), in *Standard Edition of the Complete Psychological Works of Sigmund Freud*, vol. 14, ed. and trans. James Strachey (London: Hogarth Press, 1953), 243; and Freud, "The Ego and the Id" (1923), in *Standard Edition of the Complete Psychological Works of Sigmund Freud*, vol. 19 (1923–25), 3–66.

20. Judith Butler's initial framing of her theory, but not her only discussion of it, is in *The Psychic Life of Power: Theories in Subjection* (Stanford: Stanford University Press, 1997).

21. Eng and Han, "A Dialogue on Racial Melancholia"; Anne Anlin Cheng, *The Melancholy of Race*.

22. An overview of some of the ideas involved in African American experience of melancholy is in Margo Natalie Crawford, "The Twenty-First Century Black Studies Turn to Melancholy," *American Literary History* 29 (2017): 799–807. I draw here especially on the literary interpretations of Jermain Singleton, *Cultural Melancholy: Readings of Race, Impossible Mourning, and African American Ritual* (Urbana: University of Illinois Press, 2015); and Joseph R. Winters, *Hope Draped in Black: Race, Melancholy, and the Agony of Process* (Durham: Duke University Press, 2016).

23. A study joining psychoanalytic and neuroscientific insights (re the subgenual cingulate and amygdala) on this point is Robin L. Carhart-Harris, Helen S. Mayberg, Andrea L. Malizia, and David Nutt, "Mourning and Melancholy Revisited: Correspondences between Principles of Freudian Metapsychology and Empirical Findings in Neuropsychiatry," *Annals of General Psychiatry* 7 (2008): special section, 1–23.

24. Julia Kristeva, *Black Sun: Depression and Melancholia*, trans. Leon S. Roudiez (New York: Columbia University Press, 1989), 12.

25. Singleton, *Cultural Melancholy*, 57.

26. That insight, as it recently has been applied by literary scholars, originated with Butler.

27. Greg Forter, "Against Melancholia: Contemporary Mourning Theory, Fitzgerald's *The Great Gatsby*, and the Politics of Unfinished Grief," *differences: A Journal of Feminist Cultural Studies* 14 (2003): 140.

28. Ibid., 137.

29. This is one of the central arguments in the writing of Singleton and Winters.

30. Winters, *Hope Draped in Black*, 21.

31. Eva Tettenborn, "Melancholia as Resistance in Contemporary African American Literature," *MELUS* 31 (2006): 107.

32. Crawford, "The Twentieth-Century Black Studies Turn to Melancholy," 801.

33. Singleton, *Cultural Melancholy*, 56.

34. Tammy Clewell, "Mourning beyond Melancholia: Freud's Psychoanalysis of Loss," *Journal of the American Psychoanalytic Association* 52 (2004): 59.

35. Winters, *Hope Draped in Black*, 243.

36. Judith Butler, interview with David W. McIvor, "Bringing Ourselves to Grief: Judith Butler and the Politics of Mourning," *Political Theory* 40 (2012): 411.

37. Singleton, *Cultural Melancholy*, 2–3.

38. Singleton, *Cultural Melancholy*, 13; Crawford, "The Twentieth-Century Black Studies Turn to Melancholy," 802.

39. Ranjana Khanna, *Dark Continents: Psychoanalysis and Colonialism* (Durham: Duke University Press, 2003), 25. On Africa, see also Meg Samuelson, "Melancholic States: Statist Mourning and the Politics of Memory in Post-Conflict Fiction from Southern Africa," *Journal of Social Studies* 115 (2007): 43–67.

40. Singleton, *Cultural Melancholy*, 10. Singleton's doctoral dissertation, on which his book is based, foregrounded this aspect of African American experience, emphasizing the transmission of melancholy through ritual practice (Singleton, "Cryptic Conversations: Melancholy, Ritual, and the [African American] Literary Imagination" [PhD dissertation, University of Minnesota, 2005]).

41. Singleton, *Cultural Melancholy*, 10.

42. Amadi Ozier, "This Body Still Has Time: Jermaine Singleton's Cultural Melancholy: Readings of Race, Impossible Mourning, and African American Ritual," *Social Text*, August 31, 2017, https://socialtextjournal.org/this-body-still-has-time-jermaine-singletons-cultural-melancholy-readings-of-race-impossible-mourning-and-african-american-ritual/.

43. Clewell, "Mourning beyond Melancholia."

44. Kristeva, *Black Sun*, 11; Eugene D. Genovese, *Roll, Jordan, Roll: The World the Slaves Made* (New York: Vintage Books, 1976), 3.

45. Freud, "Mourning and Melancholia," 243.

46. Eng and Han, "A Dialogue on Racial Melancholia," 59.

47. Cheng, "The Melancholy of Race," *Kenyon Review*, n.s., 19 (1997): 51.

48. Cheng, *The Melancholy of Race*, 10.

49. Gillian Straker, "Race for Cover: Castrated Whiteness, Perverse Consequences," *Psycho-analytic Dialogues* 14 (2004): 405–22. See also Danyela Demir, "Melancholia of the Privileged: White Trauma, Refused Identification, and Signs of Mourning in Sarah Penny's *The Beneficiaries*," *Wasafiri* 34 (2019): 9–15.

50. Melanie Suchet, "Unraveling Whiteness," *Psychoanalytic Dialogues* 17, no. 6 (2007): 874.

51. Delia Caparoso Konzett, *Ethnic Modernisms: Anzia Yezierska, Zora Neale Hurston, Jean Rhys, and the Aesthetics of Dislocation* (New York: Palgrave, 2002), 80.

52. Kenneth Alan Adams, "Psychohistory and Slavery: Preliminary Issues," *Journal of Psychohistory* 43 (2015): 112, 111.

53. Jacqueline Dowd Hall, " 'You Must Remember This': Autobiography as Social Critique," *Journal of American History* 85 (1998): 442. An essay by descendants of slaveholders treating their experience of repressing the trauma of slaveholding is in David Pettee and Susan Hutchinson, "Ghosts of the Masters: Descendants of Slaveholders Reckon with History," accessed July 7, 2021, https://comingtothetable.org/wp-content/uploads/2019/08/Ghosts-of-the-Masters.pdf.

54. Veronica T. Watson and Becky Thompson, "Theorizing White Racial Trauma and Its Remedies," in *Unveiling Whiteness in the Twenty-First Century: Global Manifestations, Transdisciplinary Interventions*, ed. Veronica Watson, Deirdre Howard-Wagner, and Lisa Spanierman (New York: Lexington Books, 2014), 247.

55. Ibid., 249.

56. Jenn Williamson, "Traumatic Recurrences in White Southern Literature: O'Connor's 'Everything That Rises Must Converge' and Welty's 'Clytie,' " *Women's Studies* 38 (2009): 747.

57. Watson and Thompson, "Theorizing White Racial Trauma and Its Remedies," 248.

58. Ron Eyerman, *Cultural Trauma: Slavery and the Formation of African American Identity* (New York: Cambridge University Press, 2001), 1.

59. Dominick LaCapra, "Trauma, History, Memory, Identity; What Remains?," *History and Theory* 55 (2016): 391.

60. Bill Nichols, "Waltzing with Bashir: Perpetrator Trauma and Cinema," *Studies in Documentary Film* 8 (2014): 83, 84. The context is contemporary Israel.

61. Beschara Karam, "The Representation of Perpetrator Trauma in *Forgiveness*," *Communicatio* 45 (2019): 74. The context of Karam's phrasing of this idea is that of an African scholar referencing Raya Morag's *Waltzing with Bashir: Perpetrator Trauma and Cinema* (New York: Palgrave, 2012), a closely argued critical overview of the trauma of the perpetrator set in a discussion of media and the repressed guilt of Israeli soldiers.

62. Robert Gellately, "The Third Reich, the Holocaust, and Visions of Serial Genocide," in *The Specter of Genocide: Mass Murder in Historical Perspective*, ed. Robert Gellately (New York: Cambridge University Press, 2003), 241–64.

63. Andrew Ross, who opposes the use of the term *hatred* in this context, criticizes the expression as a stereotype in *Mixed Emotions: Beyond Fear and Hatred in International Conflict* (Chicago: University of Chicago Press, 2014), 154.

64. See 217n172 on the usefulness of the term.

65. Jeffrey Prager, "Danger and Deformation: A Social Theory of Trauma Part II: Disrupting the Intergenerational Transmission of Trauma, Recovering Humanity, and Repairing Generations," *American Imago* 72 (2015): 151, 153.

66. Amy Louise Wood, *Lynching and Spectacle: Witnessing Racial Violence in America* (Chapel Hill: University of North Carolina Press, 2009), 44, 47, 24; and Donald G. Mathews, *At the Altar of Lynching: Burning Sam Hose in the American South* (New York: Cambridge University Press, 2018).

67. Singleton, *Cultural Melancholy*, 121.

68. John Corrigan, *Emptiness: Feeling Christian in America* (Chicago: University of Chicago Press, 2015).

69. There is a growing scholarly literature on this, which began to claim a place in the discussion of American religious history in the 1960s and has been advanced by numerous recent studies, bookended by Randall Balmer, *Thy Kingdom Come: How the Religious Right Distorts Faith and Threatens America: An Evangelical's Lament* (New York: Basic Books, 2006); and Anthea Butler, *White Evangelical Racism: The Politics of Morality in America* (Chapel Hill: University of North Carolina Press, 2021). The popular press in the United States has begun to write pointedly about it; for example, Carey Wallace, "White American Christianity Needs to Be Honest about Its White Supremacy," *Time*, January 14, 2021, https://time.com/5929478/christianity-white-supremacy/.

70. Butler, *White Evangelical Racism*, 2.

71. Robert H. Wiebe, *The Search for Order 1877–1920* (New York: Hill and Wang, 1967), 113.

72. Benjamin Tompson, *New England's Crisis* (Boston: John Foster, 1676).

73. In addition to the several interpretations I discuss here, see the discussion of immigration and nationalistic Republicanism in Susan-Mary Grant, "When Is a Nation Not a Nation? The Crisis of American Nationality in the Mid-Nineteenth Century," *Nations and Nationalism* 2 (1996): 105–29.

74. Renée Bergland, *The National Uncanny: Indian Ghosts and American Subjects* (Hanover: Dartmouth/University Press of New England, 2000), 2 5.

75. Ibid., 22, 14.

76. Alan Trachtenberg triangulates between immigration, Indians, and identity in analyzing the literary and material culture of the period (*Shades of Hiawatha: Staging Indians, Making Americans, 1880–1930* [New York: Hill and Wang, 2004]).

77. Sarah Rivett, "The Spectral Indian Presence in Early American Literature," *American Literary History* 25 (2013): 626.

78. Michael A. Hogg, "Self-Uncertainty, Social Identity, and the Solace of Extremism," in *The Claremont Symposium on Applied Social Psychology: Extremism and the Psychology of Uncertainty*, ed. Michael A. Hogg and Danielle L. Blaylock (Oxford: Wiley-Blackwell, 2012), 19.

79. Carroll Smith-Rosenberg, *This Violent Empire: The Birth of an American National Identity* (Chapel Hill: University of North Carolina Press, 2010).

80. Ibid., 467, x, 466, 302–5.

81. Ibid., 205.

82. Robert Hale, Commonplace Book, Harvard University Archives, Cambridge, MA, 1720.

83. M. F. Thalheimer, *The Eclectic History of the United States* (Cincinnati: Van Antwerp Bragg and Co, 1881), v, 22.

84. John Moses, *Illinois, Historical and Statistical* (Chicago: Fergus Printing Company, 1889), 35.

85. Daniel Dorchester, *Christianity in the United States* (New York: Hunt and Eason, 1890), 26.

86. George Turner, *Traits of the Indian Character* (Philadelphia: Key and Biddle, 1836), 18.

87. George D. B. Pepper, "Address at the Annual Meeting of the Maine Branch of the Women's National Indian Association: Portland, Maine, January 24, 1887," Books and Publications 88, Special Collections, Bangor Public Library, Bangor, Maine, 4.

88. Rufus B. Sage, *Rocky Mountain Life* (1857; repr., Boston: Estes and Lauriat, 1880).

89. "What Will Become of the Indians?," *American Catholic Quarterly Review*, October 1886, 11.

90. "Foreign Missions," *New York Evangelist*, March 10, 1870, 41.

91. Rev. R. J. Creswell, "Protestant Indian Missions," *Independent*, November 27, 1890, 42.

92. Thomas C. Moffett, *The American Indian on the New Trail: The Red Man of the United States and the Christian Gospel* (New York: Missionary Education Movement of the United States and Canada, 1914), xi.

93. Smith-Rosenberg, *This Violent Empire*, 212, 435. My understanding of the importance of the spoiling of racial distinctions overlaps in some ways with Smith-Rosenberg's, but I am more interested in how that process took place simultaneously with the ideological assertion of the permanence of racial categories. The attachment remained, it remained dysfunctional, and it led to violence. Serial perpetration, as surely was the case with white massacres of Indians, is driven by continued attachment to the target group even as there is a growing sense that the group has come too close, that is, has invaded.

94. Jack Jenkins, "Jan. 6: A Timeline in Prayers," *Religion News Service*, January 6, 2022, https://religionnews.com/2022/01/06/jan-6-a-timeline-in-prayers/.

Conclusion

1. Quoted by U.S. Representative Jamie Raskin, January 6 House Select Committee proceedings, live broadcast, CNN, July 7, 2022. Those phrases had been in use for several years in Canada, Australia, and the U.S.

2. Andy Humbles, "GOP Roger Stone to Speak in Mt. Juliet about His Renewed Christian Faith after Pardon," *Tennesseean*, August 11, 2020, https://www.tennessean.com/story/news/2020/08/11/roger-stone-speak-mt-juliet-his-renewed-christian-faith/3342621001/.

3. Roger Stone, video testimony exhibited at January 6 House Select Committee proceedings, live broadcast, CNN, July 12, 2022.

Index